Finding My Way to
Moose River Farm

Living with Animals in the Adirondacks

Anne T. Phinney

Finding My Way to Moose River Farm
Living with Animals in the Adirondacks

Anne T. Phinney
Copyright ©2013. All rights reserved.

First Paperback Edition, August 2013
Cover Photograph by Michele deCamp

Published by
MOOSE RIVER FARM
Old Forge, NY 13420
www.mooseriverfarm.com

Printed in the United States of America
by Patterson Printing, Benton Harbor, Michigan

ISBN 978-0-615-81579-4

Finding My Way to Moose River Farm

Living with Animals in the Adirondacks

Anne T. Phinney

DEDICATION

To Rod,
for building, maintaining and sharing
the life I always dreamed about.

ACKNOWLEDGEMENTS...

For four years, I wrote *Finding My Way to Moose River Farm* in relative isolation. When I began to tell friends and family that I was writing a book, a whole wave of supporters cropped up to offer encouragement and advice. To their undying loyalty and faith in me I owe a debt of gratitude. It gave me the courage to move forward and complete the manuscript.

Thank you...

To my editor, *Paula Roy* for spending a long winter engaged in my life; helping to produce a clearer, stronger and overall, better book.

To *Rod Phinney* for building me my dream...twice.

To author, *Constance McGeorge* for her timely advice.

To Nancy Best and the staff of Nancy Did It! for their graphic vision.

To my mother, *Barbara Lane* who read the first draft with nothing but positive constructive criticism. To my sister *Sue Sutter* for her glowing compliments. To *Lisa Eklund* for promoting my blog entries in an effort to help me get the word out. To *Michele deCamp* and *Jean Risley* with whom I have shared my horses for decades and continue to do so. To *Cindy Diver* who inspires me through lightness and darkness. To *Lori Sheckler* with whom I shared my childhood and my dreams. So glad she is living hers. To *Vicky Brazell* and *Irene Aloisio* with whom the stories will continue. To *Diane Williams* who gave me my first long term horse care experience on which I have been hooked ever since. To *Missy Elleman* who is always there for my animals and for me. To all of my nieces and nephews who love animals and with whom I have shared these adventures. To all of my *MRF riders* with whom I share a passion for horses. To my *Town of Webb School students* for constantly reminding me how it feels to be a kid!

Finally, to *Summer's Promise* who brought me great joy.

CONTENTS...

Morning Begins...

Morning on our Adirondack farm just outside of Old Forge, New York, begins at 5:30 a.m. A radio broadcast of bleak world news invades the silence of our room. I have trouble processing the information as I assemble my thoughts for the coming day. I can't understand how so much turmoil can occur in the world. What I do understand is that God appears to be shining down on me as my thoughts drift. At this moment, I am waking in my warm bed with my soul mate still asleep beside me. Three dogs also begin to stir in the darkness of the room. Two West Highland terriers, Nina and Niles, stretch and yawn as they prepare to leap off the bed. A black-and-tan smooth Dachshund named Huxley peels his toasty body away from my side and emerges from under the covers. He is planning his morning attack in which he wraps his whole wiener body around my neck, his version of an alarm clock. This assault can be a bit abrupt, but this morning I welcome his embrace as I recall how his arrival years ago melted my heart after the loss of our first generation of dogs. Besides, it sure is more uplifting than the radio news.

At 5:42, I can procrastinate no more. Lifting the covers, I prepare for the cold air of the room to blast through my flannel pajamas. The first steps to the bathroom are wrought with pain and stiffness. My arthritic hips are a loud reminder of forty plus years riding horses, a privilege that makes me determined not to give in to these signs of aging. Quickly, I exchange my pajamas for fleece pants, a fleece turtleneck and a wool sweater. I stop back at the bed where Huxley prepares for me to scoop him into my arms and carry him down the stairs that he refuses to descend on his own. At the bottom of the stairs, he begins to wriggle in anticipation of his feet hitting the floor. Once on the ground, he scampers through the kitchen to the back door. The Westies are already waiting there. Despite the abrupt change in temperature as the door opens, all three bolt down the steps, through the snow and out into the yard, barking and sniffing at messages left by wildlife visitors the night before. Huxley, meanwhile, has only one mission: to relieve himself quickly and sprint back to the warmth behind that door.

While the dogs are outside, I return to the kitchen to prepare their breakfast. Movement in the living room is accompanied by a low one syllable grunt.

"Good morning precious girl," I coo from the kitchen.

"Ump," replies Fiona, our sizeable, house trained Pot Belly pig who is curled up on a cozy dog bed in front of the fireplace.

Huxley is crying outside now for his breakfast, his body shaking from the cold. When I open the door, he zooms past me to the kitchen, then devours his breakfast in seconds. Afterwards, he leaps onto his dog bed where he whines again for a blanket to be placed over his trembling body.

Covered in snow, the Westies return from their morning patrol of the backyard. Niles scratches at the door so that I will let them in. With an air of confidence, they trot into the kitchen, shaking the snow from their Teflon fur. Niles chews at the snowballs frozen to his paws. When he is finished, he stares at his food for several minutes before eating it tentatively. Nina eats with gusto, then settles herself into a kitchen cabinet that we converted into an enclosed dog bed.

My own routine continues. I have to make two sandwiches, but I am out of turkey cold cuts. Luckily, I have some hardboiled eggs that I quickly begin to chop in a bowl, evoking fond memories of my grandmother with whom I shared egg salad sandwiches while we solved the problems of the world from her backyard. She recently passed away at the age of one hundred and ten. Next, there are two water bottles to fill and my lunch to pack. After rummaging through the refrigerator for a zucchini and some tofu, I chop them both into small pieces and scatter them on the lid of a discarded cottage cheese container. I carry the dish to a heated cabinet in the "animal" room.

Bending my stiff body down to open the door, I chant, "Good morning Rosemary," to a twenty-four-inch long iguana. She stretches her torso up so I can scratch the molting skin around her ears. I place the dish in the corner of her cabinet and hold her face between my hands, stroking her with both thumbs. It saddens me to see her all alone in the cabinet. I reflect on a time many years ago when I was allowed to include animals in my sixth grade classroom. Then many children cared for her and in return received love from this not-so-cuddly creature. I finish my stroking and close the cabinet doors so that the dogs can't invade Rosie's food dish.

Now it is time to get out to the barn. I check the outdoor temperature on my husband Rod's weather station next to his chair in the living room. It is minus six degrees this morning. Yes, that is bitter cold, but it is an improvement over yesterday's temperature of minus twenty three degrees. I beckon to the pig stirring on the dog bed in the living room.

"Fiona," I call. "Come Piggily. Time for your breakfast. Come, come, Pigiletto."

"Ump, Ump, Ump," she grunts as she lifts her bulk, blanket and all, off the cushion where she slept in front of the fireplace last night. She marches through the kitchen, stopping for a long drink that practically drains the community water bowl before heading out the back door. Her food is waiting in a rubber dish at the bottom of the steps. With a few happy grunts, Fiona's daily routine has begun.

With my coat, boots, hat and gloves in place, I am also ready to go outside with Fiona. After her breakfast, she stops to clean up stray seed under the birdfeeder. Then she and I make our way out to the barn. The cold air blasts our faces. I can't wait until spring. Winter in the Adirondacks is very long; and since it is only February, there is still a lot of winter left. I act as Fiona's plow through the several inches of snow that have accumulated overnight. By walking first, I lower the height of the snow so her belly will not freeze. She grunts softly with each step she takes behind me.

At the barn, I reach for the light switch and am greeted by a high pitched whinny from the last stall on the right. Sandi, a small Trakhener gelding, is hungry. He reminds me not to forget him back there in the far corner. Some of the other horses greet me with low rumbles, indicating that they too are hungry. I begin my ritual distribution of hay to each stall. This is when I make my daily inspection of each horse's condition and appetite, both indications of how they are feeling today. When I lift the lid on the grain bin, Fiona is at my side as if on cue. She grinds her snout into my ankle, a signal for me to drop a handful of sweet feed on the floor for her. The horse's grain is already pre-measured from the night before to save precious time and to assure prompt service. I am relieved to witness each horse dive into the grain with a healthy appetite.

Next, I hear a soft bleating from the eleventh stall. Three goats jump up to peer over the door. They are hungry too. After feeding them their own grain ration, I close the bin. Fiona has finished her handful of grain and is now making her rounds, checking out the stalls of the horses who sling feed out of their bins. I hear her protest with high pitched squeals when Easau, a bay gelding, lowers his head to sniff at her.

I check the clock to assure myself that I am still on schedule before I begin cleaning the first of ten stalls. Mucking stalls is, for me, a form of meditation. At this hour of the morning, just ninety minutes before I begin my professional day, the mindless chore allows my thoughts to simmer as I plan for the coming hours at school. Before I know it, I am emptying the wheelbarrow on my final trip to the manure pile behind the barn. I check every water bucket to make sure it will last the morning and split up a flake of hay for the goats.

"Have a good day, my loves," I sing before turning off the light switch and heading back to the house.

Fiona, who is still busy cleaning up bits of grain on the barn floor, begins to mumble in short contented grunts. Left in the dark, she trots to catch up with me. The bitter cold forgotten, I have had my barn fix, as satisfying as a hit that calms the hard-core drug user. The difference is that my dose results in an appreciative and healthy high.

Across the driveway, I see the sun hoisting itself up over the trees. Its arrival begins earlier each morning now, a true sign that the days are heading toward spring. A mourning dove calls overhead, breaking the eerie silence of the past three months. I smile thanks to God, who has blessed me with these gifts. I deeply appreciate where I am today, on a beautiful horse farm in the Adirondack woods. My childhood dreams have come true beyond my expectations. It is no accident that I am here. Years of hard work, determination, and blind faith have paid off. Still I am amazed at how my life has turned out.

Part I

Youth

Finding My Way to Mountain View Farm

CHILDHOOD FRUSTRATIONS...

Before Moose River Farm there was Lakeview Farm on Sixth Lake in Inlet, New York, our home for the first eighteen years of marriage. And before Lakeview Farm there was a childhood of longing for a life lived with animals. Little did I know during my childhood that the seeds of these future homes were being sown through decisions and choices I made along the way. Fifty years later it is perfectly clear that I am living the life that is meant to be mine.

The path to this extraordinary life meandered through a long childhood marred often by frustration and misunderstanding. As the youngest of four children spaced two years apart, I was at a disadvantage from the day I was born. Yes, every child can recite the disadvantages of her placement in the birth order, but being the youngest of so many is anticlimactic. My sister Sue claimed the first girl position four years earlier. My oldest brother, George, began elementary school on the day I was born. He would probably complain that my arrival overshadowed the first day of his full-time academic career. This fact robbed me of being the first at anything. Perhaps my brother John, two years older than I, felt the same way at times, but he was the typical third child, amicable and easy to please.

Our mother stayed at home with us despite the Bachelor's degree she received from Elmira College in 1953. Her own parents were graduates of Mount Holyoke and Dartmouth Colleges. Her mother had worked as a bacteriologist for five years before she married and raised a family in the early 1930s. My mother worked briefly, although she would hardly call her experience a career. Once she married our father, her role as wife and mother prevented her from pursuing a career. I have often wondered if motherhood was enough for her. She raised us with little help from our father. Although he did not know how to handle small children, he loved us dearly.

He was able to immerse himself in a successful career as a salesman of pneumatic and electronic control instruments for the steel industry.

Eventually, he became Vice President of Sales for Moore Products Company, thus utilizing his engineering degree from Cornell University.

Golf provided him with much needed stress relief so he played as often as he could, three or four times a week during the good weather months. Typical of fathers in the 1960s, he did not interact closely with us. He dedicated his working life to providing a private college education for each of his four children. My brother George and I were also given a graduate school education. We all entered the workforce debt-free thanks to our father's hard work.

We were raised just a few miles from the Philadelphia city line in Jenkintown, Pennsylvania. My father had been raised nearby and brought my mother there to live after he finished his stint with the U.S. Army at Fort Hood in Killeen, Texas. She had been raised in upstate New York, just twelve miles from Lake George in the town of Hudson Falls. Unfortunately, Hudson Falls had nothing to offer a pretty young girl after college graduation. She had spent her teenage years trying to escape her hometown by taking summer jobs as a resort waitress on nearby Schroon Lake or in Maine. Moving to a Philadelphia suburb suited her just fine, although it moved her far away from her parents, which made visiting them difficult while raising four children.

My mother loved animals and had spent her childhood longing for a dog. Her father, a nattily dressed bank president, refused to allow the family to have a dog. She claimed she understood how much I wanted a horse, but I could not equate the longing for a dog with the ache I had for a horse. Only in the last few years have I begun to think that she probably did understand how I felt.

My father was sympathetic to animals, but I am not certain that he actually spent much time considering them. He grew up with a dog; there are pictures of him throwing a ball for a collie named Pat. However, Pat's care in terms of feeding, walking and grooming came from my father's family housekeeper, Edie. My father did show devotion to my two childhood dogs, a collie named Bonnie and later a golden retriever named Penny. He played with and loved these dogs, but took little part in caring for them.

Finding My Way to Mountain View Farm

The day our collie died suddenly from a stomach rupture while we were vacationing with her at the sea shore, my father cried and cried in a way that I had never witnessed before in all my fourteen years. I remember how uncomfortable it was to watch this man weep over our beloved dog. I wondered if my own death would provoke the same intensity of emotion. Now, with adult insight, I believe that he didn't know how to show affection without appearing weak. Since his sudden death from a heart attack in 1993, I actually feel his presence in a warm and calming manner, particularly when my own anxiety begins to worry me with the "what ifs" of my future.

These five people lived alongside me as I sprouted awkwardly through childhood with a wicked case of self-consciousness that I inherited from my mother and an obsession with horses that matched my father's obsession with golf. The combination made it difficult for me to feel part of any peer group. My friends were prettier, skinnier, and more athletic than I was, a typical teen sentiment as I now know.

But all this changed when I was with horses. With horses I exited the prison of my psyche and physique. With horses I enjoyed being in the company of creatures who didn't care about my appearance. With horses I was happy. I inhaled their wonderful aroma, ran my fingers through their plush coats, and brushed my lips across the soft spot between their nostrils. Horses soothed the frustration I felt at home. I lived in the moment only at the barn and spent the rest of my time counting the hours and minutes until I could return. Luckily, I was able to "belong" in various barns along the way. Each one developed my level of horsemanship and character, thus preparing me for a future lived with the animals I so desperately wished and prayed for.

The daily request for a horse of my own was always turned down, no matter what conditions I promised to maintain at my end of the bargain.

"Can I have a horse? I promise I will keep my room clean for the rest of my life. Please!!!!"

"No."

"Can I have a horse? I promise I will not ask for anything more for my birthday or Christmas for the rest of my life. Please!!!!"

"No."

"Can I have a horse? I promise I will never ask for clothes, records, or any other pets, ever. Please!!!!"

"No."

And so the scenario continued. Alone in my room, I cried often in frustration. Nobody seemed to understand that I was not a spoiled child asking for something that caught my fleeting attention.

I prepared my life to include horses by researching, learning and immersing myself in all that I could about them because I knew there was a lot more to owning one than riding it every day. The care of horses requires more knowledge than riding demands. I learned anatomy; I read about every lameness, blemish and disease that specifically afflicts horses. C.W. Anderson's sketches of thoroughpins, bog spavin, bone spavin, ring bone, founder, and poll evil are etched in my mind after all the time I spent quizzing myself from his book *The Complete Guide to Horses*. *Veterinary Notes for Horse Owners* occupied a permanent position on the table next to my bed, a bible for all that I needed to know. This book even had a chapter about equine care after a nuclear bomb attack, something to consider seriously during the Cold War of the 1970s. No other title excited me more than Margaret Cable Self's *A Horse of Your Own*, which I consulted often to reassure myself that I would be a knowledgeable horse owner at some point in my future. If only I could have seen into my future, I might have enjoyed my childhood more. I might have allowed myself to live in the moment as my teen years poked along.

To soothe the ache for horses, I spent lots of time in my room writing about them. Sitting at my antique slant-top desk while Barbra Streisand, The Carpenters, and the Bee Gees provided the soundtrack of my adolescent years, I wore down hundreds of my father's number three pencils in an effort to get the story right. Although my novels focused on horse ownership, there was always a menagerie of animals that accompanied the main character, usually a girl my age, on every adventure.

In one story, my wealthy main character, Linda, who graduated from college brilliantly early, headed for South Africa to work with her uncle, a game warden who also bred Thoroughbreds for the racetrack. After a year of adventures among African wildlife, Linda returned home to England with a lion cub and one of her Uncle's racetrack rejects. Once trained by Linda, the colt, (black with four white socks and a white blaze on his face), named Sir Dominic, won an Olympic gold medal in show jumping with Linda in the irons, of course. The lion, Figaro, matured into a spectacular specimen who followed Linda everywhere she went along with her two little Dachshunds, a giraffe, and an assortment of goats. It was a marvel that the lion never ate the goats, but he was so well trained and loved his mistress so much that the thought never crossed his mind. After Linda had accomplished a lifetime of achievements before the age of twenty-six, she met and married a rock star.

As silly as the plots of these adolescent tales were, writing them provided an escape from the world that adults controlled. On paper I could own horses, lions and lots of dogs. They could go everywhere with me, well behaved as a result of my gifted training methods. Through my words, I could live in my own Peaceable Kingdom.

Horseitis...

Although I love all species of animals, I burn with a passion for horses. I am not certain when the addiction began because I don't remember a time when it wasn't there. However, I do remember my first pony ride at age five; the smell of him, the clip-clop of shod hooves and the squeak of the saddle. Charcoal was the name of the black pony on which I took my first ride while we vacationed in the Pocono Mountains in August, 1966. After that first encounter, I was hooked. I had to find more opportunities to be around horses.

The next summer my parents sent Sue and me to Lost Acres Day Camp, which specialized in horseback riding. During the fall and spring months, that same camp offered trail riding on weekends. Every Saturday morning, we woke up anticipating our day at the barn. My mother ceremoniously wrote the ten dollar check that provided us with transportation to and from the barn plus the long awaited ride on horseback. With lunches packed, we were sent on our way.

The barn was a revolving door of horse flesh. Every week there seemed to be new additions to the herd as others disappeared. It was heartbreaking to arrive and discover that Jojo, or Brand X had been hauled off to the auction. However, Stormy and Flash had arrived to take their place. I remember a foal named Rusty whom I adored. He was my first experience with baby horses. I taught him how to lead with a halter as I volunteered to take him out on the grass to graze.

We returned home late in the afternoon, exhausted and full of talk about the horses and barn activity. Our jeans smelled of leather and manure. That aroma had to last me through the week until the next Saturday when I was anointed again.

When my sister entered high school, her passion for horses began to wane as boys entered her life. I continued to go to the barn, but it wasn't the same. Her absence made it difficult to discuss the events of the day at home. There was nobody else to share horses with in my family.

When Lost Acres Day Camp eventually closed, all the horses were sold. Many years later, I drove by the property and reminisced about my budding equestrian career. The next couple of years were horseless, but I never lost the desire to find them again. There was a small farm on the way to my Grandparent's house, just a few miles from where we lived. It appeared as an anomaly in the suburban sprawl of Wyncote, Pennsylvania. Every time we drove to my grandparent's house, I craned my neck out the car window to catch glimpses of horses. There was always a gray goat on the lawn, and occasionally I caught sight of a swishing tail or stomping foot by the barn. The sightings made me desperate to find whole horses again.

In the spring of 1974, my mother found an ad in the *Times Chronicle*, our local newspaper, for Was-A-Farm, a riding camp that was starting up at that very farm in Wyncote. She called to set up an appointment to check it out. The call proved to be an opportunity to have horses in my life.

Finding My Way to Mountain View Farm

Diane Williams was the most independent teenager I had ever met. At age sixteen, she began her own day camp for horse-crazy children. Diane had grown up on her family's Was-A-Farm with horses. A local horse dealer, Mr. Scarlett, had set up an arrangement with Diane that enabled her to collect some horses for the summer and sell them in the fall. Mr. Scarlett spent most every Monday at the New Holland Horse Auction in the Amish country of Lancaster County. He loved horses and despite the slim pickings at New Holland, Mr. Scarlett had a keen eye for picking those with potential. Each week he arrived home with a couple of sorry looking ponies or horses in his rickety horse trailer. Diane spent the summer fattening up and training these horses in her camp program. At the end of the summer, she sold the horses, making quite a profit after settling up with Mr. Scarlett.

Many of his purchased horses arrived freshly gelded and from the race track. After a couple days of rest to heal and adjust to new surroundings, the geldings were put into training. I don't remember there being any rogues over the years that I rode at Was-A-Farm. They weren't necessarily well schooled, but they did not have behavioral problems. After eight weeks of working consistently in the ring, they became lovely lesson horses. We campers enjoyed every minute of time spent with them.

Was-A-Farm Day Camp was heaven on earth for me. There, I could immerse myself in horses and learn, learn, learn. Diane was my hero. Little did I know that her independence was the result of growing up in a family very different from mine. The horses provided her with an escape. Diane was a survivor who was left to figure life out on her own. At the time I thought she was the luckiest girl in the world; I would have given anything to trade places with her. Little did I know that she would have gladly traded places with me.

After my first summer at Was-A-Farm, I spent the fall taking weekend riding lessons from Diane. All week long, I counted the hours until it was time for my lesson. What sustained me through the week was the aroma that my shirt and jeans had absorbed. They lay on the back of a rocking chair in my bedroom where I could sniff them and smell horses. This was aromatherapy before anybody coined the phrase!

Diane had a beautiful dark roan Quarter horse mare named Missy who three years earlier had given birth to a long-legged chestnut colt named Merrylegs. To say that Missy was a handful was an understatement. Her constant jigging around the ring twisted my organs into knots. Her canter, however, was as smooth as glass and worth the bouncy wait. The only thing I dreaded about the canter was that it marked the end of my lesson that always came too soon.

The following summer, my mother sent me to a riding camp in New Milford, Pennsylvania, just south of Binghamton, New York. Camp Equinita was the sister camp of the well-established Camp Susquehanna and had a wonderful reputation for competitive riding. The property sprawled out on top of a mountain with breathtaking views that I remember vividly thirty-five years later. The distance from the lush riding fields and outside hunt course to the quaint waterfront required several miles of walking per day. Since the barn was at the bottom of the mountain and required three trips a day up and back leading the horses on foot, we campers were kept in top physical shape.

It was exciting to know that I would be with horses every day for an entire month and that I would be assigned one of my very own to care for daily. I arrived for the second four-week session at the end of July. Two hours after my parents dropped me off and settled me into my tent, I was introduced to my assigned horse.

His name was Never Never Land, a great big full bodied bay Sabino Paint cross with four high white stockings and a bald face. He was beautiful, and for me it was love at first sight. Every morning I was responsible for fetching Never from the fifteen acre field, where he spent the night with the entire camp herd, and leading him to his stall for breakfast. While he ate grain and hay, I groomed and checked him over from his nightly turnout.

At Equinita, it occurred to me that not everybody who loved to ride horses was devoted to caring for them. Many of the campers possessed impressive riding skills after the expensive training that they engaged in throughout the year. But that training did not necessarily include or encourage connecting with the horse once the rider dismounted. The younger

Finding My Way to Mountain View Farm

girls, aged 8 to 11, still appeared to be obsessed with horses, preferring to hang out at the barn rather than at any other spot on the enormous camp property. One of the eleven-year-olds who frequented the barn grew up to become accomplished actress Laura Lynney.

I couldn't connect with the older girls who were more impressed with the boy campers and less enamored with the equines. Luckily, two of my tent-mates, Pamela Narins and Carolyn Morgan, did share an all-consuming interest in horses with me. The three of us spent the month of August thoroughly engaged with horses. We never complained about barn chores and always tried to extend our time with horses at the expense of missing an arts and crafts activity or swim lesson to do so.

Although I cared for Never daily, he was not necessarily my mount every day in a lesson. There were others that I rode including Cocktail, Majorette, Senior Prom and New Moon, to mention just a few. My four-week camp experience flew by quickly. All too soon it was time to say an emotional good bye to Never as well as to the other horses.

Returning home with no riding prospects in sight was depressing. I had had a taste of caring for a horse and I wanted more. To make matters worse, I also had to face ninth grade with all of the challenges to an adolescent who struggled to fit in with her peers. Instead of expressing thanks for this wonderful camp experience, I retreated to my room and wept incessantly for the loss of horses yet again.

There to console me was the soothing voice of Barry Gibb, oldest brother of the group, the Bee Gees. Their music from the early and mid-seventies, years before the falsetto voices of Saturday Night Fever, comforted me through some of the most difficult periods of my adolescence. To me, Barry was more than feathery good looks and a flashlight smile. He was a consummate musician who wrote his own lyrics, composed the melodies and accompanied the iconic tunes with his own guitar playing. After my tears were spent, I lay on my bed in a trance. Barry's lyrics beckoned to me from the stereo I had recently inherited from Sue who was packing for her freshman year at college.

"*So darliiin'.....yooooou run to meeee.*"
    or

"…In the morning of my life
The minutes take so long to drift away
Please be patient with your life
It's only morning and you've still to live your day"

To ease horseitis, my parents signed me up for weekly riding lessons at a barn owned by Mr. Scarlett's son. Rich Scarlett ran a reputable riding stable with large classes and very "broke" horses. He also offered the opportunity to compete in horse shows. Every Saturday morning through the fall, winter and spring, my mother drove me seven miles through more than fifteen traffic lights out into the vanishing countryside for my one-and-a-half-hour horse fix. Her effort got me successfully through a rough year, but left me craving more time spent with horses. How was I ever going to satisfy my need to be with them more than once a week? The answer arrived by mail in the middle of May.

After several years of running her own riding camp, Diane Williams was headed off to college. She sent me a letter asking if it would be possible for me to care for her mare, Missy, while she was away. That meant daily treks to her barn, which was not too far from my house. I could walk, ride a bicycle or drive. Finally, I was going to have a horse to ride every day. Life was looking up. That summer I attended Diane's camp for the whole season and entered tenth grade with a horse to care for. My confidence and self-esteem were on the rise.

Caring for a horse agreed with me. My commitment was not as much a surprise to me as it was to my parents. Missy's daily care had to be incorporated into my schedule; I had to arrange all other activities, with the exception of school, in consideration of the mare. At the very least, I needed to arrive once a day to clean her stall and turn her out for a few hours. The shortening fall daylight hours made this a challenge, but somehow it all worked out. I was happier than I could ever remember.

Diane even allowed me to take Missy to a few horse shows. I don't remember that Missy was a star in the local show ring, but competition did give me a goal to work toward in terms of my riding, particularly jumping, and that was enough for me at the time.

The only setback occurred in late February when Mononucleosis invaded my body, forbidding me to be around horses. An enlarged pancreas is one of the symptoms of Mono and the doctor's orders prevented me from risking injury. During this time, another child, desperate for a horse of her own, was assigned to Missy's care.

Mono knocked me down for a solid three weeks. Unable to eat or remain upright for any length of time, I simply gave in to the illness and stayed in bed. Fifteen pounds melted off of my frame and zapped any strength that I had built up by working in the barn. When I felt up to it, my mother drove me to the barn to visit Missy and the other horses, hopeful that the fresh air and company might promote my recovery. Of course, just inhaling the wonderful smells of barn and horse worked wonders.

Five weeks later and well into spring, I was back at the barn caring for Missy with the strength and vigor I had possessed earlier in the school year. The lengthening days allowed me to spend more time riding her and conditioning her for the coming show season. However, something had changed. Carol, the young teen assigned to Missy's care in my absence, was left without a horse. Her parents also denied her a horse of her own so Diane's barn had become her "Mecca" for exposure to horses.

I liked Carol and I liked spending time at the barn with her. We shared the care of Diane's horses, working together amicably until Diane returned from college in mid-May. Carol and I wondered what Diane would do with us now that she was home and could take over the care of her own horses. Little did I know that Diane was just about to change my life forever with a decision she made that spring. To this day I am ever grateful for her wisdom and ability to stand up to my father.

"Now that you have cared for my horses this year, it is time that you had your own horse," exclaimed Diane.

I could not have agreed with her more, but there was one large obstacle standing in my way. Without my father's blessing and financial assistance, horse ownership was out of the question.

As my tenth grade year ended, Diane began making plans for the coming camp season at Was-A-Farm. Recognizing that I was rather old this year to be a camper, she incorporated my horse care skills into a "counselor in training" position. She also made an effort to speak to my father on a number of occasions about the issue of horse ownership. I always made myself scarce when she spoke to him, fearing that he might say something embarrassing. Therefore, I have no record of their conversations. What magic combination of words had she assembled to elicit the response I finally got to hear the last time I pleaded with my father for a horse of my own?

Horses and Heartbreak...

"Ok,..." he said softly. "You can have a horse."

His eyes looked straight at me as I searched his face for some misunderstanding of the words. As I realized their meaning, the words began to soothe me like antacid on an upset stomach. In fact, I didn't even need to hear them again, for I had heard those words clearly in my imagination often enough. The words came from my father who had denied the possibility of there ever being a horse in our family. His concerns about expense, time, commitment and lack of knowledge had prevented him from being able to agree to my pleas. I have never been truly certain why he changed his mind, but perhaps observing a daughter who dedicated 150% of her life to borrowed horses may have contributed to his assent.

It was mid-June. Tenth grade was finishing up. For the first time in my life, the summer stretched ahead of me with the prospect of shopping for a horse that would belong only to me. While I helped out with the chores at Was-A-Farm Day Camp, I could work off the board for my horse and spend seven days a week getting to know him. Life just couldn't get any better. Even the second statement that my father uttered after saying I could have a horse of my own couldn't deflate my excitement. Who cared that the horse would have to be sold before I went off to college in two years? Two years is an eternity to a fifteen-year-old. Cloaked in youthful elation, I could not foresee the lessons I was soon to learn.

Many secrets about the person I was and wanted to become when I grew up hid in the desk in my bedroom. Among sappy manuscripts, autobiographical scribbles, and ill-proportioned illustrations, there was a list of over one hundred horse names that I had collected over the years. Perhaps my true love of writing stems from the clever combinations of words used to name race horses and show horses. Who can deny that Secretariat became a lovely word once it was associated with greatness? Idle Dice and Jet Run labeled two of American show jumping's greatest athletes. My list included such goodies as Night Wing, Sir Dominick, Tesseract, (from a Wrinkle in Time), and Elgin.

At the top of my list was the name Beaushannon, borrowed from a dun mare named Taffy Beaushannon that my sister Sue rode at Lost Acres Day Camp one summer. I loved the sound of her whole name, although in the barn we just called her Taffy, leaving the name Beaushannon for my horse.

Beaushannon was the first horse to arrive on trial for me in Diane's barn. Trial is not a word that a horse-starved teenager fully understands. I first laid eyes on him just after midnight in one of the dingy stalls behind the auction block at the New Holland sales barn in Lancaster County, Pennsylvania. He shared the small stall with two other geldings that Mr. Scarlett had purchased earlier. Tattoos under the horses' top lips explained that all three had probably come from failed attempts on the racetrack prior to New Holland's Monday sale day for horses. As if that wasn't enough stress, all three stood traumatized from the crude method of gelding or castration without anesthesia that had taken place the day before. Although stallions run cheap through the auction ring, they must be gelded before being broken as riding horses. Mr. Scarlett's connections at New Holland made it possible to have the horses gelded before he brought them home to Wyncote.

Despite the trauma Beaushannon had endured, I could tell that he was beautiful even under the dim light from a single dusty bulb hanging above the stall. The brand new, vivid blue halter that hung around his head contrasted starkly with his dull, dirt encrusted coat. His long stringy mane hid a thin neck that pronounced his youth. Behind the tattooed lip, a nubby incomplete set of teeth indicated his age as between two and three years.

Mr. Scarlett had purchased the horse for me to have on trial through the summer months. With no pressure, I was to take my time getting to know the horse and begin his training. After a vet check later on, I could decide if I wanted to keep him. If not, Mr. Scarlett would take him away and find another horse for me to try. This is the most intelligent way to buy a horse, although a teenage girl's heart may disagree.

We arrived with Beau and the other two geldings back at Diane's barn shortly before 2:00 a.m. Once we settled them into stalls of their own, we all headed home to bed. Despite a lack of sleep, I was back at the barn early the next morning, excited to see my new horse in daylight. My mother and sister accompanied me on that first morning, sharing my enthusiasm for the potentially good looking gelding. A sudsy bath removed the caked-on filth from his body and the dried blood from his hind legs. The sun revealed a striking blood bay coat with four high white socks. Large brown eyes separated by a narrow blaze extended down the front of his narrow face. This beauty was mine.

Beau and I spent the next week getting to know each other as the lazy summer days flew by. Due to his recent gelding, I couldn't ride him right away, but I did begin to lunge him in an effort to reduce the swelling that replaced the space where his testes had been. At first he appeared listless, no doubt due to a combination of all the stresses he had recently suffered. Time, rest, and love were the healing ingredients necessary for Beau to reach a point where I could start riding him.

Ten days later, I was ready and excited to begin training my new horse under saddle. Race horses, although broke to carry weight, have no concept of a rider's leg against their sides. Therefore, most of my first under-saddle training sessions were spent showing him what my lower leg meant. With Diane's experience and help over the next few days, we got Beau to comply with the wishes of my lower leg. Eventually, he was able to trot from my leg and did so willingly and obediently. But as his training progressed and we asked him to trot for longer intervals, hidden injuries from the race track began to surface in his hind legs, particularly his hocks. At first the lameness was a step here and a step there with long intervals of soundness in between. In time these intermittent steps of soreness became a blatant bilateral lameness complete with heat and swelling.

Diane arranged to have her veterinarian come out to examine Beau. Old Doc Rile's years of practicing veterinary medicine were a testament to his experience with horses. Since he had seen it all on the race track, we were sure he would get to the bottom of the gelding's physical troubles. The vet recommended rest and deemed Beau sound except for his hocks. He hoped that with time and patience, the gelding might work through the old injury.

By August Beau's issues had not resolved. After a week or two of rest, we began with light work, but heat and swelling returned anytime the training went beyond ten minutes at the trot. With the first day of school only three weeks away and Beau's physical capabilities a big question mark, the inevitable became clear. He was not going to be my horse.

Dr. Rile made a final diagnosis, declaring that Beau had chronic inflammation in both hocks, probably due to torn cartilage in the joints. The prognosis was not good news for a teen who had two years ticking away to realize the dream of owning a horse that she could ride. On that same day, Diane made arrangements with Mr. Scarlett to come and take Beau away.

I was devastated. The thought that Beau would not work out had never really occurred to me after I fell in love with him under the dirty light bulb at New Holland. He had been my dream come true. I had already dared to dream further of the day that I could finally ride in a show on my own horse, a horse who was living flesh and bone and wore the name from the top of my coveted list. How could this be? I had already spent ten years feeling the ache of not having a horse. Now I had lost a real horse, my horse. And what would become of Beau? Who would buy a horse with such a prognosis? The guilt of letting him down began to take hold and the combination of loss and betrayal sent me into a spiral of tearful, teenaged despair.

I arrived home later that afternoon and fell apart in front of my parents. Perhaps my mother understood how I was feeling as she had witnessed the love I felt for this horse, finally my own. My father was not as sensitive.

"We can't have this display of emotion every time a horse doesn't work out for you or when we get rid of it," he stated sternly, unaware of the power in those words.

Suddenly, I became very aware that what he meant was; "We are not going to stand for your emotional outburst when it comes time to get rid of the horse before you go to college." At that moment I began to hear the ticking of the clock that was chiseling away at my two year chance to realize my dream. It was already August. I didn't have a horse yet and already he was worried about my emotional state after I said goodbye to my dream, two years away.

Over the next few days, I brooded over my loss but tried to busy myself with activity at the barn. Diane, my sister, Sue, who was working as the Arts and Crafts counselor, and all of the campers were sensitive to my loss. Some of the boarders offered their horses for me to ride. Their gestures were a testament to how a "barn," so connected by the love it shares for horses, rallies around one who is suffering.

As camp came to a close, Diane, exhausted from the responsibility of so many children and horses, began preparing for the school year at West Chester State College. Mr. Scarlett collected the camp horses that Diane had not sold; and the barn, now home to fewer horses, prepared for the coming fall. Although Diane was busy with her life, she still made time to look for suitable horses for me. She even convinced my father to drive down to West Chester to look at two geldings that she knew were for sale.

The two horses were housed at a boarding stable that specialized in fox hunting. Not surprising, both horses were fearless and packed around the ring dutifully. Unlike Mr. Scarlett's auction purchases, these horses had pedigrees and price tags that stretched to four digits. My father took these numbers as an insult to his hard work to finance four children's college educations. It became unclear why we had even driven so far to look at horses that he had no intention of buying. It also wasted Diane's time, making her wonder what it was we were looking for. As the child caught in the middle between my father and Diane, I took the blame and guilt head on, feeling terribly trapped and uncomfortable between these two adults.

Just before Labor Day weekend and the first day of school, Diane called me to come to look at a horse that she thought I should consider. With renewed hope, I returned to the barn to see my horse. What I saw was Brutus.

Brutus was a huge 16.3-hand strawberry roan, part-draft horse that Mr. Scarlett had kept around for years. The gelding had a bald face with blue eyes and four white stockings that went well up past his knees and hocks. His bones were long and thick while his disposition was quiet, almost vacant. His long ears drooped at half-mast from his enormous red speckled head. Brutus was sound as a dollar. On such a physique, a chronic lameness would never stand a chance.

The gelding attended the same YMCA camp each summer and returned home to be leased out over the winter months. That way Mr. Scarlett still owned Brutus but didn't have to care for him. Of course if anybody wanted to actually buy Brutus, eight hundred dollars would complete the deal.

I had met Brutus a few times before this night in Diane's barn. Frequently, he waited behind Mr. Scarlett's tack store where one strand of electric wire provided a holding pen for horses on their way to new homes or back to New Holland. Brutus was there between gigs as a lease and camp horse. In all fairness to Brutus, I have to say that today I would welcome him with open arms to my farm. Brutus would have been a great, safe horse to ride anywhere. But for a young girl who had just had her heart broken by a gorgeous thoroughbred, Brutus was not what I had in mind on the rebound from my break-up with Beau.

Barn friends who had gathered to see me lay eyes on "my horse" for the first time noted the disappointment on my face. What was I to do now? As hard as I tried, I could not fall in love with Brutus. Diane, now only hours from returning to school, was not pleased with my ingratitude. She had done all that she could to find and provide horses for me. My youth not only prevented me from considering her side of the situation but also kept me from acting graciously. Understandably, this was her last attempt to help me. From now on I was on my own to find the horse of my dreams.

The school year started the day after my sixteenth birthday, and still there was no horse to come home to in the afternoon. To make matters worse, I was now a new student at a small Quaker school, Abington Friends, having left the large public school and many friends behind. My siblings had flown the coop to college or careers. For the first time in my life, I was an only child with too much time on my hands and no barn affiliation. All I had was a tote full of grooming brushes and a beautiful leather bridle that Diane had given me in appreciation for my help at camp. What I didn't have was a horse to use them on. Not to mention that the two years my father had proclaimed would end with the sale of the horse were dwindling down to 23 months. Where was my horse? Why wasn't this a happy time for me? How on earth was I going to find a horse without Diane's help?

SUMMER'S PROMISE...

"Go get the *Times Chronicle* and start looking," pleaded my mother, referring to our local newspaper and completely ignoring my protest that good horses aren't sold out of a newspaper.

"All of them have something wrong, so only people who don't know look for horses in the paper," I reasoned all-knowingly.

"Well, how about the *Philadelphia Inquirer*? Perhaps somebody reputable is advertising a horse today in a bigger paper." Ignoring my eye rolling, she encouraged me to look in the paper, any paper.

"By just looking, you are not committing to anything. Nobody will ever know," she promised, referring to the unwritten laws that horsemen abide by so that they don't seem ignorant. Buying a horse out of the newspaper just wasn't done if one wanted to be considered a knowledgeable horseman. Thankfully, my mother didn't care about unwritten rules and regulations. She just wanted a solution to end my misery at starting a new school with no friends and no prospects of a horse. It was unbearable for my mother, who had taken the full brunt of my sulking since my father was away on a two week business trip in Houston, Texas. My dilemma was far from his thoughts; he was occupied with the risks of maintaining clients for his company.

Finally one evening, I reluctantly took the paper and pencil that she handed me and began the taboo task of looking in the paper for a horse. There were many "horse for sale" ads in the *Times Chronicle* that week. Many of them appeared to be written by people who understood what the buyer would want to know. They used educated horsy terms like, "green broke," "working hunter," "swaps leads," and "in the ribbons" to describe Thoroughbreds, Quarter horses and Welsh ponies. The rather high prices indicated that they knew what they were talking about as well. My father and I had never discussed price; but since I was paying for half of this horse, I knew I could only afford $500.00. The rest of my carefully saved income would have to support half of this horse's monthly expenses.

Then the following ad caught my attention:

Registered Saddlebred Chestnut Mare,
4 yrs, 15.2 H, good mover, green broke over fences,
Huntingdon Valley Green Hunter Reserve champion,
$800

Perhaps it was her jumping experience, appropriate size and youth that attracted me, because her American Saddlebred breeding was the antithesis of what I was looking for. Apparently, this horse had never been trained in the various high stepping gaits of the typical Saddlebred horses with which I was familiar. With drying tears tightening the skin on my face and resolve in my voice, I allowed my mother to make the call that would change my life.

Within twenty-four hours of the phone call, my mother and I found ourselves standing in the lower level of an old stone foundation bank barn that had been turned into a tidy horse stable. Six stalls lined the interior stone walls of an area that had probably accommodated milk cows in the last century. Although the work area of the barn was well-lit, the stalls on the perimeter were so dark that it was difficult to see their occupants. Mr. Palermo, the owner of the horse we had come to see, began to elaborate on the mare's qualities. It was hard to concentrate on what he was saying while my eyes strained to make out her form in the darkness.

"She is very shy around men," he chuckled, jiggling the U-bolt that once unlatched would flood the stall with light from the work area and reveal the chestnut mare.

She was standing in the far corner with her head down. Her shiny rump greeted us with evidence that she had just been groomed. With gentle coaxing from Mr. Palermo, she turned to face us. Without a word, my mother and I knew that she was the one. Her glossy red coat fit snugly over a well-conditioned physique. Two scrubbed high white socks gleamed from the cannon bones above her oiled hind hooves. Her soft brown eyes and beautiful face enhanced by a lightning-bolt shaped star between her eyes took my breath away.

Mr. Palermo respectfully allowed us to look her over out in the work area once she was secure on cross ties clipped to either side of her halter. Under the bright light, we could see all of her. Afraid to speak for fear of my emotions getting the best of me, I stood close to her, stroking her head and neck. She stood quietly, showing no concern for the stranger who had stepped into her space. My mother touched her and talked to her softly.

Under saddle she proved wise beyond her four years. She walked, trotted and cantered with the gentlest of aids or signals from my hands and legs. We even jumped a couple of cross-rails that were set up in the Palermo's ring. After the ride, I washed her down and brushed her before putting her back in the dark stall. It had been weeks since I had been in the presence of horses, let alone cared for them. This encounter made me realize how much I missed them. As we prepared to leave, Mr. Palermo, who also recognized this match between horse and human, mentioned one small problem.

"A lady did come out to try the mare yesterday," he admitted sheepishly. With a slight hesitation he continued, "She liked the horse a lot and was going to make arrangements to have the mare vetted at the end of next week. To be honest, the lady rode the horse like a sack of potatoes despite telling me how good she was."

My mother and Mr. Palermo did not miss the disappointment that darkened my expression. This lady had inquired about the mare first and was entitled to a first refusal. Of course, if her vet found something wrong

Finding My Way to Mountain View Farm

with the horse and she decided not to purchase the mare, why would I still want to buy her?

Mr. Palermo tried to comfort us, adding quickly, "I know she was looking at other horses on the same day. Maybe she liked one of them better and isn't interested in the mare by now. I have her number, so I will give her a call and…"

"What if I leave a down payment on the horse tonight, right now?" my mother interrupted with a strength I rarely witnessed in her. "I will make the necessary arrangements with our vet; and if she passes, I will make up the difference." Of course the first person to put down actual payment claims the prize.

With a satisfied smile, Mr. Palermo accepted my mother's offer. Before I could grasp what had just happened, the check was written, Mr. Palermo shook hands with my mother and we were on our way home in the car. I had just found the equine love of my life, thanks to a timely ad in the *Times Chronicle* newspaper.

The next week was a blur of activity that focused on the purchase of my horse. First, my father, still working in Houston, had to be informed that we had found a horse that seemed a good fit for me. My dad didn't trust a complete stranger to whom he was about to write a check for hundreds of dollars. He remained skeptical about a young girl's dream horse, a notorious money pit to any father who, worn down by pleas and promises, finally agrees to a purchase.

"Call John Lynam," he instructed my mother over the phone.

Mr. Lynam was the golf pro out at Old York Road Country Club where my father religiously tended to his golf addiction. Not a country club in the normal sense, "York Road," as we referred to it, was a golf course for those who ate, slept and breathed all things golf. No extravagances went along with membership. We really weren't "the club" type of family and he was not interested in pretending that we were.

Mr. Lynam and my dad had been friends for decades, sharing their passion for golf and a sense of humor. Apparently, Mr. Lynam had grown up with horses and knew quite a bit about them. He had even purchased one that he rode in his spare time. These facts told me that they must have shared many conversations about horses over the years. Why would my Dad talk to anybody about horses if he wasn't even interested in them? Grown-ups!

Mr. Lynam agreed to meet my mother and me at the Palermo's barn the next evening to offer his opinion about the mare. I was resentful that my Dad was willing to take the word of this would-be cowboy over the word of his daughter.

After exchanging pleasantries with Mr. Palermo and my mother, Mr. Lynam approached the mare as she stood quietly on the cross-ties under the fluorescent lights of the barn's work area. He stroked her and stood at her head, observing the connection between her neck and shoulder. He ran his hands over her body, gently squeezing here and there, checking for a reaction. The mare stood, succumbing happily to the gentle massage his inspection provided for her.

Silence filled the barn as he moved his hands down each one of her limbs, continuing to palpate the tendons and joints. He picked up each hoof and examined the frog and angle of the sole. Then Mr. Lynam gently flexed the joint in each of the mare's legs to see if she reacted unfavorably to the torque. Still no reaction. After a fifteen minute inspection of her entire body, Mr. Lynam asked to take the mare outside where he could watch her walk and trot. Mr. Palermo obliged by leading the mare out into the driveway with my mother, Mr. Lynam and me following behind. Mr. Lynam took the lead rope and began to walk the mare in a circle around him. Then he clucked at her to trot on the small circle in both directions before turning to my mother who was waiting for his opinion.

"Seems like a very nice horse, Bobbie," he affirmed in his low voice. "I think you have found a horse that will serve your daughter well. Everything I see pleases me."

With Mr. Lynam's approval, my father was ready to give his consent to the purchase. The next step was to schedule a pre-purchase exam with a veterinarian. Dr. Rile was unavailable, but another local vet agreed to have a look at the horse the following Tuesday afternoon.

My mother kept me busy through the weekend by taking me to Mr. Scarlett's tack shop to buy a used saddle and some other supplies that I would need for my new horse. At our local Good Will thrift store, we found an old wooden trunk to serve as my tack box once my mother spray painted it blue, my favorite color. The grooming equipment from Diane fit nicely into the box. I hoped that the beautiful bridle would fit the mare as well.

After a thorough veterinary exam of her eyes, lungs, limbs and way of going at the walk and trot, the mare passed with flying colors. Horse ownership was now just one detail from coming true.

It had been close to one week since that fateful encounter with the classified section of the *Times Chronicle* led me to the horse of my dreams. All of the pieces were fitting into place neatly except for a barn in which to board her. We weren't really sure where we stood with Diane at the moment. My mother had called her for an opinion of the mare after our first visit to check her out. Diane was encouraging although understandably cautious as she tried to picture an American Saddlebred jumping a course of fences. Her barn was undergoing a major upheaval with several of my peers moving their horses out to new boarding stables. This meant that a couple of little girls and their horses were left behind in Diane's barn. Although my allegiance was with Diane, I wanted to be with the girls who were closer to my own age.

Until we located a new barn that could accommodate several additional horses, I found a temporary boarding situation just a few miles from where the mare was living. It was the end of September. Although the days were cooling down, my mare could spend the month of October sharing a stall with a pony that would live outside during the day and in the stall at night, while my horse lived out at night and in during the day. With this last detail in place, we made plans for Mr. Palermo to deliver the mare to the barn on Thursday afternoon, just one week and a day after my mother had called to inquire about her. This time there was no trial, no false hope, and no devastation. There was, however, one more agonizing long day at school to suffer through before horse ownership became reality.

The mare's registered name was Kate's Promise. Mr. Palermo's daughter, (whose name was not Kate), had changed the mare's name to Sweet Promise. That name didn't do much for me, although I did like the name Promise and thought that it was fitting considering the whole horse buying experience of the last four months. Still, I wanted the name to fit better. Consulting my collection of names didn't help. Not one of them fit with Promise.

Late in the afternoon when the horse trailer finally wobbled and squeaked down the gravel driveway, it occurred to me that all the turmoil of the past summer was finally coming to a peaceful end. As the horse of my dreams stepped off the trailer and into my life, I spoke her name under my breath for the first time. My Summer's Promise.

The next day my father returned, exhausted from his two week trip to Houston. Although a whole roll of film recorded the arrival of my new horse, the digital age was still decades away, preventing me from sharing pictures with my father upon his return. Instead, he planned to stop at the barn the following day after his golf outing. I tried to describe what Promise looked like in case I had not arrived at the barn yet to introduce them.

When he arrived home from golf the next day, he wasn't sure that the horse he had seen in the paddock was ours. No one around the barn could set him straight so he had to wait until he could describe the horse he had seen to me.

"There was a brown horse, all alone, eating grass in front of the barn," he described.

"That was Promise," I said casually. "The others are turned out together in a field behind the barn and she is either in a stall all day or in the front paddock by herself."

"That's our horse?" he questioned in disbelief. "That is a beautiful horse. I can't get over how beautiful that horse is."

His words made me beam with pride for my horse, my beautiful horse.

A HORSE OF MY OWN...

Volumes have been written about the relationship, both thoughtful and disturbing, between girls and horses. Since I know the bond personally, I can only describe it as magical on so many different levels. Horses are gregarious by nature and typically like to be in the company of their humans. They are also extremely humbling to the human ego through their honest reactions to what is asked of them. The latter fact needs to be considered often when working with an animal that weighs, on average, 1200 pounds. Luckily, I had learned so much prior to purchasing Promise.

Promise and I thrived in our relationship. I kept her immaculately groomed and cared for. My monthly income from babysitting and cleaning cat kennels was only enough to provide rough board for her. That meant I was responsible for her daily care, including stall cleaning, and feeding. This constant contact with her taught me so much about her and, therefore, more about horses in general. I regularly practiced leg wrapping, mane pulling, clipping, lounging, bathing, and formulating her nutrition. I kept impeccable records of her deworming schedule, shoeing schedule, veterinary care and expenses so that I could monitor my finances closely.

Riding and training Promise was a joy, although at times I was frustrated by her reaction to my aids. I was too young and inexperienced to understand that a horse's honesty prevents it from misbehaving unless it simply doesn't understand what the human is asking it to do. When this occurs and the horse has had enough, its behavior can become dangerous enough to injure the rider. Luckily, I never pressed Promise to that point. But to say that every day was a perfect ride isn't true either. She was just enough of a challenge to keep me interested and motivated to get it right.

Horse shows are a wonderful measure of riding progress. Promise and I attended many horse shows in those two years before college. Usually she made me proud; but because I could only afford to work with an instructor occasionally, we didn't have the edge that the professionally trained competition enjoyed. Promise and I won a respectable rainbow of ribbons, including blue ones. There were even occasional championships and reserve championships, but honestly, winning was not my first priority in owning a horse.

As I write, I remember most clearly the magical moments between just Promise and me. On summer afternoons when the horses refused to stay outside bothered by bugs in the uncomfortable heat and my chores were all caught up, I loved to sit in her stall and look at her as she munched through a pile of hay. The rhythmic sound of her grinding teeth and the swish of her tail at the few flies that found her there gave me a sense of peace. She was beautiful with her round, copper body that, when illuminated by the sun, shone with dapples. She was a reflection of who I wanted to be. This nurturing experience did wonders for my character as I was experiencing, in a sense, many facets of motherhood in a healthy way.

At a time when many girls experience a sense of self-loathing, horse ownership elevated my self-esteem. With Promise I did not fixate on my looks or weight. I had little interest in clothes or hairstyles, and shopping wasted the time when I could be out at the barn with Promise and the friends who shared my all-consuming interest.

Among those people who shared my love of horses at the barn was Lori Alosi. Lori was two years younger than I. She had three much older siblings and was the apple of her father, Tony's, eye. He lavished her with all that he could afford from the income he earned as a bakery delivery man in Philadelphia. Lori grew up in a "twin" or duplex in the Northeast section of Philadelphia, far from any place where horses could live. Her mother Thelma took care of the house, while Tony worked over sixty hours a week to provide for his family. Lori attended a strict catholic school from kindergarten to graduation and then followed me to Centenary College the year after I graduated. Although now we live hours apart, Lori and I have remained close friends for more than thirty-five years due, no doubt, to our love of horses.

Tony had a passion for small ponies. At one time he owned five, which he boarded ten miles from his family's home out in the country. Lori received her early horse education at this farm owned by a cowboy friend of her father. He practiced the let-the-ponies-fend-for-themselves form of management. The number of days that passed between human visits to the farm did not concern the cowboy. Since the ponies were tethered out on grass and the cowboy didn't geld the stallions, it wasn't a surprise to find newborn foals accompanying mares when somebody did get around to checking on the horses.

The property also housed over one hundred fowl. The flock included everything from bantam chickens to a huge Toulouse goose named Hector who patrolled the property with the vigil of an armed security guard. The cowboy didn't actually live on the property, but at any given time a

Finding My Way to Mountain View Farm

number of different families and individuals took up residence in the various rental houses that dotted the acreage where the ponies lived. They came and went like the wind, leaving behind unpaid utility bills and no forwarding addresses. Only the animals suffered when the electricity and water were shut off by the utility company.

Lori's father loved to visit his ponies on the farm. One of the perks of his delivery business was collecting the stale bread left over long after "sell by" dates had passed. Frequently, he arrived at the farm with his delivery van stuffed full of loaves of old crumbly bread. With a cigar clenched between his teeth and his little beagle Daisy at his side, Tony emptied bags and bags of old bread onto the ground where his ponies could gorge themselves. This custom was always questionable to me, given that a horse's digestive system is one of the most delicate set of organs known to man. However, I don't remember the ponies suffering ill effects from these gluttonous meals.

As Lori grew up and began to see the pony farm for what it truly was, she begged her father to allow her to move her pony to a boarding stable. She had outgrown the small ponies that her father kept, so he purchased a large pony for Lori around the same time that I found Promise.

By the end of October, my peers from Diane's barn were ready to move to a boarding facility farther away in Fort Washington, Pennsylvania. The local train made it a doable distance on a daily basis. Promise and I moved to the new barn just before the November winds raced across the greater Philadelphia area, dragging winter along behind.

Triangle Acres had been a day camp in the same era as Lost Acres. Therefore, the two camps had competed for campers from the same area, offering horseback riding as their most popular activity. The property was spacious with large pastures surrounded by a hodge-podge of barbed wire and mesh wire fencing. Years of neglected vegetation had grown thick around the fences in most places. The centerpiece of the property was a flat two-acre field that contained a variety of old jumps badly in need of paint and repair. Trails twisted through the property, providing options for every ride.

It was here that I met Lori. Her new large pony, a dapple gray mare named Just Be Nimble, was her best friend and most prized possession.

Nimble lived in a field on the farm, full time with three other horses. Lori lived about an hour away, making daily visits impossible for her. She made up lost time every weekend when she spent two whole days at the farm with Nimble.

Lori and I rode Nimble and Promise together all over Triangle Acres, basking in our mutual adoration for our horses. During the show season, Lori's father hauled Nimble and Promise in a blue stock trailer to horse show venues all over Montgomery County. He spent the day preparing a buffet of food for us on a portable grill that fit snugly in the van. Sausages, hot dogs, pasta and bread kept us fed throughout the long day at the show.

Lori and I cheered for each other, always showing support whether or not our rides went well. In a barn full of competitive teenage girls who didn't always want each other to do well in competition, this was a refreshing feature of our friendship.

What Nimble lacked in her plain conformation, she made up for in athletic ability. She could jump the moon if Lori asked, often besting well-bred Welsh ponies in her division. However, if Lori wasn't paying close attention as they passed the in-gate, Nimble might ditch the course and head for the exit! Thirty-five years later we still chuckle, but at the time Nimble's antics humiliated Lori. She does admit that the pony toughened her as a rider, a resiliency that helped her while training her current ex-racehorse, Baby Face.

After graduating with a degree in Equine Studies from Centenary College, Lori established a career in the bakery industry. Her life has ridden a roller-coaster of phases including the loss of both of her parents, health setbacks, several job changes, and one sadly failed marriage. Through each of these challenges, two things remained constant, giving her strength and a will to keep going: her sense of humor and her horses. She has successfully kept horses through it all and today, happily remarried, lives on a small farm in Boyertown, Pennsylvania, with two horses. She remains my closest childhood friend with whom I shared an indelible part of growing up.

My first Christmas with a horse of my own is one of my favorite memories. It was the first Christmas in ten years that I didn't need to look out the window to see if Santa had left my heart's desire on the lawn. I can still visualize the pile of gifts among discarded wrapping paper: a brand new blue halter, lead rope, blanket, saddle nameplate, leg wraps, and first aid items, all for my horse. Later that afternoon, I packed it up in the car, and we drove out to celebrate with Promise. She was wrapped in her new blanket and snug in her clean stall when I hugged and kissed her goodbye, never remembering a time when I felt so happy.

One day in the middle of January, I needed to visit Mr. Scarlett's tack shop for a saddle repair. One of the older girls from the barn drove her car while several others came along for the ride. We parked the car at the rear of the store to see if Mr. Scarlett had any horses in the paddock. There, to my surprise, stood a familiar friend with a thick, dull winter coat. I climbed under the strand of wire and walked over to him. When I spoke softly, he alerted to my approach.

"Beau, oh Beau, how are you?" I whispered as I stretched my arms around his neck and pressed my face against his jowl. "My boy, how is my good boy?"

He closed his eyes as I stroked his face and kissed his muzzle. My heart, now clenched in a vise, wrung out tears as I held onto him. For a brief childish moment, I wondered if I could swing the financial obligation of two horses. After several more minutes and one more squeeze, I climbed back under the wire feeling sad and uncertain about his future. I never saw Beau again.

Eventually, spring began to bloom all over southeastern Pennsylvania; it was time to look forward to the riding season. Winter riding was sporadic since there had not been much snow, leaving the frozen ground too uncomfortable for hooves without shoes. In early April, after Promise's feet were newly shod, we began daily training. Lori and I also began to pencil in horse shows on the calendar when tragedy struck.

One afternoon in the middle of May, I arrived at the barn and went to fetch Promise from the field where she and another horse, Brandy, spent their days. As I approached her, I could tell that something was not right. She was standing with her left hind leg raised. The closer I got, the more grotesque the scene became. Blood poured down her leg at the front of the hock and a three inch wide flap of skin hung half way down her sock. The rest of the afternoon blurred as I waited for Dr. Rile to arrive. In the meantime, I followed his instructions to wrap her leg with cold wet towels. This task required me to get close to the gaping wound that yawned in my face, forcing me to look at the tendons and various structures that should have been kept safe and clean beneath her skin. All I could think about was an infection creeping in to end my horse's life.

Dr. Rile removed the wet towels and began to examine the wound on Promise's leg. As he scrubbed and irrigated the large opening, he asked me how she had injured herself.

"To be honest, I don't have any idea," I said wondering for the first time how this had happened. "She was grazing in the middle of the large field out behind the barn when I found her like that."

"Could she have put her leg through that old fence somehow?" he asked, referring to the mish mash of barbed wire that surrounded parts of the fields. Since most of the fence was overgrown with vegetation, it never occurred to me that she could get hurt by it.

"I'll have to go down there to see if some of it is exposed." I answered.

Dr. Rile finished cleaning the wound inside and out before beginning to suture. He was concerned about a torn tendon but remained hopeful that it would heal with time. After suturing up the flap of skin, he showed me how to dress the wound. On top of the dressing I was to apply my well-practiced standing wrap. He taught me to apply a hock wrap above the bandage to keep the dressing clean but allow Promise to flex the joint. Then he showed me how to apply a spider bandage over the entire leg, fashioned from an old clean towel with strips cut on either end. Starting from the top, he tied each pair of strips and tucked them into the set below. When he was finished, her whole leg was encased in a tight white towel with knots of tied strips forming a tidy row of bumps from top to bottom. He left me with a list of instructions for changing the dressing and bandage every three days. Promise was put on a course of antibiotics and given Bute for pain. What he couldn't give me was a favorable prognosis that included my ever riding her again.

"Time will tell," he said, as he closed the door on his Volvo station wagon and prepared for his next call. "I'll be back in three days to have a look under that dressing." With that he wished me luck and drove away, leaving me with my damaged horse and broken heart.

"Time will tell," I thought to myself.

Grounded by Promise's injury over the next eight weeks, I became her dedicated caregiver. My daily trips to the barn included medicating and checking the elaborate layers of bandages and leg wraps, making certain that they stayed in place and that she wasn't trying to rip them off with her teeth. Every third day, I peeled everything off and scrubbed the area liberally with Betadine. Then, I reapplied the dressing and the elaborate sequence of bandages. Luckily, Dr. Rile arrived to help several days after the injury. The wound looked gray and shriveled, but he was confident that blood still flowed to the area. Because it was fly season, keeping the wound covered at all times was essential as nothing prevents wounds from healing more than a bunch of flies irritating the flesh.

Dr. Rile came several more times to inspect the wound and to cut away the extra granulated tissue called proud flesh, which formed as a result of moisture around the wound area. Because there was such a large opening in the tissue, Promise's body was trying to fill it in too quickly with proud flesh. As the wound continued to heal over the next several weeks, we reduced the dressing and bandages until she just needed a light polo wrap around the hock to keep a small piece of gauze in place. Eventually, she returned to the large field for turnout after being confined to a small medicine paddock where she was discouraged from racing about.

Finally, after eight weeks of painstaking care, I was given the go ahead to leave the bandage off and to begin riding her lightly. From the first ride, she showed no signs of discomfort or lameness in her hind left leg. In fact, through the whole healing process she never once took a lame step. Now in the middle of July, Promise and I were back in training mode.

Although I had searched the fence line after Promise's injury, I never found so much as a patch of fur or piece of skin along the few areas of exposed barbed wire. To this day I have no idea how she tore such a huge hole in her left hind leg. An ugly scar remained to remind me of lessons learned during that first summer with my horse.

ONE YEAR DOWN AND ONE TO GO...

The rest of that summer was uneventful for Promise and me. We were together every minute, riding the trails, conditioning in the ring or just hanging out in her stall or field. Away from the barn, I worked hard for the income necessary to maintain my half of my horse. Babysitting the four children of a neighborhood family provided me with a significant portion of Promise's cost. I also cleaned cages and enclosures for a woman who bred show cats in our neighborhood. She hired me when I was twelve years old and kept me gainfully employed until I graduated from high school.

College was twelve months away; my "two year" agreement about life with Promise was half-way over. My parents and the school guidance counselor were pressuring me to begin considering and visiting colleges. The thought of giving up the horse that gave me so much joy was, quite frankly, unthinkable. How could I give her up? She was part of me like an arm or a leg. In fact I would have gladly given either an arm or a leg to keep her. However, what would I do with her while I was away? I didn't have a barn in my back yard to house a horse while a neighborhood child, crazy for horses, took care of her. Who would buy her? Worse yet, what if the person who did buy her didn't take good care of her? What if the person lost interest and neglected her care or left her at a boarding stable, never coming to brush her or ride her? What if, like Beau, I never saw her again?

Reluctantly, I went back to school in September, dreading the college search. Not only did I not want to say goodbye to Promise, but I also didn't know what I wanted to study at college? Biology? Teaching? Pre-veterinary science?

As if driven by our inevitable separation only ten months away, I dove even deeper into life at the barn. Lori and I attended horse shows just about every weekend that fall. When the high school yearbook pictures were taken against the lovely fall foliage on the campus grounds, I arranged for one of the older girls at the barn to trailer Promise to school for my picture. She made me proud as my classmates gathered to greet her and watch us pose for the photo shoot.

Finding My Way to Mountain View Farm

"We need to start looking, honey," my mother said gently, approaching the subject I had managed to avoid until late October.

"I know," I choked before dissolving into tears, fearing that my father would hear my forbidden display of emotion.

The next week I met with my guidance counselor, advisor and both parents to discuss college plans. Earlier in September I had met with my advisor, Mrs. Mosley, a wise middle-aged Quaker woman who knew all about Promise and her looming sale date. Mrs. Mosley was also my English teacher who recognized that I loved to write. At this meeting, she asked the most obvious question.

"Can you take a horse to college with you?"

"No way! It would be very expensive and there is no way that my father is going to send me to college with a horse. I mean there is no way."

This time my father never uttered any profound words and I never really asked any direct questions. Something must have changed in him during the college planning meeting and suddenly going to college was looking up.

"Where is the barn?" my dad asked the young coed who was taking us on a tour of Rutgers University Agricultural College.

My dad was asking about "the barn" at every college we visited. He wanted to know where it was, how the students got there and how much it cost to board a horse. Dumbfounded, I didn't dare ask why he wanted to know those things.

When we toured Cornell University, his Alma Mater, the condition of the barn raised some concern about safety for the horses. Cornell had one of the best polo teams in the Ivy League despite the state of its facility. In 1988, a state-of-the-art riding facility was built on a larger piece of property, but this was 1979 when it appeared that little financial consideration was allocated for the Oxley Polo Complex.

Again I kept my mouth shut and dropped my jaw when he asked one of the barn girls if there were other riding stables in the Ithaca area. She sent us out to Asbury Hill Farm in Freeville, about ten miles from Cornell, a farm well suited for horses. Not fancy, but practical with facilities that kept horses happy and healthy. Gary Duffy, the trainer at Asbury Hill, spoke horse language that I was familiar with, and the whole farm felt like a good fit to me. Of course the monthly board was more than I had ever paid on my fixed income so I wondered what we were doing out here anyway. Still, my father said nothing.

Our next college visit took us to Hackettstown, New Jersey, to Centenary College, a small private women's school. Although the agricultural college at Cornell was now my first choice, Centenary offered a program that intrigued me. Plus, if Cornell didn't feel the same way about me, I needed a back-up school. Centenary offered a degree in Equine Studies. Who knew that such an opportunity existed? Just imagine studying horses in a classroom with hands-on lab activities in a brand new barn facility. Where the Cornell barn suffered neglect, Centenary's barn shone with well-designed stalls, board fencing and two efficient wash stalls with hot and cold running water. Each school horse, donated to the program by various individuals who received a favorable tax write off, was round and shiny, reflecting the staff's commitment to care.

Centenary's main campus was exactly thirty minutes from the barn by car. There, too, I felt comfortable with modern dormitories and the Victorian styled Seay building that dominated the small campus. Centenary's student population totaled about 500 where Cornell's student population across the seventeen different schools totaled over 18,000. With so many factors to consider, I was relieved when the decision was essentially made for me, allowing me to participate in both of these educational experiences.

When all was said and done, Cornell deferred my acceptance, encouraging me to attend another school for two years. If I maintained a grade point average above 3.6, I was automatically accepted to Cornell in my junior year. This provision allowed me to attend Centenary's Equine Studies program and graduate with an Associate's degree before arriving at Cornell.

So there was life beyond high school graduation after all. Since that fateful meeting among my parents, the guidance counselor and advisor, my experience was going to include a horse at college. Not just any horse, mind you, but the one that I had dreaded having to give up. No longer did

Finding My Way to Mountain View Farm

I hear the doomsday clock of her sale date ticking away. Instead I saw horses in a future where I was going to study and learn even more about them. With riding lessons three days a week, I was sure to receive a much needed boost to my training abilities. With college plans in place and relief at knowing I could keep my horse, I was able to enjoy the rest of my senior year of high school.

Approximately one year after Promise and I moved to Triangle Acres, word spread through the barn that the property had been sold to a major land developer. This news did not come as a surprise. All of Montgomery County's farmland was under constant threat of development as more and more people wanted to live in the country. Town planning boards were busy carving up beautiful tracts of fertile farmland so that developers could come in and build, build, build. Although the sale price was never revealed, I imagine the land was sold for several million dollars, a deal that the owners could, understandably, not refuse. We were put on notice that, come the following May, we needed to find other boarding arrangements.

With this certainty in the near future and the added expense of gas money now that I was driving myself, I decided to ask Diane if I could bring Promise to her barn to board over the winter months. Come spring, I planned to join my fellow crew from Triangle Acres once we had located a new facility that fit our budget.

Diane agreed. On December 1, I moved Promise to Was-A-Farm. It felt good to be back there in control of my own hay and grain purchases while knowing that Promise was close to home. On one unusually warm sunny day, I rode her home to my house on Wooded Rd. in Jenkintown, making her stand with her head at the kitchen window to get my mother's attention. Mom and I spent the afternoon watching her graze on our lawn. I wish I had taken a picture of her through the window that I ran to every Christmas morning.

Although, I was back at Was-A-Farm, I saw very little of Diane. She was a senior in college, like my sister Sue, and rarely came home except when her horses needed hay or other supplies. Our relationship was cordial and respectful, but I couldn't help feeling cautious as well. Two decades would pass before Diane and I experienced a most profound reunion.

Until that time however, we spent twenty years wondering whatever happened to each other.

By the end of March, one of the snowiest and coldest winters on record finally loosened its grip. Promise and I celebrated the end of our second winter together looking forward to changes that signaled the arrival of spring. Arrangements had been made to move the Triangle Acre boarders, including Lori and Nimble to a farm between Broadaxe and Ambler.

Hedgewood had been leased for years by a local trainer and his girlfriend; but for some reason, he had left, leaving her to dissolve the lucrative clientele left behind before disappearing herself. In the meantime, the property was purchased by a couple who had recently moved back to the Fort Washington area from the music scene in Los Angeles. Their plan was to subdivide the sprawling twenty-five acres and make millions by developing it. For whatever reason, they were in no hurry and agreed to allow six teens to keep horses at the farm. We agreed to care for their two older geldings, a small pony and two Thoroughbred broodmares who recently returned from a breeding farm in Virginia.

In addition to the five horses, there was a large wether, or neutered male goat, left behind by the fleeing trainer and his girlfriend. Pierre became my best friend. Unfortunately, no one else at the barn appreciated his goat-iness. While horses are friendly and wait to be told what to do, goats are dictators who behave based on their own needs, rarely considering others in the decisions they make. But they are full of fun, and I have always been partial to those characteristics that make a goat a goat. Pierre realized that I understood goats. He followed me frequently out into the cornfields on foot or behind Promise as I rode. I made an effort every day to spend quality time with him, allowing him to roam freely around the barn and property while I rode or worked with Promise. Of course he urinated and dispensed an endless trail of "nanny raisins" all over the barn floor, usually just after it had been swept. He stood on top of tack boxes where the boarders kept their horse supplies. If the spirit moved him, he peed a huge puddle. It's not surprising that he was the least popular animal on the farm.

One day I convinced Lori, now with her own driver's license, to take him with us in her car to McDonalds where we planned to pick up lunch.

Reluctantly, she agreed. Her tack box was a frequent target of the goat's assault. Pierre seemed pleased to join us for the ride and willingly jumped into the backseat of Lori's old station wagon. The minute the window was lowered, Pierre, stuck his head out and enjoyed the breeze that blew his ears straight back.

"Blah, blah, blaaaah," he bleated to every passing motorist.

Our plan was to use the McDonald's drive-thru window so we didn't have to leave Pierre alone in the car. Of course the reaction from the employee was exactly what we had hoped for. She called all of her colleagues to come to have a look at the unusual customer at the drive-thru window. They gave Pierre a complimentary apple pie that he devoured eagerly. Next he tried to join Lori in the driver's seat to see if any more apple pies were forthcoming. She held her temper while she shoved him back into his seat. Then she gave me the "why did we bring him with us" face.

Back to the barn we drove, less than two miles away. Of course just as Lori signaled a right turn into the barn driveway, Pierre began to pee all over the backseat. Goats urinate and immediately dispense fifty little "raisins" as well. This may have been the first time that Lori was truly mad at me and rightly so. Thirty years later we laugh about it, but it was no laughing matter each time she pointed out the lingering stench that plagued that old station wagon.

In another incident Pierre, fond of climbing the steps up to the apartment adjacent to the hayloft, somehow got locked up there. He must have been up there for hours, trying to figure out how to solve his dilemma. I was downstairs cleaning my stall when out the window I saw a huge body fall to the ground from the hayloft doors above. Fearing it was a human, I ran out into the driveway, afraid to look. Standing under the hayloft door was Pierre, his legs splayed, shaking his head and appearing a bit disoriented. He had finally given up hope that he would be rescued and leapt out the window. After another minute or so, he went about his day as if nothing had happened. I never discovered how he got locked into that apartment, but I sure had my suspicions.

My Horse Goes to College...

Too soon summer ended; it was time to enter a new phase-college life. Only a year before, I had dreaded this change. But now, thanks to my father, I was on my way to study horses in an academic setting, and Promise was coming with me.

Centenary opened my eyes to so much that goes on in the horse industry, both positive and negative. My freshman class of fifty young women ran the gambit from backyard horse owner to a Medal Maclay competitor and all levels in between. Although I had some showing experience, my horse could not begin to match the quality of many of the horses that were boarded by students in the barn. Girls discussed their custom made riding boots, terms of their horses' insurance policies and the number of trainers they had worked with over the years. Although Promise was not the expensive show horse that many of these girls possessed, my relationship with her was uniquely close. Many of my classmates only connected with their horses while sitting in the saddle. Somebody else had always been paid to handle all other aspects of the horse's care.

At Centenary I rode many other horses in addition to Promise. As a result I collected a whole "toolbox" of knowledge that I couldn't learn from riding only one horse. Eventually, other students were encouraged to ride her so that her training could benefit from a higher level of experience. Three lessons a week greatly improved my riding skills and developed a whole new philosophy about how to control the horse.

There were opportunities to ride with famous equestrians who came to give clinics on a regular basis. Karen Healy, Ray Francis, Anthony D'Ambrosio, and Susan Harris were among some of the more well-known clinicians. They were all good friends of the Director of Equine Studies.

The Director was a phenomenon of the 1970s hunter-jumper circuit. In her career she had participated in judging, timber racing, show jumping and training. She was the toughest woman I had ever met. Her talent as a trainer and knowledgeable horsewoman served me well in my two years as a student at Centenary because she forced me to grow and to

Finding My Way to Mountain View Farm

take my riding more seriously. One of her suggestions was to sell Promise so I could upgrade to a horse who would take me places in competitions. I was not sure if this was a compliment to my riding potential or an insult to my horse. But the fact that Promise and I were together forever was clear to me and nobody, not even the Director, was going to make me consider severing that bond.

As a student, I gave the Director ultimate respect and absorbed everything she taught me. As a result, my horsemanship skills and confidence with horses grew. My affection for them never abated, thanks to the constant reminder from Promise that it was my love for her species that brought me to this level. But I began to accept that horses were a commodity in an industry that generated millions of dollars each year. I was beginning to explore a world that required keeping emotions in check and displaying a practical approach to riding, assessing horses' needs and accepting their limitations as well as their capabilities.

Through this education I understood the concept of slaughter as a solution to the problem of unwanted horses. The problem was created by people, not the animals themselves. There are worse things for a horse than being killed and harvested for meat. Neglect and abuse are not acceptable alternatives. For whatever reason, physical or behavioral, a horse may need to be disposed of. That was the way the livestock industry worked. Since horses are livestock, slaughter is an acceptable as well as necessary part of the equation.

At this same time, it became clear to me that slaughter would never be an option for my horse. I could only guarantee that she would never die this way by keeping her until her natural death or the decision to have her euthanized humanely would need to be made. I also vowed that none of the horses in my future would face slaughter. That vow was extended to all of my future animals, as I began to picture living my childhood dream in my adult future, not just with horses but with other species as well.

For two years at Centenary I trained to become a tough and practical horseman. I learned to drive a tractor, assess lameness, teach riding, and manage large numbers of horses. Luckily, I forged three great friendships that kept me grounded along the way.

As I moved into our room freshman year, May Hoholick was lying face down on her bed playing Solitaire. She had grown up in New Jersey not too far from Centenary. Her gentle, quiet nature and closeness to her family appealed to me. Although May had taken riding lessons for a few years, she had not spent a great deal of time around horses. With her eagerness to learn and her genuine affection for animals, May became a respectable horseman, finding work with polo horses after graduation. We remained roommates for two years and good friends ever since.

Michelle Hofling grew up eventing in New Hampton, New Hampshire, with horses on her own farm. She shared her passion with two sisters and her mother, while her brother and father tolerated horses but never took to them the way the girls in the family did. Michelle, like me, had attended a small private school before arriving at Centenary, not yet ready to tackle the larger populations of a major university. Unlike me, she had left her horses at home, but knew they were being well cared for by her family while she was away. In her sophomore year she brought a borrowed horse named Kibaba Moon to school with her. Kibaba and Promise became paddock pals during turnout.

After graduation, she became a working student of Olympic Three-day event rider, Denny Emerson, where Michelle aspired to ride at the Preliminary level. She purchased a horse to take her to the top. For several years Michelle trained diligently toward her goal. Eventually, she was married and raised two girls in Maine.

Missy Elleman also grew up in New Jersey in the center of the junior equitation industry. With a dysfunctional family much like Diane's, Missy also buried herself in horses to survive. She rode in the prestigious Maclay division, which qualified her for two finals at Madison Square Garden. Her natural talent has served her well as she has spent her entire career training horses and riders since graduating from Centenary.

Although there were many other unforgettable women I met at Centenary these three have remained part of my life ever since. Together we survived and thrived at Centenary.

Where Centenary excelled with horses, it fell desperately short in social life. In the early 1980s, there were no cell phones, texting, and social

Finding My Way to Mountain View Farm

networking to connect us despite physical distances. When Centenary emptied out on Friday afternoon, students headed home to friends and parties; those of us left behind found little to keep ourselves busy after we met our academic obligations. I began to work at the barn on weekends to pass the time and earn much needed income to help support Promise's upkeep. Because my weekday schedule permitted me to spend only two hours a day at the barn, weekend work allowed me to participate in Promise's care, a task I missed.

By the end of freshman year, the Director began to notice my dedication to the horses and my hard work toward becoming a better rider. She had high expectations for her students and was not impressed by humble beginnings with horses. The Director was more impressed by riders with experience at the upper levels of competition. When she began to offer opportunities for me to ride horses with more sophisticated training, I took it as a compliment. What I lacked in experience I made up for in drive. I was determined to ride at a level based on "feel" of the horse between my hands on the reins and my leg.

By the time sophomore year began, my riding had greatly improved. As a result the Director selected me to compete as a "point" rider at many intercollegiate horse shows. That means that my competition placings were generated into team points. Although the results were forgettable, recognition of my ability in the saddle was quite motivating.

Burgess Meredith spoke at Centenary's graduation in May, 1981. He had just finished filming Rocky III in which his character (Rocky's trainer, Mick) dies. Very much alive, Mr. Meredith, challenged us to go forward and live life to the fullest while pushing ourselves to be the best that we could be. With my Associate's degree in Equine Studies and a grade point average above 3.6, Promise and I headed off to Cornell University where life was about to become a whole lot more exciting.

In the small world of the horse industry, I was not surprised to learn that the Director and Gary Duffy were friends. Although I had met Gary briefly while touring Asbury Hill Farm during a college visit two years prior, it was the Director's good word that got me into the barn. Asbury Hill Farm was a private barn with no Cornell affiliation. Most of the boarders were local adults and children who trained fancy horses with Gary to show at recognized horse shows. Many even traveled with their horses to Florida in the winter to compete on the Sunshine Circuit while avoiding the miserable central New York winter weather.

The facility was neat and tidy with several grass turnout paddocks that surrounded large open spaces for riding. A well maintained outdoor ring sat on top of a knoll above the barn. This ring was not useable for a good portion of the year that I was in Ithaca. Most of my riding took place in the indoor arena that, again, although not fancy, served a useful purpose.

The farm's insurance plan required supervision on the premises twenty-four hours a day, seven days a week. Therefore, a three bedroom apartment served as housing for a revolving door of residents who traded rent for "barn watch." The cast of characters who lived in that apartment during my time at Asbury Hill could provide enough drama for a whole series of books.

A few of the boarders belonged to college students, like me, from Cornell or nearby Ithaca College. The owners were good riders but not necessarily horsemen who lingered in the barn to help with chores. They came to the barn when they could find time in heavy academic schedules, rode their horses and disappeared quickly afterwards. I needed the barn, often staying longer than I should have. Perhaps it is no wonder that my grades suffered with my priorities out of order. The fact remains that the barn kept me sane and safe when the pressures of trying to fit in academically and socially made life difficult.

With two years of maturity and college experience under my belt, I arrived at the New York State College of Agriculture at Cornell University to major in Animal Science. Nothing could have prepared me for the academic expectations of Cornell, least of all Centenary. Although Centenary could claim rock star Debra Harry, (from the musical group, Blondie) as its most successful graduate, Cornell had graduated top officials in every industry in the country, including medical research, politics, education, and finance to name a few. Achieving academic success was about to become my greatest challenge. It took a whole lot of restructuring and prioritizing even to entertain the chance of graduating. After a rocky start

Finding My Way to Mountain View Farm

and emotional upset that alarmed my parents enough to drive four hours to help me pull it together, I did succeed, graduating respectfully with nothing but passing grades.

Eventually, I found a niche at Cornell with people who did not share my all-consuming interest, but who still valued my friendship. On campus I was forced to broaden my perspective. Most of my acquaintances were not horse people. They had other interests including academics and socializing. Broadening my horizons made it easier to join in.

In doing so I stepped outside the horse industry and turned around to look at it from a new perspective. It stared back at me in the form of a Venn diagram with two intersecting circles. The section on the left contained the horses themselves in all colors, shapes and sizes. The section on the right contained all the people associated with horses including trainers, veterinarians, blacksmiths, grooms and riders. And in the middle where the two circles overlapped was a big fat dollar sign. When I stared at the circle on the left, my heart felt full and content; but when I stared at the circle on the right, I felt anxious and disconnected. Exactly what it all meant, I didn't really know.

JOB OF A LIFETIME...

When spring break arrived in March, 1982, I began to think about a job for the summer. I had spent the past two summers as a "glassware cleaning" technician at McNeil Laboratories in Fort Washington, Pennsylvania. There, within the windowless walls of McNeil, I washed glassware for all of the research laboratories. The job was lucrative and interesting as I observed many commercial laboratories in the throes of groundbreaking drug therapy development.

I also witnessed research that required the use of live animals. I have been conflicted on this subject ever since. We humans owe a debt of gratitude to the millions of animals who sacrifice their lives to provide necessary testing for every drug, medical procedure and piece of medical technology that we depend on today. I accept that animal testing is a necessary and a vital factor in the research equation, but we need to do more to make these animals' existences as pleasant as possible in exchange for the sacrifice they make.

After two years at McNeil I was ready to spend the summer outdoors in the fresh air, if only I could find the right job. Thanks to my Dad, the perfect job was only one interview away.

F. Eugene Dixon, a Philadelphia philanthropist who owned a portion of the Philadelphia 76ers Basketball team, also provided considerable financial support for world class show jumpers and Dressage horses as well as for race horses. He lived with his family on an estate that he inherited from his uncle, George D. Widener, in the early 1970s.

Erdenheim Farm, (German for earthly home), was a 400 plus acre green oasis just beyond the city limits of Philadelphia. Wissahickon Creek meanders through the farm's pristine pastures. The property was a collection of facilities including a beef farm, sheep farm and horse farm. Widener purchased the farm around 1912 and used it to raise and train race horses. In the 1980s the racehorses were long gone. The facility housed show jumpers in what had been the stallion barn, Dressage horses in the training barn and a potpourri of retired horses and ponies across Stenton Avenue in what had been the mare barn. An indoor riding ring had been added to the farm much later to accommodate the training of show horses rather than race horses.

Dixon's daughter, Ellin, was busy training her Dressage horses with the help of top trainer Gunnar Ostergaard. Olympic rider Michael Matz trained show jumpers for other clients as well as for Mr. Dixon at Erdenheim.

Unlike most world class riders today, Michael came from humble beginnings. He grew up in Reading, Pennsylvania, the son of a plumber; he only began riding horses after an accidental encounter with them in his mid-teens. However, his natural talent and attention to detail established him in one of the greatest show jumping careers. Before he retired to train racehorses full time, Michael had competed in several Olympic Games, World Cups and other international competitions.

My father just happened to know the woman who worked as Mr. Dixon's private secretary. While I was growing up crazy about horses, she used to tell my father that I should work at Erdenheim Farm someday.

In April, 1982 Michael Matz was looking for a summer employee to help out in the Jumper barn.

On a promising spring day, I drove out to Erdenheim to meet Michael for an interview. After conferring with a groom in the Dressage barn, I found Michael riding in the indoor ring. Not wanting to disturb him, I was relieved when he brought his big shiny chestnut stallion down to the walk and approached me as if he had been expecting the interruption. His friendly Hollywood smile put me at ease as we made our introductions.

"The job requires cleaning stalls and grooming the horses every day before and after they're ridden," he stated, still mounted on the large stallion who was now dozing peacefully in a large sun-spot at the arena's doorway. "Do you ride?" he added as an afterthought.

"Yes," I responded, unaware that I would actually get to ride horses and be paid for such a pleasure here at this beautiful farm. Then I offered him a brief synopsis of my educational experience.

A few minutes later, I thanked him as he returned to his training session. I lingered at the rail to watch this exceptional athlete, now my employer, at his craft. I had seen Michael ride many times over the years at the Devon Horse Show and the American Gold Cup. In my adolescent years, I had even been brave enough to approach him for an autograph. But at this moment, I watched him through the eyes of a horseman who was really beginning to understand the rider's role in the saddle. His lean long-legged frame remained soft and light. With perfect timing, Michael's body whispered an appropriate aid that politely asked the horse to transition into the canter. In addition to Michael's perfect position, I was taken by the steadiness of his hands on the reins. The whole atmosphere in the ring at that moment remained focused, calm and successful. I wondered how many different horses he had ridden in his lifetime to develop such a gift. After spring break, I returned to school with enthusiastic anticipation of my summer job, which would begin shortly after Promise and I returned home at the end of May.

In 1982 spring finally took hold of Ithaca after two late April snowstorms. To catch up, the sun came out and kept the temperatures well into the 70s throughout the two weeks of final exams. My classmates and I used our breaks from studying to explore the natural wonders of the gorges that carve out the unique landscape that is Ithaca. Then, with my first year at Cornell having ended satisfactorily, I was on my way home to work in an elite show jumping barn.

Promise was going to be boarded for the summer across the street from the former Hedgewood, (now completely leveled and awaiting construction of many cookie cutter homes), at Willow Lake Farm, a boarding and breeding facility with lots of trails to explore along with an indoor ring and several outdoor rings. With so many housing developments destroying farm land, the option to board in somebody's backyard and take care of my own horse was not possible. Plus, the long hours at Erdenheim kept me from spending endless hours with Promise. Willow Lake was not far from Erdenheim so I could make the trip after work every day. Unlike my schedule at McNeil with weekends off, Erdenheim required a six-day work week with Mondays off. The chance to work with these elite horses was worth the sacrifice.

My first week working at Erdenheim Farm got underway just before Memorial Day weekend. During the summer months, the show jumpers traveled a circuit of competitions all over the northeastern region of the country. After each show, the horses returned to the farm for a few days of rest before hitting the road again for a new venue. Not all the horses attended every show, so some of the grooms had to remain behind to care for those left at home. In addition to working with the jumpers, Michael was beginning to dabble in the racing industry. He kept a couple of race horses who were recovering from injuries at Erdenheim.

Although I worked in the Jumper barn, I was in charge of the recovering race horses and two retirees who resided in the Dressage barn where Dixon's daughter Ellin also kept an impressive collection of Dressage horses. Here I began to connect with Dressage and gravitate toward the training methods used to produce horses that appear to dance when ridden correctly. Through osmosis in the presence of these great equine athletes, I began to get it.

While working at Erdenheim Farm, I also became impressed by the rhythm of routine that ticked away each day. I witnessed the effect of

 Finding My Way to Mountain View Farm

this significant detail in calm and happy stallions who worked under saddle agreeably. In exchange the horses received elite care from grooms who tended to their every need while keeping them impeccably polished and conditioned.

My job began at 6:30 each morning when I turned out my charges in their assigned paddocks. Then I cleaned stalls, a task that took considerable time due to the depth of shavings or straw used for bedding. After my assigned horses were tended to, I made my way over to assist with the chores at the Jumper barn. An endless amount of laundry including saddle pads and leg wraps needed to be sorted through, folded or rolled. We cleaned saddles and bridles daily, along with draw reins, martingales, and tendon boots. There was always hay to stack, a floor to sweep, or cobwebs to clear; by the end of the day, which included a visit to ride Promise, I was completely worn out. On days when Michael didn't ride, we finished at the barn by 11:00 a.m. Then we each took turns coming back to the barn to "pick" stalls and feed the horses in the late afternoon.

My favorite assignment was taking care of the retiree barn on weekends when old man Fenton had his time off. Fenton had been a jockey and exercise rider in the 40s and 50s during the Widener racing days. I don't think he was as old as he looked, but certainly a lifetime caring for and riding horses had hung extra years on his frame.

The retiree barn housed some of Erdenheim's most legendary equine prize winners, including show jumper Mighty Ruler and an ancient white pony that had collected ribbons for Ellin when she was a child. Three white geldings of various sizes rounded out the herd. The retirees lived outside most of the summer, but they returned to the barn to be fed in the afternoon so they could be examined carefully every twenty-four hours. The old stone barn provided a welcome escape from the hot sunny fields where the horses spent their days. I loved to study the architecture of the barn with its heavy wooden stall doors and cobblestone aisle that was always a challenge to sweep after I dispensed hay to each occupied stall.

The office served as a museum for some of the accolades awarded during Erdenheim's racing era. There were moth eaten wool blankets or coolers and a few tarnished silver trophies on display around the room. No doubt this memorabilia meant something to Fenton, but to me they appeared rather sad as they sat aging under layers of dust that had accumulated over the years.

Two of my charges included pensioners who should have resided in the retiree barn across the street. One, an old jumper named Grande, had won the American Gold Cup in the early 70s. Although he had been a talented bay Hanoverian gelding, he looked like a pregnant broodmare. He also had an extremely large head that earned him the affectionate nickname, "Big Head." Now he spent his days as a babysitter for some of the younger horses who found solitary turnout too stressful. Grande's good nature had a calming effect on each pasture-mate, encouraging the horse to graze peacefully in the paddock.

The other retiree that I cared for was an aged black Thoroughbred stallion named Jaipur. This son of acclaimed sire Nasrullah became famous after running one of the most impressive horse races ever witnessed at the 1962 Travers Stakes at Saratoga Race Course. He and Ridan battled it out all the way from the starting gate until a photo declared Jaipur the winner at the finish line.

It surprised me that Jaipur was not very big, only 15.1 hands. However, each morning when I turned him out in his own lush pasture, he proved to me how quickly he could accelerate from a standstill. Once he heard the click of the metal clip on the lead rope, he bolted with all his might, crow-hopping on arthritic hind legs before settling down to graze after the effort.

Every afternoon Jaipur and Grande, along with the young race horses, were brought back to the barn with a stop at the grooming stall to be vacuumed and brushed. I marveled at how well Jaipur tolerated all of my fussing over him since he was not a cuddly horse. Race horses experience so much activity before they retire from the track to the breeding shed. Jaipur seemed to accept all aspects of handling; aside from his exuberance at turnout, he was always the perfect gentleman. Once impeccably groomed, Jaipur was returned to his own stall. There was always a chance that Mr. Dixon might pay a visit to the barn in the evening to show off the horses to dinner guests or other visitors, and the horses were expected to look sleek and shiny for the viewing.

In addition to Jaipur and Grande, there was a five year old Thoroughbred stallion named Royal Rouge (Rougey). Unlike the two retirees, Rougey's robust long legged physique and 16 plus hand height suggested the power and speed that he was bred for. Unfortunately, his typical "champagne-stem-glass" ankles were ultimately his undoing. While Rougey was recovering and rehabilitating from a tendon or joint injury, his future was being considered for other equestrian disciplines besides racing. Needless to say, I fell in love with him. His dark bay, almost black, coat with no white markings presented a striking picture of the equine athlete. In addition to his care, I was asked to ride him daily. The goal was to teach him how to carry himself. Athletically speaking; I encouraged him to push off of the ground with his hind legs instead of pulling with his front legs. Rougey, therefore, was schooled in a frame propelled by his hindquarters. Riding him was a huge treat that I looked forward to every day despite the way he sometimes pulled at the reins like a freight train.

In addition to the equine characters that I cared for were the human characters that I worked with at Erdenheim Farm. There were eight of us who groomed horses for Michael. Many of my co-workers were gay men who regaled the rest of us with hysterical tales of their escapades. I received quite an education as I cleaned stalls and rubbed on horses. Edited versions of their stories provided me with anecdotes to share at the dinner table with my own family.

Then one Sunday in mid-June, The *Philadelphia Inquirer* Magazine published a shocking article about a devastating and fatal disease that appeared to be plaguing the gay community. The article pointed an accusing finger at patrons of the bathhouses and other communal gay hangouts. This was one of the first exposés written about AIDS. Looking back, I think that my parents, although concerned, handled the situation with dignity and grace. They certainly wanted me to be aware of their concern for the fact that I worked alongside men at high risk at a time when very little was known about how AIDS spread from bloodstream to bloodstream. They wanted me to be careful. They also respected the fact that I truly cared for these people who shared my love of horses. Sadly and not surprisingly, a handsome Dutch groom, who was particularly gifted with horses, succumbed to the disease a few years later.

Although working for Michael proved to be the equine job of a lifetime, it was his barn manager who had the most profound influence on my future with horses. Karen Golding was a thirty-two-year-old English woman whose gentle nature combined with immense knowledge and experience around world class horses. She was a pleasure to work for due mostly to her lack of ego. Karen offered her knowledge willingly. I tried to absorb everything she taught me about bandaging, tail pulling, feeding, saddle fitting, tendon boots, polo wraps, shoe studs, banking stalls, and much more.

Many grooms at the world class level are discouraged from displaying affection toward the horses in their care. Karen was the exception. Her love and devotion for the great Jet Run was no doubt one of the reasons he thrived in the sport. Although Michael as Jet's trainer and rider certainly felt a special bond with the horse, Karen was Jet's "mother." She knew the leggy bay gelding inside and out and had traveled all over the U.S. and Europe with him as his exclusive caregiver. Long after he retired, she still made frequent visits to Erdenheim's mare barn where Jet, Mighty Ruler and Grande spent their last years together. With Karen's blessing, Jet was euthanized at age 28.

In 2007, Karen was the first groom inducted into the Show Jumping Hall of Fame for her years of dedication to the horses of the sport. Today, Karen works as a Federation Equestre Internationale, (FEI) chief steward at horse shows up and down the East coast and Europe. In 2010, I reconnected with Karen so that I could write her story for *Practical Horseman Magazine*. It was a great privilege to tell about her incredible life and career with horses.

After a successful and educational summer working at Erdenheim, Promise and I returned to Cornell for senior year. Maturity played the biggest role in my continuing success at Cornell. In Ithaca, I was forced to stand on my own two feet and advocate for myself. It was here that I began to realize that life after graduation was a big question mark that included Promise. What would happen to us? Where would we go? Could I keep her forever as I had vowed to do? I was going to have to face so many decisions in the next year, and I wasn't even sure what I wanted to do with my degree. For the first time in my life, there was no specific plan on the horizon as there had been after high school. The future was full of unknowns. In the fall of my senior year, I further complicated all of these uncertainties when I adopted a four- month- old Dachshund puppy.

And Now We Are Three...

When I was growing up, my family was large-dog territory. My parents and siblings never considered having a little dog; they attached negative labels such as yappy, snappy and awful to such an animal. Our neighbors, the Putneys, had a Chihuahua named Tiny Tim who jumped at the back door when the bell rang. We were certain that he remained suspended in air for a few seconds to bark out the window before dropping to the ground and launching himself again.

No one in my family had anything positive to say about poor Tiny. My mother could not say his name without a tone of disgust. In truth, I thought Tiny was so adorable that I loved to hold him on my lap. Because he lived in a perpetual state of shivering, his body, with its short coat, was always toasty warm against me.

After Tiny, the Putney's moved on to a pug named Princess. Aside from snorting and wheezing through life, Princess was also a cute little dog. After Princess, there was a Shi-tzu named Tigger. It occurred to me that the Putneys' were onto something. They had a closer relationship with their little dogs than my family had with our large dog. Nobody at our house snuggled with the dog. Nobody.

So began my fascination with small dogs, particularly Dachshunds. I loved their long sad faces and their sleek coats, so horse-like. Of course there would be no Dachshunds in our house. My family shopped for a golden retriever in the summer of 1975 after the sudden death of our nine year old collie, Bonnie. If I thought I could have changed the collective family mind to think about getting a little dog, believe me, I would have.

So Dachshund ownership was put on the "When I am an adult I will have…" list, (as sacred as the one that contained possibilities for my future horses' names) and stored in my desk. I knew there would come a day when I could sit with small dogs on my lap in the evening after a long day spent with horses.

Eric was a leftover. His three siblings found homes before they were eight weeks old. Eric grew quickly, and in no time the adorable eight-week-old puppy was four months old. The breeder kept him in a kennel so that she didn't have to address his housebreaking needs. Meanwhile, a new litter of "Dachsie" puppies was on its way, so all of the breeder's energy was directed toward the expected babies.

When the fall semester of my senior year began at Cornell, I moved into an apartment with three roommates. Our new-found independence led us to live off campus in student housing at the bottom of Stewart Avenue in College Town. It just so happened that the apartment allowed pets.

Two weeks into the school year, I was asked to housesit for a friend of a boarder at Asbury Hill Farm. The homeowner arranged for me to meet some of her neighbors since I would be living in the house with a large orange cat named, Max for four weeks. As Eric's breeder was one of the neighbors, it did not take long for us to connect my love of Dachshunds with a little leftover liver colored puppy in her kennel. We arranged a time for me to meet him.

Keep in mind that, although I had always wanted a Dachshund, I had never actually had one or seen a puppy of the breed. My only experience, up close and personal, was with Ursula, a liver colored Dachshund that belonged to a friend from Diane's barn. I wanted Ursula to like me and I tried desperately to befriend her. However, she was always leery of strangers and curled her lip in a growl to prove it. I loved her sleek look. Despite her cantankerous personality, I still wanted a Dachshund of my own.

Now close to four months old, the puppy was really a gawky teenager. The first thing I saw was the bump on the top of his head. Then he raised his head, alerted by my approach to the kennel where he lived. His large head was dominated by two almond shaped brown eyes. Dachshunds have very long pointed noses as adults, but this puppy's snout still had not reached its full potential. His short stubby front legs turned out so that his feet stood at forty-five degree angles. The expression on his face looked pitifully sad, a look that all Dachshunds have perfected to tug at unsuspecting human heartstrings. His shiny body enticed me to stroke him, confirming how smooth and wonderful he felt to touch. A familiar feeling swept over me, reminiscent of the immediate connection I had made with Promise on that fateful day only five years before.

In hindsight it might have been more considerate of me to discuss the arrival of a dog with my roommates prior to arriving home with him two days later. They were very supportive but nervous about all the destruction for which puppies are notorious. I reasoned that since I would be living out in Cayuga Heights for the next four weeks, the puppy's training and routine would be well established before I moved back into the apartment.

Max, the cat, accepted our presence in his house amicably as Eric and I began our life together. While Max's people toured the northern Canadian Provinces, collecting checkmarks in their field guides from flashing glimpses of rare bird species, Eric endured a crash course in housebreaking and manners. Max's owners had given me permission to keep the puppy with me while I was house sitting, but I still owed it to them not to leave any signs that a puppy had lived there.

Committed to will power and strict rules, I began training him that first night. I put Eric in the bathroom along with his little blanket and a few chew toys. Next, I kissed him goodnight, shut the door and left. Then I tiptoed down the hall to the room assigned to me, flicked off the light switch and climbed into one of the twin beds. As I lay there waiting for sleep, I kept wondering what he was doing. It was so quiet! Was it really going to be this easy? Lucky me, I got the dog that...

"Oom, oom, oooooom," came the whimper from down the hall followed by, "Owww, owowow, Oowww." Then there was silence. After a few minutes, the howling began again. My heart broke for the little being sitting all alone on his blanket, no doubt wondering where he was and why he was suddenly all alone again.

"Don't go to him. He will be all right. He has to learn," I recited over and over in my brain as I lay wide awake, desperate to sleep so that I could function in the morning. Eventually, he did settle down and we were both able to sleep a few hours before the early morning sun poured through the windows. Eric had survived his first night. He was overjoyed to see me when I opened the bathroom door and lifted him from the floor. In my arms he was warm and wiggly. His long nose poked at my face and neck as he tried desperately to lick me.

"Where have you been?" his darting tongue seemed to ask. Outside, tiptoeing through the morning dew, he tended to his business before zipping around the yard with a wild case of the "crazies" spurred on by his release from the bathroom prison. Dachshunds are full of exuberance and interest in the world around them. However, they love nothing more than to be close to their special person. After his penned-up energy was spent, he curled up tight to me on the couch and rested quietly while I tended to my reading assignment on pig breeding.

As he lay with his eyes squeezed shut, I abandoned my required reading to study his tiny form nestled by my hip. My hand could not resist caressing his smooth coat, especially where it glistened on his long ears. I couldn't resist palpating the little black toenails that punctuated the ends of his pudgy paws. This was my dog, a small dog who would forever remain the size of a puppy I could hold in my arms.

For the next two or three nights, Eric and I went through the same routine. I placed him on his blanket in the bathroom, closed the door and crawled into bed. Just as I was about to drift off to sleep, Eric began to whine and whimper pathetically. Eventually, he quieted down and I was able to get at least two or three hours of sleep. In the morning he was overjoyed to see me. I was exhausted.

On school days I had to keep him in the bathroom for the hours that I went to class. I never had to leave him longer than three or four hours at a time, but I still felt guilty. Finally, Eric took care of the matter himself.

Five or six nights later, while I was preparing for bed, brushing my teeth and washing my face in Eric's bathroom, I left the door open so that he could have just a few more minutes to run up and down the hallway. I was only half aware of him as he entered and exited the bathroom repeatedly. When I eventually tuned into what Eric had been busy doing while I was preoccupied, tears welled in my eyes.

My puppy had made several trips back and forth from the bathroom to the bedroom. With each trip he had carried and deposited one of his toys by the bed. On the final trip he had dragged his yellow blanket to the room as well. He was clearly communicating that too much of his time was spent waiting for freedom from the bathroom prison. Sadly, I carried all of his hard work back to the bathroom and assembled it for the night. The image of his confused expression when I turned off the light and closed the door burned in my mind as I pulled the covers up to my chin and prepared for the whimpering routine to begin. As I lay there waiting for the inevitable, I wondered why I felt that my puppy had to stay in the bathroom all night. What exactly was I accomplishing by forcing him to wait in that lonely room? It was bad enough and unavoidable to leave him in there during the day. Wasn't I throwing away valuable hours of our life together? When the whimpering began a short time later, I did not grit my teeth and repeat my affirmations of strength until he quieted down. This time I climbed out of bed and hurried down the hall to the bathroom. Without saying a word, I opened the door and tip-toed across the cold floor. After I scooped him up in my arms, I carried him down the hall to the bedroom and placed him on the bed. Then I crawled back under the sheets and settled on my side. Eric curled up behind my knees on top of the blanket. I glanced at his silhouette against the moonlight that sneaked in the window. His little head rotated like a periscope as he absorbed the view in his new location.

Just as I was about to drift off to sleep, Eric raised himself up on all four feet, then slowly moved toward my head that was peeking out at the top of the blanket. With his nose he pushed his way under the sheets and turned around so that his head was just below my chin. Next, he pressed his toasty body up tight against my chest. As I instinctively wrapped my arms around him, my heart filled with love for this little being who had only viewed the world from the inside of a cage and a dark bathroom. At last it became clear to me why I had a dog. For the rest of his life, he slept under the covers, close to me. The warmth that radiated from his body gave me comfort and a good night's sleep.

He was my little dependent who gave me good reason to stay home to study. My daily routine now included responsibility for a little dog who relied on me to provide food and comfort. As a pet owner, I had to consider him in every plan that I made. Unlike Promise, whose daily visit was scheduled into my day, Eric had to be considered all day. He was my constant companion when I wasn't attending classes. Occasionally, I took him with me to class where he would curl up on the seat next to me, remaining quiet as a mouse during the lecture, despite the frowns of the academic professionals. Eric went to the barn with me every day. Several dogs attended the barn regularly and Eric soon became a member of the pack. Gary had a Jack Russell Terrier named Lammy, and there was also an older black Lab named Cubby whom Eric looked forward to visiting with most of all.

Cubby's story began one day when she showed up at Asbury Hill Farm during one of its horse shows. It wasn't the performances of the lovely horses that attracted her but smell of burgers and fries that wafted across the fields from the food truck. Nobody seemed concerned about the presence of the friendly English style Lab who graciously consumed anything offered to her and begged for more. Everyone assumed that she belonged to one of the farms attending the show. After the food truck shut down and the last van had pulled out of the parking lot, Cubby lingered in the driveway, wondering where the bounty of gastric delights had disappeared. That's when my friend Lisa took notice of the dog.

Lisa Eklund was the barn manager at Asbury Hill Farm when I was a student at Cornell. Six years older than I, Lisa had graduated from Oneonta College with a degree in English before taking the job at Asbury Hill. She was Gary's right hand, for which he owes her a debt of gratitude for years of dedication and friendship. She has ridden the ups and downs of the horse industry, finally settling in at SUNY Morrisville where she is an Assistant Professor in Equine Studies. The position allows her to work with horses professionally while pursuing other interests.

Lisa had grown up with a horse of her own; and, like me, couldn't seem to get them out of her system. She and I became close friends over the two

Finding My Way to Mountain View Farm

and half years that I lived in Ithaca. We socialized with the same circle of friends, both at and away from the barn. Lisa attended Rod's and my wedding, but within a few years I lost track of her. Fifteen years later, I found her again, living not too far outside of the Adirondacks. We have been in close contact ever since.

Everyone assumed that Cubby had been left behind by competitors who packed up all their gear but forgot one of their passengers. After a few phone calls, it became apparent that Cubby was a local resident who was in no hurry to leave at the end of the day. Lisa took Cubby home with her. After a few days of investigation, she determined that Cubby lived down the road from the farm with the father of the dog's mistress. However, the young girl was away at college and although Cubby was provided with food and water, she was otherwise ignored.

The family accepted Lisa's offer to take the dog; and for two years Cubby accompanied Lisa wherever she went, including to a smorgasbord of horse show venues throughout the northeast. Cubby became a regular attendee at every food tent, working the crowd with her docile, loving personality. Needless to say she kept up a hefty physique from rewards of generous helpings.

Lisa gave Cubby the best years of the dog's life and was understandably shocked when months later, the young mistress asked to take Cubby back. Thankfully, Gary Duffy stepped in and voiced his strong opinion about the wonderful life that Cubby was living with Lisa. Two years later, at age eleven, Cubby died of cancer.

Late spring, 1983, was time to plan for the upcoming summer. Since I was returning to Cornell in the fall, I made the difficult decision to leave Promise behind at Asbury Hill Farm. Finances were now even more of a consideration in my future decision-making plans since graduation loomed ahead in January. A woman named Gail, who worked as a public librarian, had agreed to lease Promise through the summer months. She had been riding Promise in her weekly lessons with my friend Lisa as her instructor and vowed to visit Promise several days a week to keep an eye on her and to keep her fit with frequent riding. I was confident that Promise would receive excellent care. Horseless for the first time in six years, Eric and I headed home for the summer.

I had been asked to return to Erdenheim Farm and happily accepted the offer. With anticipation of another great working experience with horses, I began my job in late May. Arriving at Erdenheim I discovered that nothing had changed from the previous summer. The same grooms, the same quality of horses and Michael's impeccable attention to detail were all in exactly the same place they had been the summer before.

However, something inside of me had changed. I was confused about why I wasn't feeling as inspired by the opportunity to work a second summer at the Jumper barn. I was beginning to comprehend the great divide between very wealthy horse owners and people like the grooms and me who loved horses, but would never compete on, least of all own, the quality of horseflesh that resided at Erdenheim. The owners who came to ride horses that were trained by Michael were not necessarily horsemen interested in caring for their horses once they had dismounted. Like many of my classmates at Centenary and several of the boarders in Gary Duffy's barn, their endless financial resources allowed them the luxury of purchasing expensive animals. But these riders/owners relied on other people to care for their horses.

Now that I had put away my childish view of horses as pets, I was forced to accept horses as an industry fueled by checks and balances. Competition was the barometer that determined the net worth of the animal despite the degree of talent possessed by the rider. On the verge of financial independence, I needed to figure out where my niche with horses was going to fit into this equation. If my career didn't focus on horses, what would I do with Promise? How could I afford to keep her on the income from an entry-level position in a yet to be determined career? These questions haunted me as the summer months pressed onward toward my final college semester.

In the meantime, I did the best that I could with my job. One of my charges was a little unnamed bay filly who had spent months recovering after having a bone chip removed from her knee. In addition to her daily care, I was also assigned the task of lightly breezing or galloping her out on Erdenheim's one mile training track. This was new territory for me and to be honest it was the first time that I had ever been frightened on top of a horse. Up until this time, I would have boasted that I felt more comfortable sitting in the saddle dealing with horse antics than standing on the ground at the other end of a lead rope. But galloping at twenty-five to thirty miles per hour ignited anxiety as I was forced to surrender total control to the horse. All I could concentrate on was the possibility that she was going to trip and fall. Surely I would break my neck on impact with the ground. Relief flooded my extremities every time a session ended and Michael was satisfied with her performance for the day.

Knowing that I was without a horse of my own for the summer, one of my favorite jumper grooms, Jimmy Herring, volunteered me to ride Michael's accountant's gelding. The horse was boarded at the Mounted Police barn in Fairmount Park, just a few miles from Erdenheim. Twice a week I was paid to take Equity, a large chestnut warmblood-crossbred for a ride through the park. Once again I couldn't believe I was actually going to be paid for the experience of riding a safe and easy horse through one of the most well-maintained city parks in the country. There was no turnout at the police barn. Therefore, my two outings a week were the only times that Equity was out of his stall. My empathy for this dear horse prevented me from ever missing a ride. I could not accept the thought of him spending endless hours in a stall with no prospects of getting fresh air.

LEARNING TO FLY...

The summer did distract me as I worked with the Erdenheim horses. Because the indoor ring at the farm had an insulated roof to prevent loud noises from spooking the horses, it was a prime site for nesting birds. Early in the summer, the underside of the roof was full of sparrows and starlings that dove in and out through the large doors to bring food to their young. It was not uncommon to find casualties of these nests after they tumbled thirty feet to the sand footing below. We found most of the babies dead or near to it; and although the Dressage grooms and I tried to coax them with food and water, the ones who had life in them succumbed within hours of our rescue. It was depressing as we counted nine dead baby birds in the early weeks of the summer. One day a baby starling was brought to me from the indoor ring.

"Another one?" I whined, not wishing to witness the death of yet another baby bird. This time I was not going to invest any more emotion in a doomed baby. I wrapped it in a towel and left it in a bucket in the warm end of the feed room. In the morning I planned to remove the tiny carcass and put it in the manure pile. The next morning, the little starling startled me when I peeked into the towel and found myself staring into his large yellow beak, gaping with anticipation of food!

"Now what am I supposed to do?" I wondered out loud. I still had to walk Grande over to the barn for babysitting duty and turn Jaipur and the filly out in their paddocks. There was no time to tend to this little fellow for at least forty-five minutes. I lifted him out of the towel and held him up for a better look. His pin feathers stuck straight out all over his bony little body. The stretchy sheathes that bound the feathers as they matured were flaking off into the palm of my hand. The feathers on the top of his head had already shed their casings, giving him a slick sheen above protruding eyes. The bright yellow beak dominated his face, making his overall expression look pouty. At the moment, he was holding his beak open and bobbing his head up and down, trying desperately to get someone to poke food into his mouth. His tiny body felt cool to the touch. I decided to stash him in my shirt while I tended to my immediate chores. That would give me a chance to think about what to feed him when I finally got caught up with my work.

Tucking my shirt into my jeans allowed me to place the little bird, now wrapped in a paper towel, above my belt where he could benefit from the warmth of my body. He remained quite still while I went about beginning my work day. The time allowed me to put together a plan for the little bird's meal. I had a tuna fish sandwich in my lunch bag. I was pretty sure that starlings that frequent trash dumpsters probably prefer an omnivorous diet. Since he was a juvenile, protein would be the most important nutrient. Besides, the only other items in my lunch were a banana and some cookies.

Once the horses were secure in their paddocks, I was able to tend to the baby starling now beginning to wiggle under my shirt. After dissecting my tuna fish sandwich, I held a small chunk in front of his beak. The reaction was immediate. As if I had tripped some kind of trap, the gaping beak sprang open and begged for the fish. I poked a piece in. The baby bird snapped his beak shut and began to bob his head up and down, gulping at the mouthful. In no time, the beak gaped for more of the lifesaving fish. I poked more fish into his mouth and continued until he stopped asking for it. Then I filled a cup with water and carefully dripped some onto the end of his beak. Once again the beak sprang open and the head bobbing began as he appeared to "gargle" the water. Once he'd had his fill, I wrapped him in a terry cloth towel and placed him back in the bucket. So began one of the most extraordinary bonds that I have ever shared with an animal.

I called him Peeper because of the constant peeping noise he made whenever I talked to him or lifted him out of his bucket. The baby starling imprinted on me immediately after that first feeding. He didn't seem to care that I was not a real bird nor did he care that his original nest had been replaced by a metal bucket. He was easy to please as long as he was fed and watered regularly. Later that first day, I purchased hamburger and fed it to him raw by rolling little pieces into "worms" that slid down his throat more easily. "Eat like a bird" did not apply to Peeper. He ate a lot and he ate often. As a result, he grew quickly. When his pin feathers were finally released from their bindings, their dark sheen revealed itself.

He lived in his bucket for several weeks, accompanying me to work and home every day. He got mixed reactions from my co-workers, having endeared himself to the Dressage grooms, (all women), who asked about him often. The Jumper grooms were not as impressed and wondered why I was going to so much trouble to save a bird that hung out around the garbage dumpster. They had a point, but to me he was a living creature that needed my care. I was not capable of turning him away. I should mention that I was never sure of Peeper's gender, but I referred to him as "he" for the duration of the summer.

Eventually, Peeper began to spend a lot of time flopping about in the bucket, exercising his wings. I knew that eventually he would need to learn to fly. Since his mother was not around to teach him, I had to figure out how to provide the necessary lessons. In the meantime, he liked to practice perching on the handle of the bucket as it hung on a nail in the tack room of the Dressage barn.

As Peeper began to make more and more appearances outside of the bucket, I had to supervise Eric's intense interest in our new family member. I am not certain what he would have done if I left him alone with the baby bird, but I was not about to find out.

In the middle of the summer, I was able to take three days off from work to visit with my family who were vacationing at the seashore in Avalon, New Jersey. Peeper, Eric and I drove for two and half hours in sweltering heat to arrive at the cottage that my parents had rented on the bay. All of my siblings were visiting as well, including Sue, her husband Steve, and their cat Bruce. I hung Peeper's bucket on a nail in the screened porch where he could watch swallow and seagull activity outside. Of course Bruce thought that having a bird indoors to watch was a marvelous idea. With tail twitching, the cat spent hours staring at Peeper through the sliding door, planning to pounce on him the moment somebody opened it.

While at the seashore, I taught Peeper to fly. Standing out on the pebbled yard by the dock, I began by throwing him gently into the air about two feet above my head, forcing him to use his wings to soften his landing on the ground. From the first throw, Peeper knew just what to do. After a few days, he was able to remain in flight for a short distance before landing. At this time he began to utter his unique raspy version of the adult starling. He knew that it brought "Big Bird" mother running to rescue him when he had flown a little too far away for comfort. After three days, we were on our way home and back to work at Erdenheim.

Peeper's growth over the three-day vacation could have been measured in leaps and bounds. Once back at the farm, he wanted to fly all the time. His newly discovered mobility stirred a mixture of emotions in me. From the moment I discovered him alive in the bucket on the second day, I accepted the fact that if he made it to adulthood, I would have to let him go back into the wild where he belonged. Of course my heart was not convinced that this was a good idea.

Over the years, I had had the opportunity to rehabilitate all kinds of wildlife, including squirrels, a raccoon, and a number of baby birds. Aside from the raccoon, all of them eventually died from digestive distress brought on by ingesting the wrong formula or food. The deaths of these animals broke my heart. Peeper was surviving; if all continued to go well, it wouldn't be too long before he left the nest.

Now that he could fly, Peeper's care became a whole lot easier. The farm had no cats and was far enough away from the road that I did not worry about mishaps. When he wasn't resting on his bucket, he flew in and out of the barn through the windows and doors. His distinctive raspy voice made it easy to locate him in the large sycamore trees that kept the barn cool under their shady leaves. He was free to discover his own dietary needs. I was never sure what he found to eat around the farm, but I limited his hamburger meals to twice a day.

Starlings are opportunists. Since Peeper had no fear of humans, he assumed that everybody enjoyed his company. The Jumper barn grooms were beginning to warm up to him now that he confidently landed on the shoulder of anybody who called to him. But Peeper didn't always wait for an invitation.

"Anne," Michael yelled from the jump field where he was schooling a small chestnut warmblood named Chef. "Come get your bird!"

Dropping the pitchfork I was using to clean stalls, I ran out to the field. There sitting on the brim of Michael's ever-present baseball cap was Peeper. He was taking a rest from flight practice and seemed to enjoy the bouncy lift that Chef was providing for him. Michael was smiling as he leaned down over Chef's shoulder so that I could pluck Peeper's stubborn claws from the hat.

My favorite memory of Peeper that summer was the walk over from the Dressage barn to the Jumper barn every morning to turn Grande out. While I led the big horse from his left side, Peeper would follow in a sweeping motion, stop briefly to sit on a fence post, then swoop to catch up with us. Eric trotted along at my left, always keeping a safe distance from Grande's huge feet. With the early morning mist lifting off of the green grass, our little procession felt like a scene from a Disney movie.

At the end of the day, I simply had to call Peeper from wherever he was exploring and haul him home in the bucket. Once at home, he flew around the yard until I called him in and put him to bed in the bucket for the night. Then one night, he refused to come down from a large pine tree in our backyard. I called and called and he squawked and squawked but refused to budge. I had no choice but to surrender to his wishes. After a night with little sleep, I went outside through the back door to leave for work. Peeper swooped down to the bucket when he spied it in my hand. Once we arrived at Erdenheim and had been through our usual routine of turning Grande out and feeding Peeper, I decided to leave him at the farm for good. No longer was I going to call him down to the bucket as I prepared to leave for the day. There were too many dangers in my suburban neighborhood if he should decide to stop coming when I called him. At Erdenheim he would be much safer. A huge flock of starlings resided at the farm; some of them, no doubt, were Peeper's relatives.

Sadly, Eric and I returned home without Peeper that afternoon. Once again, I worried about him all night. The next morning I arrived earlier than usual, unable to prolong my reunion with the little bird. There in the driveway as I pulled in was Peeper, waiting for breakfast. And so we established a new routine: Peeper greeted me every morning in the driveway and escorted me immediately to the refrigerator where I dispensed his hamburger "worms." Then he went on about his day as Eric and I went on with ours. Occasionally, we saw him and occasionally he visited by landing on and grasping the forelock of a horse that I was vacuuming. After we chatted briefly, he was off on another adventure. By now I was resigned to his independence and thankful that I had experienced raising this extraordinary little being. Then one night there was a terrible storm.

It was actually the leftover from a hurricane that had battered the Carolinas a day or two before attacking the Philadelphia area. Gale force winds along with thunder and lightning downed trees and power lines, causing electricity outages all over the city and outlying areas. By the time I arrived at the farm the next day, the storm had abated, leaving debris in its wake. Erdenheim's spectacular driveway lost two large sycamore trees and several concrete posts along the fence lines. Tree limbs scattered all over the property required days of attention from the farm's maintenance crew. The horses had fared well in their stalls all night; and aside from a few broken panes of glass in the barn windows, there wasn't much damage.

When I drove up the driveway, I was only mildly concerned when Peeper's silhouette did not appear to greet me. I figured that he may have been too terrified by the storm to come out yet. After surveying the damage around the farm with the other grooms, I began to look for him in the trees where he now made his home. Nothing. I began the routine chores of my job, calling Peeper from every new location that I worked in. Still no response.

All day I called for him, seeking high and low for any nook or cranny in which he might have sought refuge. Eventually, the other Dressage grooms joined in the search. Early in the afternoon, I began to fret. Was this how it was going to end? Did we make it this far for him to blow away in a great storm?

By late afternoon I had to accept that he was gone and that our story ended here with a tragedy. Not knowing what had happened to him was the worst part for me. Perhaps I could deal with anything that had closure. Sadly I prepared to leave for home.

"Anne, he's out here," called one of the Dressage grooms, as I was just about to get in the car. "He's out here in the window."

Eric and I ran back into the barn. There, perched on the window sill looking no worse for wear, was Peeper.

"Where have you been?" I scolded him. At the same time I felt great relief. The answer remains a mystery, but at least he was safe.

The storm proved to be a pivotal point in rearing Peeper. Afterwards, he occasionally met me in the driveway upon my arrival each morning but rarely showed interest in the raw hamburger. He was, after all, an adult starling now and he didn't need his mother anymore. He still liked to visit me from time to time in the wash stall or while I was riding the filly outside. But I was able to accept that he was living independently. He was part of an enormous flock of starlings that perched on the chain link portable paddock fence outside the Dressage barn. His voice remained distinct among the mass of squawking birds. I loved to approach the flock and watch as all but one single bird flew away. Then Peeper would jump on my head before flying off to join his extended family.

All too soon, the summer came to an end. It was time to say goodbye to Erdenheim Farm for the last time. I said goodbye to Peeper too, knowing that he was all grown up. Now the rest of his life was up to him.

Graduation and Independence...

Just before Labor Day weekend, Eric and I made the four hour trip north to Ithaca to begin our final semester at Cornell. Promise had fared well all summer at Asbury Hill Farm. After having ridden the filly and Equity all summer, it felt good to ride her again. More than ever, I depended on my time with her to keep me grounded and squelch the anxiety beginning to surface as my uncertain plans for after graduation drifted closer. So many questions needed answers, and I wasn't really sure where the answers were going to come from.

It was clear after my summer at Erdenheim that a career with horses was out of the question. I did not want to spend my life grooming other people's horses, and I certainly didn't have the drive or the talent to train riders. The horse show industry was a complete turnoff as I began to realize that horses were not going to provide the bread and butter for my future daily life. Realizing that fact, I also knew that owning one or more horses would be very expensive unless I found a job that provided above and beyond what horses cost.

By November I had made the decision to leave Promise in Ithaca until my life had some tangible direction after graduation in December. To keep my finances in check, I moved her out to a farm on the southern end of Cayuga Lake where she received daily turnout and a stall at night. Other than that, she lived in the rough. No grooming, no riding, no handling of any kind. She more or less waited there until I was ready to include her in my future plans. Promise was only ten years old at that time and still had lots of years ahead. The vow that I had made about keeping her forever was still important to me. There were lots of older horses on the farm, including Lisa's aging gelding Faila, to keep her company while she waited for me to figure out how I was going to fit her into my independent life.

After final exams in December, I packed the car with Eric and everything else that had helped me survive at Cornell, except for Promise. Then I drove home to face the future. Six dismal months passed before I made two decisions that sent me on my way to the life I had imagined in my childhood dreams.

ABOVE. *My first ride was in the Pocono Mountains on a pony named Charcoal.* (1967)

My sister Sue, (sitting on Taffy), and I attended Lost Acres Day Camp for many summers. (1971)

Finding My Way to Mountain View Farm

Diane Williams gave me, (sitting on Merrylegs), the opportunity to care for her horses while she was away at college. (1977)

BELOW. *Never Never Land was my assigned horse at Camp Equinita.* (1975)

ABOVE. *Finally, in the fall of 1977, horse ownership became reality when Summer's Promise became mine.*

Promise, Mom and me. (1977)

Finding My Way to Mountain View Farm

My future brother-in-law, Steve holds my hen named Chicken while I kiss her. (1979)

BELOW. *My high school yearbook picture.* (1979)

OPPOSITE TOP. *Pierre the goat visited my family's kitchen one day.* (1979)

OPPOSITE BOTTOM. *Promise, my Dad and me.* (1982)

BELOW. *Sue and Steve visited me at Erdenheim Farm where I groomed and rode some lovely horses, (Royal Rouge), in training with Olympic show jumper, Michael Matz.* (1982)

Promise and me at Asbury Hill Farm in Freeville, NY, near Ithaca. (1982)

Finding My Way to Mountain View Farm

ABOVE. *My sister Sue holds Eric at a safe distance from Peeper.* (1983)

LEFT. *Eric and Luther, my first generation of Dachshunds.* (1985)

Part II

The Adirondacks

Finding My Way to Mountain View Farm

DESTINY...

Tranquil describes my impression of Raquette Lake when I saw it for the first time back in June of 1984. After driving for more than an hour on the remote stretch of Route 28 that crosses the Adirondack Park from Warrensburg in the east to Alder Creek in the west, I finally caught a glimpse of my destination. A sign posted against the backdrop of shimmering water and mossy green mountains confirmed my location. So breathtaking was this scenery I just had to pull over and get out of the car to take in the view. Despite a light drizzle of rain, several black flies swarmed my face. Little did I know, standing there by the side of the road, that I was staring out at my future beyond a summer job at the Raquette Lake Girls Camp. There was no way for me to interpret the faint whisper in the tall pines and spruce trees along the edge of the lake as a welcome home. But for the first time since graduating from Cornell six months ago, I did feel calm and settled. Perhaps I belonged here. Once I got back in the car, Eric pressed against my leg as we continued on our way into the future that began when I accepted a job as the riding instructor for a girls' summer camp in the Adirondacks.

The Raquette Lake Girls Camp, with its clusters of rustic buildings and a multi-million dollar view of Raquette Lake, spreads out over the southwestern shoreline between the sleepy Raquette Lake village and Cortland State College's outdoor teacher center. The camp's waterfront encompasses over 1500 feet of prime lakefront property that includes an impressive labyrinth of floating swim docks. Additional docks stretch out into the water; an extensive fleet of ski boats is tied neatly to them while tidy rows of canoes and sailboats rest on the beach. The camp is a "candy store" of high end activities that entice parents from the pages of the New York Times Magazine's famous camp issue published every winter. The expensive tuition allows children to create pottery in a state of the art studio, act in elaborate stage productions and dine on three delicious meals a day.

In 1984, horseback riding was an elective activity that required an additional fee. Fifteen young girls were signed up to ride, and I was responsible for scheduling and teaching the lessons. I also cared for the three horses leased for the summer to accommodate the program. Since I was arriving sight unseen, I decided to leave Promise at home that first summer because I had no idea what kind of facility the camp had for horses. This was long before it was possible to peruse a website or check out pictures on Facebook. Despite missing Promise, I knew I had made the right choice.

The prestigious Raquette Lake Girls Camp's equestrian facility was nothing more than a sagging shed that served as camp storage for most of the year. It had four standing tie stalls and an open space that I turned into a grooming area. The ring/paddock was full of stones and old wood chips, an attempt at creating footing, I suppose. The ring gravitated on a forty-five degree angle with a post and rail fence that defined the space. In the middle of the ring were two large boulders and a few smaller boulders piled together. This was the area where I was expected to teach children how to ride.

The horses, which had arrived a day or two before me, consisted of two Quarter Horse mares that, unquestionably, had passed their 20th birthday and a small, youthful Appaloosa gelding. They were not emaciated, but they had no muscle tone. The mares seemed exhausted, but the little Appaloosa had fire burning in his eyes.

As I assessed my working conditions, it hit me. One year ago, I had been working for show jumper and trainer Michael Matz, an Olympian and consummate horseman. I had handled and ridden some very fine horseflesh and had viewed the horse industry from its highest peak where the horses were afforded the best care. A year later, I was in charge of three horses and a whole camp riding program in the middle of the Adirondacks. How had I ended up here?

AFTER GRADUATION...

The events of the last six months leading up to my job in the Adirondacks were, frankly, uneventful. After graduation I began to fear that I was headed on the fast track to nowhere, least of all to any recognizable path to realizing childhood dreams.

Finding My Way to Mountain View Farm

I had arrived home from Cornell in December, just before Christmas, with a car full of college memories that were neatly unloaded and stacked in the basement for whatever was to come next, perhaps independence. But independence required income and a job, neither of which I had at the moment. The holidays provided a week or two of distractions as our family gathered to celebrate. By New Years, my siblings had all returned to their lives. When the holiday decorations were put away in that musty basement closet, it was time for me to do something. What?

My résumé was organized, typed and awaiting distribution along with proof of my recent Cornell degree in Animal Science. But what was I to do with it now? The year was 1984, long before the internet made searching for job opportunities as easy as it is today. Once again I turned to the *Times Chronicle*, and the *Philadelphia Inquirer*, this time to find the perfect job that would provide me with the income and dignity required to live the rest of my life. Unfortunately, neither paper was able to work the magic that the *Times Chronicle* had when I discovered Promise in it six years ago. Independence required hard work, determination and many follow up phone-calls.

With my father's guidance, I began to apply for jobs in the field of pharmaceutical sales. The two summers that I spent at McNeil Labs had at least provided me with some exposure to how a pharmaceutical company operates. I applied everywhere and beat the pavement all winter with a fair number of interviews. You name it, Ortho, Shering Plough, Smith Kline Beckman, Pittman Moore and a number of smaller animal product companies all granted me first interviews that raised my hopes. It didn't take me long to figure out how the job game was played at these prosperous companies. Although my education and experience with animals were impressive, the fact that I was not a young male with at least five years of experience in sales prevented me from landing an entry level position.

In the meantime, I took a part-time job conducting market research over the phone at a company called the Data Group. The job was challenging as I had to use my communication skills to convince people to stay on the line long enough for me to conduct my survey and reach my quota for the evening. The eight hour shifts were long as I sat within the three walls of a small cubicle. My neck ached from pinching the phone between ear and shoulder while entering the data collected with a pencil on the various forms provided. Under these uncomfortable conditions, I conducted interviews on a variety of topics. One night I collected data from the head of the household about his or her knowledge of network news.

> *"Who would you be more likely to trust: Tom Brokaw, Peter Jennings or Dan Rather?"*
>
> *"On a scale of one to ten; a ten meaning all the time and a one meaning never, how would you rate your viewership of NBC News?"*
>
> *"How would you describe your knowledge of foreign affairs? Would you say you are very knowledgeable, somewhat knowledgeable, hardly knowledgeable or not knowledgeable at all?"*

The next evening I might be requesting input from the female head of the household.

> *"Which brand of chocolate chip cookies do you associate with giving your family nothing but the best? Friehoffers, Mrs. Fields, or Nabisco"*
>
> *"On a scale from 1 to 10, how often do you buy cookies in a supermarket?"*
>
> *"How often might you use a packaged cookie mix to bake cookies for your family? Would you say often, somewhat often, or never?"* The job kept me occupied as the dismal winter months passed slowly by.

In the middle of January, six weeks before her due date, my sister Sue gave birth to her first child, a girl named Amy. Thankfully, Amy's early arrival was only complicated by a week-long stay in the hospital to make sure her lungs were functioning properly. My family rejoiced in our tiny wrinkly pink addition. Six weeks after her birth, I traveled to New Hampshire to meet her for the first time and was not prepared for the impact that this little baby would have on my life.

Amy and I hit it off immediately. I was fascinated by her and could hardly wait for her to wake up from naps so that I could engage her in a babble of conversation. Neither of us could have guessed at that time that she was destined to grow up with a passion for animals, especially horses. Through Amy and two more nieces, (my brothers' future daughters), my siblings began to empathize with a young girl's addiction to horses. These three girls' passions for horses have provided some justification for my own within our family. After a week-long visit, I arrived home to pursue the dismal job market once more.

Eric prevented me from falling into total despair. By tending to his daily needs and spending all of my non-working time with him, I survived. His constant presence and loyalty provided a spark of hope that, eventually, I would figure out some kind of future out for all of us. My parents had warmed up to Eric, somewhat. My father teased me about his tiny size, but I think he got a kick out of watching the puppy play with our aged golden retriever, Penny.

I missed Promise terribly over the long winter. Horses and horseback riding seemed so frivolous and childish at the moment. I began to wonder if I was still a horse person. It had been a long time since I had dreamed about a life with animals. To dream of a life that, in reality, required financial resources I didn't have, also seemed naïve and childish.

By the end of March, the bleakness of winter began to green into spring. As the days lengthened and brightened with the sun, Eric and I spent more and more time outdoors. I still continued to apply for every sales position listed in the newspaper and went through the motions of interviewing to no avail.

Memorial Day weekend marks the opening of the Devon Horse Show, one of the most prestigious as well as oldest hunter/jumper venues in the country. Showing at Devon is a huge accomplishment let alone winning or placing in any of the divisions. The horse necessary to compete at Devon is pricey and meticulously trained by those who work in the industry. Gary Duffy was bringing several of his clients from Ithaca to Devon for the week and asked if I would work as a groom for him. He also offered to transport Promise down with the show horses.

She had survived the winter well from all the reports that I received. I had gone back to visit my apartment-mates and Promise once during the winter. Although it had been wonderful to see my horse, visiting my friends was confusing and anticlimactic. My future felt stalled.

I agreed to both offers and found a farm with a large pasture willing to board Promise for the summer. Three other horses lived in the pasture as well, so Promise would not be alone. This situation was certain to buy me some more time as I continued to work on my job prospects.

I looked forward to working at Devon, although I knew from experience that working for Gary meant long hours at the show grounds. My job included feeding, bathing, lunging, mucking, and tacking up the horses, (making certain the saddle was snug and the bridle immaculate), so that the owners could concentrate on nothing but competing against some of the best horses in the country. In other words, I was in charge of everything for the horses except riding them in the prestigious Devon classes. The job paid well and only lasted for the ten day duration of the show.

Several days before Devon began, Gary arrived at the show grounds with the horses, including Promise, in the large eight horse trailer owned by Asbury Hill Farm. I had arranged for a local trainer to pick my horse up and deliver her to the farm where she was to be boarded. I drove down in my own car ahead of time to greet Promise whom I hadn't seen for almost four months. The show grounds pulsated with activity as show horses were unloaded from huge fancy tractor trailers and secured in their temporary accommodations. All of the horses were sleek, shiny and fat with conditioned muscles.

Gary's horses were already settled in their stalls when I located them among the labyrinth of stables.

"Promise, where are you?" I called.

A low nicker identified the location of her stall. Unlatching the door, I barely recognized my horse. Her dull winter coat still clung to her frame so late in May. When I reached out to touch her, static electricity made clumps of hair literally jump onto my hand. Her mane was long and stringy

Finding My Way to Mountain View Farm

and the whiskers on her muzzle and around her eyes resembled the limbs of a daddy-long-legs. Although Promise was in good flesh and her feet were trimmed, her appearance stung me. How had I neglected her all winter? The contrast to the beautiful pampered specimens strutting about the show grounds made her condition look that much bleaker.

Promise settled into her new pasture home easily and, thankfully, got along well with the established herd. In addition to my horse, a Morgan gelding, an ancient Shetland pony and a retired race horse resided in the field. They lived outside all year long with only a stand of oak trees to provide shelter from the elements. There was an old bank barn on the property with stalls inside, but the thick cobwebs hanging throughout made it clear that horses hadn't entered the barn in years.

Once my obligation to Gary's horses at the Devon Horse Show was completed, I was once again unemployed. I continued to apply for jobs and interview, but there was nothing promising on the horizon. In the meantime, and as a result of my daily visits to see her, Promise began to bloom into the horse I had purchased almost seven years ago. With daily grooming, her coat began to shine. I pulled her mane and trimmed the whiskers on her face to a more tidy length, trying not to shave them off completely. Eventually, I began to ride her around the farm and in the woods. This always made me feel a bit guilty. I had no right to "play" with my horse without a steady income with which to support her. My savings from the Data Group were dwindling. How long was this guilty feeling going to last? I needed to get going with my adult life and the achievement of those hazy dreams.

In mid-June, I interviewed for a job in the animal testing/care department of a local company. The job paid well, complete with pension options, and full medical and dental benefits. Unlike the sales positions that I had been interviewing for all winter, this job did not require my pressed brown suit. Instead I arrived in a pair of khaki chinos and a polo shirt tucked in at the waist.

After interviewing with human resources, I was given a guided tour of the facility by a young female employee. She led me from room to room where various animals were participating in controlled studies.

There was a bin on the floor about ten inches high with a mesh cover to prevent escape. Inside the bin several rabbits were held in place by harnesses that prevented them from any movement at all. Their eyes were being tested for reactions to a chemical. A technician was responsible for applying the chemical to their eyes with a dropper; the harness prevented them from rubbing their eyes if and when irritation occurred. Next there was a cage with several baby pigs that were being tested for skin reactions from specific products that the company wished to market as well. The results of these tests eventually provided the text printed on warning labels.

I could barely breathe as I toured the facility. The young guide seemed indifferent to the suffering of these poor animals. Perhaps that full benefit package prevented a young woman from remembering that she couldn't bear to see animals suffer. There were thousands of mice and rats participating in tests all over the facility.

After forty-five minutes, the tour finally ended and I was free to go. I barely made it through the door labeled "Animal Care" before I burst into tears. No matter what the income was, I could never become that young woman, resigned and indifferent to the sacrifice animals make to improve our lives. It is hypocritical to feel this way when every day I use products that have been tested on animals. I'm not sure what the answer is. Perhaps keeping ourselves aware and appreciating the sacrifices made by lab animals will have to do for now until more humane methods become available in the future. I never did make the follow-up phone call to the company and I never heard from them again. Perhaps I hadn't hidden my emotions while I toured the facility. I needed a job, but I was not willing to compromise my respect for animals in order to be hired.

A week later and out of the blue, the Director called my home and offered me a job. Centenary College had an opening for an instructor in Equine Studies. I was flattered that she thought of me. With no other job prospects, I accepted immediately. In addition to one riding class, I was assigned to teach Theory of Equitation, Equine Lameness and Anatomy and Physiology of the Horse.

"Apparently, I'm not a salesman after all. I'm going to be a teacher." I had to say it several times because it had never occurred to me that I

Finding My Way to Mountain View Farm

was a teacher. The pay was $13,000 a year, but it did include health insurance and lots of vacation time. Perhaps I could make a little more money during the weeks off. The job didn't begin until after Labor Day and it was only the end of June when the offer was made.

"What are you going to do all summer?" the Director asked casually.

"I don't know," I stammered, still trying to picture myself as a teacher in front of a class filled with women only two or three years younger than I.

"Well, a gentleman keeps calling to see if I know anybody who will be the riding instructor at his camp up in the Adirondacks. He had a woman lined up to come but she just called him last week to say that she was no longer available and now he is desperate for somebody. Camp starts next week. I keep telling him that the college students have been gone for a month now and I don't know of anybody who needs a job. You want to give him a call and just see what the job is?"

"I guess," I answered hesitantly.

She gave me the magic telephone number that ultimately sent me on my way to the Raquette Lake Girls Camp and my future in the Adirondacks.

Within three days of my initial phone call to the camp owner/director, Eric and I were on our way to the Adirondacks. Since I wasn't sure what I had gotten myself into and had no idea what the quality of the riding facilities might be, I decided to leave Promise at home with her pasture mates. Once again I was abandoning her, but at least this time there was a plan beyond August that did include her. In the meantime, she had to wait eight weeks in the pasture until I returned.

GRAMMIE...

Raquette Lake is only eighty miles from the town of Hudson Falls where my mother grew up. Her mother was still living there when I accepted the job offer at the girl's camp that summer after graduation. Before making my way into the Adirondack Mountains I made arrangements to stay with my grandmother for one night. It was always a special treat to visit Grammie's house. She and my grandfather had collected antiques, particularly clocks, for the forty-nine years they were married. The house was full of stories that, as a child, I loved to hear over and over again. It had been a number of years since I had visited my grandmother at her home where she now lived alone among the collections that kept the memories of her husband and raising her family alive.

Grammie was thrilled that I wanted to visit, even if it was only for one night. Thus began one of the most rewarding relationships of my adult life. From that visit forward, Grammie and I became best girlfriends who spent lots of quality time getting to know each other as two women with so many shared opinions about how the world should work.

After seven hours in the car, Eric and I pulled into the driveway at 8 Cherry Street. While it seemed that the rest of Hudson Falls was crumbling into slow decline, Grammie's house, with its tidy green lawn, trimmed shrubbery and fresh coat of yellow paint, spoke of the past when Hudson Falls had been a thriving mill town. An explosion of fuchsia-colored rambling roses cascaded over a small section of fence rails that separated Grammie's property from the O'Neil's who lived next door.

Out of the car, Eric took a few minutes to sniff around the new environment before relieving himself. Satisfied that he was empty, I called him to follow me through the door next to the garage. It led us into the kitchen where the smell of Grammie's house brought back a tornado of memories. On overload after such a long trip, I had to separate them into two groups. One group included the memories from my own childhood when I visited this enchanted house with my own family; the other list included all the stories about my mother and her two brothers when they were children growing up within this space. I smiled at the mental slide show clicking in my head.

Eric and I walked through the kitchen past the old fashioned working telephone that hung on the wall by the door to the dining room. Sensing there was somebody nearby, Eric took off ahead of me, and soon I heard the lovely New England accent that had captivated my brothers, sister and me when she visited us as children. It was coming from the sun porch.

"Why hallow theya. You must be Eric."

I turned the corner into the sunny concrete porch. Two sides of the room contained windows that reached to the ceiling from half way up the walls. The windows were not insulated and therefore the room remained shut off by a storm door of sorts for the winter. In June, however, this was her favorite room in the house. She had both exterior doors open so a breeze could blow through and provide a cool escape from the muggy summer day. The vintage furniture was durable and charming: a bamboo loveseat with two faded blue cushions and a matching chair. On the footstool was her ever present cross-stitch, neatly organized with the colored floss and pattern for easy access. Her favorites at the moment were reproductions of old samplers that hung in various Americana museums around New England.

When Grammie saw me, she stood right up with the agility of a young woman rather than a fragile elder. Looking down, she made sure Eric was out from under foot before taking a step towards me. It felt so good to hug her. Her snow white hair, perfectly set from a visit to the hairdresser the day before, smelled like Ivory soap. She was only five feet and one inch tall with a large bosom and square build below. Her hands had fascinated me since childhood; but now, through adult eyes, I wondered how she still was able to cross-stitch with such limited dexterity. All of her fingers appeared to be slightly bent, but her pinkies on both hands were permanently crimped at the second knuckle. Apparently, a tight ligament was the culprit and having them clipped for cosmetic purposes was often discussed when she was a child. Thankfully, her father, a professor of biology at Brown University in Providence, Rhode Island, objected for fear that she would risk losing any use of them at all.

Grammie and I spent the rest of the afternoon and evening catching up on family news. She had prepared a delicious dinner of chicken salad and cold vegetables in an effort to ward off the summer heat in the kitchen. We sat at the dining room table and used the good sterling silverware. We drank water from pewter goblets and filled ourselves up with each other's presence.

After the long evening, Eric and I made our way upstairs. The steps were too steep and narrow for him to attempt on his own, so I carried him in my arms and placed him on the wooden floor. Immediately he took off down the hall, scattering Grammie's hand-hooked throw rugs along the way. Back and forth down the hall he zoomed, possessed by the crazies after being cooped up in the car for the long ride. After straightening the rugs, I grabbed him and put him on the bed in my mother's room.

Later, I lay in my mother's bed with Eric curled up against my side. Crickets chirped a continuous chorus outside, and a light breeze lifted the curtains at each window. I thought about Promise and wondered if she and I would ever share the carefree existence that we had known together before I graduated from college. Why had I chosen to travel so far away from her to teach children how to ride? So many thoughts swirled in my head. Eventually, the steady rhythm of Eric's breathing comforted me and I fell asleep.

The next day, Grammie and I enjoyed breakfast at the kitchen table and talked until nearly lunchtime. Finally, it was time for me to be on my way up the Northway into the Adirondacks. As an adult, spending time with Grammie left me feeling as if I had made a new friend. After a warm hug, I left her in the driveway, feeling certain that I would be back soon. As Eric snuggled against my thigh, we were off to my summer job at the Raquette Lake Girl's Camp.

LESSONS TAUGHT; LESSONS LEARNED...

I had been hired by the camp to teach horseback riding. What the riders got out of the program was going to come from me, not the condition of the riding facility. I knew it would require great self determination to produce accomplished equestrians over the next eight weeks. After all, compared to my experience working for Michael Matz and the fact that I had degrees in Equine Studies and Animal Science, I was overqualified for the job. Wasn't I?

First I needed to evaluate the horses' abilities. All three were more or less safe mounts for beginner riders. They could walk and trot with minimal encouragement from the rider's leg, but cantering up and down the slope of the ring was going to be more difficult. Having no idea what the experience levels of the campers were, I wasn't quite sure how much cantering the horses needed to do.

A day later camp officially opened with the arrival of close to 100 female campers. The next day, Monday, girls who signed up to ride paid their initial visit to the barn for orientation and scheduling. Riding should be taught holistically, I believe. It is essential that the rider and the horse share a bond. This is the difference between developing riders versus well rounded horsemen. Through brushing the horse's shiny coat, cleaning his feet with a hoof pick, and tightening the girth of the saddle before mounting up, the horse and rider become a team. Hopefully, by the time the campers were sitting on their horses, any fear they may have felt initially was replaced by confidence. At this stage the rider becomes the leader of the team and the horse, a willing partner, feels nothing but total trust in the rider. Now real progress in the art of learning to ride can ensue.

Most of the girls had never even been around horses before, let alone ridden one. However, it didn't take long for them to become smitten with the three equines. Sugar, Jimmy and Amber were the most glorious and gorgeous horses they knew because they were the only horses they knew. The horses possessed patience and gentleness, both attributes so necessary when one is becoming acquainted with such large creatures. I too garnered deep respect for my co-teachers without whom there would be no riding program at all.

As summer advanced, the girls began to take great pride in caring for the horses as well as in riding them. They were generally concerned with the animals and doted on them, preferring to stay in the barn and groom or care for them on days that it was too rainy or hot to ride. I was adamant that the horses not be overworked.

Despite their imperfections, I became quite enamored of my equine charges. The life of a school horse includes lots of unintentional tugging at the mouth and kicking at the sides. Even the most tolerant school horse will sour after a few weeks and act out with typical school horse antics. Refusing to move forward or lying down with a rider sitting on its back is a sure way to scare the rider to death. These disobediences provided me with an excuse to school them myself in the cool air of the Adirondack summer evenings. I made a compromise. Instead of working them monotonously in the ring, I rode them out along the trails.

Jimmy, the youngest and greenest of the three, was the one I schooled the most. He and I spent our evenings discovering all the nooks and crannies around Raquette Lake. We traversed the soft sand roads which led into the woods and remote areas of the lake untouched by human encroachment. We trotted the dirt road out to the dump, praying not to encounter bears along the way. We rode down into the Raquette Lake Village, composed of two churches, a library, a general store, a laundromat and a bar. Jimmy became quite the enthusiastic little trail horse. I also spent some time broadening his education by introducing him to small jumps. The rides refreshed him because they did not include constant yanking on his mouth and kicking at his sides. He also began to behave more respectfully in the ring when the campers were mounted on him. Sugar and Amber also benefited from their time on the trails. These girls didn't require as much schooling, just a reminder where their "brakes" and "gas pedals" were.

When not working with the campers or the horses, Eric and I took off in the car to explore the neighboring towns: Inlet, Eagle Bay and Old Forge. The ice cream stand in Inlet often enticed me. No wonder the combination of that indulgence with the delicious kosher cuisine at camp packed ten pounds onto my body despite the exercise I assumed was burning off extra calories.

The eight weeks at camp flew by quickly. Horses were making a difference in the lives of young girls who may not have been as horse crazy as I was at their age, but who were having a taste of that incredible relationship between girls and horses. They began to feel empathy for living creatures other than humans. The girls began to accept that manure was a constant when working with horses and learned it is not acceptable to wrinkle noses or giggle when horses lifted their tails to poop or break wind. They couldn't avoid biting flies, and they realized that having a horse step on your foot accidentally hurt a whole lot but is not the end of the world. And it began to occur to me that my connections with these young campers were not my impressive horse credentials. Instead my passion for horses and animals in general probably had the greatest effect of all.

When Thursday, my day off, finally arrived, I woke up early to care for the horses. After turning them out in the paddock with enough hay to last most of the day, Eric and I climbed into the car with a week's worth of laundry and drove for two hours to Hudson Falls.

Finding My Way to Mountain View Farm

Grammie and I spent the day on webbed folding lawn chairs in her backyard. There under the maple tree, (whose bright orange leaves had arrived in an envelope addressed to my mother each fall), we talked about every topic under the sun. While my laundry dried, we chatted about politics, religion, discrimination, music, books, stamps, art, the past, the present and the future. As we chatted, Eric explored the backyard or lay on a towel in the shade under my chair. He snapped at flies and barked at any activity in the backyards adjacent to Grammie's property.

At noon we brought egg salad or tuna fish sandwiches out to our chairs. Grammie always drank iced coffee with her lunch, no matter the time of year. I drank iced tea. She made sure there were Freihofer's crème filled chocolate cupcakes for dessert on our special day.

The conversation continued all afternoon as the sun began to sink toward the west. Her perennial garden, which included Job's Tears, Solomon's Seal, Bellwort, Columbine and wild Bleeding Heart, brightly bordered the tidy backyard. By August, orange and yellow day lilies dominated the flower garden. She had collected wild ferns from the woods and transplanted them years ago around the summer house, a gazebo type structure. Several varieties of ferns thrived under her care. She knew the name of each one.

By late afternoon, the chill from the shaded backyard sent us inside to assemble dinner. Grammie kept the fare light and easy to prepare with chicken, hamburgers or pork chops and a hearts of lettuce salad. We hurried through the first course so that we could savor dessert. Coffee ice cream was our favorite, and occasionally she sweetened the treat with fresh raspberries or strawberries from the Farmer's Market held once a week outside the Grand Union on Main Street. She refused to do the dishes until I left, not wanting to waste a moment of our visit on tasks she could easily do once I was on my way. As the sun set, it was time for Eric and me to head back to Raquette Lake, our batteries recharged and ready for the coming week. Visits with Grammie always filled me up with brain food. I departed with extra cupcakes and thoughtful information to metabolize in the coming days.

One Thursday, I snapped a leash onto Eric's collar so that Grammie and I could tour family landmarks on foot around the village. Grammie had grown up in Providence, Rhode Island, but my grandfather had grown up in Hudson Falls. His oldest sister, Mary, had been Grammie's roommate at Mount Holyoke College in South Hadley, MA. After graduation in 1921, they had remained best friends and kindred spirits. Grammie had met Mary's younger brother, Kip, only a handful of times before he asked her to marry him. The scene where he arrived in Cape Cod unexpectedly and found her on the beach is a vivid story I heard repeatedly as a child.

Grammie and I walked down to the "Main Street" house, a lovely Victorian home with a wraparound porch where my grandfather and Aunt Mary grew up with two other siblings. Its impressive elegance contrasted starkly with the Martindale Avenue house where Grandpa's father had grown up with a cow in the backyard. The dilapidated house under the hill still stood as a reminder of poor Grandpa's mother walking every day down to visit her ailing parents during her final pregnancy. Her ankles and legs had swollen to almost twice their normal size, a sad omen of her fate. After Aunt Alice was born, Grandpa's mother succumbed to blood poisoning. So many women in Grammie's stories died young, including her own mother who died after the birth of her fourth child. Many of the people in Grammie's stories still lived in New England. One Thursday, she and I began making plans to visit them on a road trip after camp ended in mid-August.

Soon it was time to say goodbye to my little herd of horses and campers. I never knew what became of Jimmy. I want to think that he found a wonderful home where he could continue his training on the trail. Sugar returned to camp the following summer, but Amber was sold shortly after she left camp and hopefully found a loving home that could benefit from her gentle nature.

When camp came to an end in mid-August, I felt blessed by the experience. I had met lots of wonderful people and learned a great deal about Judaism with its many traditions. The Adirondacks had beguiled me unexpectedly, so there was no question that I would return next summer. Eric,

Finding My Way to Mountain View Farm

my Dachshund, and I had spent every minute together, sealing a bond that I had never shared with a dog before.

Grammie, Eric and I took off on our road trip that included a visit to my sister Sue in New Hampshire. Amy was about eight months old, having changed so much since I saw her in the winter. She smiled at Eric as he licked her fingers and toes. She stared, mesmerized by Grammie who held her often and entertained her with friendly expressions and that charming accent.

We visited with Aunt Mary in South Hadley, Massachusetts, and then toured Providence, visiting Grammie's childhood haunts. The experience cemented my adult relationship with Grammie. Eric was a well behaved visitor everywhere we went, including the beach at Quonochontaug. Grammie's baby sister, Hope, and her husband Herb owned a summer home on "Quonny." It was here that Eric experienced ocean waves for the first time and barked incessantly as they chased him up the beach. His zest and energy endeared him to the many family members he met. Herb's elderly sister gasped when she saw Eric and began to cry as she reached down to stroke his velvety ears. Only two weeks prior to our visit, she had euthanized her ancient Dachshund who resembled Eric in size and color.

A week before Labor Day, I backed the car out of my grandmother's driveway and turned toward Philadelphia with Eric by my side. As Grammie stood waving from the driveway until we drove out of sight, I felt that this moment in time was more a beginning than an end. Reflecting on how far I had come since arriving home from Ithaca only nine months ago with little in the way of a future, I thought that perhaps now I was on my way. The first day of a new job that would combine my love of horses with teaching was only a week away. I had just spent the summer as a riding instructor, sharing my number one passion with youngsters. The experience enabled me to wipe the haze from my image in the mirror. Finally, I recognized the woman who loved animals of all kinds and, yes, she was still a horse person.

PERHAPS I AM A TEACHER...

The next week I was busy preparing to relocate to Hackettstown, New Jersey, with my dog and my horse. I found a room for rent in a woman's house just a block away from the college. She agreed to allow pets. The rent provided me with a bedroom and kitchen privileges. As it turned out, the woman was rarely home, so I was able to use the whole house. Eric and I could sit on the living room couch in the evenings and watch television, read a book, or cross stitch, a creative outlet I now shared with Grammie.

Promise had moved out to the college's barn at the top of Schooly's Mountain, where she was going to be used as a school horse. This arrangement made the college responsible for all of her expenses, but I still owned her. She had fared well in the pasture all summer while I was working in the Adirondacks, but I was eager to have her in my life again. Finally, the three of us, Eric, Promise and I were together once more. It still wasn't quite the "happily ever after" I had been hoping for, but it was a step in the right direction.

As my camp experience and road trip with Grammie settled into a summer memory, my new job at Centenary took hold. I rather liked teaching. It occurred to me that the more I taught, the more I learned. To teach a concept required that the teacher knows it inside and out from all possible angles.

I did my best with Theory of Equitation, which required evaluating and comparing the philosophies of many of the horse masters, including Colonel Alois Podhajsky, Gordon Wright, Xenophon and George Morris. In other words, I taught riding from a podium while students, dressed in breeches and boots and mounted on chairs, recorded my lectures in their notebooks. In addition, I was expected to expose them to the form and function of all the major pieces of tack and bits. Although I found it interesting to learn, I didn't find it particularly interesting to teach "riding" in the classroom. For me, the saddle is the best place to learn these concepts while applying them. Most of learning to ride is kinesthetic. The rider needs to feel the horse's response to her aids immediately through the levers of the tack. Then she can commit sensation to memory. Once a "feel" is established, the rider can apply support to the philosophy.

Teaching horse science courses such as Lameness, Health and Disease and Anatomy and Physiology was an exhilarating challenge. To enhance my teaching in these fields, I made friends with the local knacker, the person called upon to remove a horse or other livestock carcass from a farm. His processing plant was an anatomist's and pathologist's haven. I collected all kinds of "parts" to share with my students, providing them with a front row seat to the complex, inner workings of the animal they had chosen to study at college. I was able to handle this subject emotionally because I did not have any association with these horses; it also helped that, unlike the research animals at the chemical company, these specimens had been euthanized before they were used in my labs.

The knacker provides an extremely efficient and necessary service to a horse farm. The horse must be dead before it is collected. Then the carcass is processed into bone ash that is used for fertilizer or pet food production. In fact the knacker sold many of his products in a store at the front of the facility. His dog kibble was a premium product, and his highly effective fertilizers were sought by local gardeners as well.

I spent many a Tuesday afternoon inside the carcasses of horses where I witnessed firsthand how the reproductive organs are suspended in the lower abdomen. One cannot fully appreciate the delicate convoluted marvel that is the equine digestive system until it is manipulated by hand. It is no wonder that the horse succumbs so frequently to colic. The tendons and ligaments of the lower limbs work effortlessly to produce that floating movement in the Dressage horse or the powerful hind leg push of a show jumper. These structures are nothing short of miraculous as they assist the boney levers with efficient assistance from the major muscles of the upper portions of the legs. In terms of physics the equine limb is the perfect simple machine!

Although I thrived in the classroom, coming back to Centenary had its drawbacks. Unfortunately, I had changed from the young girl who had graduated from Centenary only three years prior to becoming an employee. Although I loved horses, I was not enamored with the horse industry now that I was a working adult. A complex world existed beyond the wealthy aristocrats who dominated the show grounds. They didn't impress me. The Director was disappointed, perhaps justifiably, by my feelings. I was supposed to be promoting the industry within the classroom to assure that the next generation of trainers, grooms, riders and everyone else associated with the industry were prepared to enter it fully educated and prepared.

As a result, I avoided the barn. Of course that meant I avoided Promise too. I taught a riding class three days a week, but I never went out to ride. Promise was receiving excellent care from the students, so I didn't actually need to be there. I gained ten more pounds. Except for my frequent walks with Eric, I was pretty sedentary.

Often, I spent time with my Centenary roommate, May, who had landed a great job and was living at home only forty minutes from Hackettstown. Missy was still in the area as well. Both of them had dogs. We loved to get together so that our dogs could interact. For me this was a more satisfying social life.

As my life got busier, Eric was spending more and more time alone in our tiny room. My parental radar worried about the solitary hours, although my schedule provided plenty of time to sneak home and tend to his needs. When I had to leave him in his crate, it broke my heart to know he was staring at the door, once again waiting for my return. Perhaps another puppy would be good company for Eric. Yes, a puppy was the perfect solution for Eric's loneliness.

Dachshund puppies are very popular and, therefore, available throughout the year. I began my search for a puppy shortly after I convinced my landlady that I would protect her house from destruction. Over the next couple of weeks, I visited lots of Dachsie litters. My heart was set on a miniature black-and-tan male. I found him in Northeastern, PA, and picked him up one Friday evening in October on the way to my parents' house for the weekend.

Luther or Ludie was only seven weeks old and no bigger than a kitten. His tiny size made him appear fragile. He was precious, and I couldn't wait for Eric to meet him. After securing Luther in a crate, I took him out to the car where Eric was all a-wiggle in the window. After setting the crate on the backseat of the dark car, I allowed Eric to jump over the seat and sniff Luther. Eric showed great interest in the puppy who stood confidently at the door to the crate, whining for acceptance. As the gears in Eric's brain began to turn, he realized that this noisy ink spot was going to come between his mistress and him. He would have to take care of this matter himself. Eric began to bark sharply at the puppy, causing Ludie to bolt and cower at the back of the crate with a pathetic yelp. I felt sorry for both of these boys who were clearly stressing each other out. There was nothing that I could do until we arrived home.

Once home I took my time to reintroduce the two dogs in the safety of the kitchen with the lights on. My mother fussed all over Eric as I tended to Ludie whose eyes swelled at the enormity of his new world.

"Who are you?" his expression seemed to ask. "What is this place? What happened to my mother? My family? My life?"

I cuddled Ludie and kissed his tiny head. His tan eyebrows worried about the stranger holding him tight. His tiny Dachshund body radiated the same heat that Eric's did through a diminutive surface area. In no time I was in love with him and so wanted Eric to feel the same way.

Eric had a different idea. He wanted no part of this intruder. He spent all day Saturday inserting himself between the puppy and me in a desperate attempt to remind me who came first. I made every effort to lavish attention on Eric. However, I also wanted to enjoy the tininess of Ludie before he quickly lengthened into an adult. If only Eric could join me in making Ludie feel secure about his place in his new pack. Instead, Eric curled his lip at the puppy and emitted a low warning growl. The puppy cowered in submission.

Several factors were failing in this scenario; over the years I have often reflected on the lessons that these two dogs taught me. I learned that animals have no concept of real time. Forty-eight hours was not long enough for Eric and Ludie to establish a relationship based on the mysteries of "dog law." Most importantly I learned that my only role in getting these two dogs acquainted was to protect Luther from any aggression that Eric might exhibit; thankfully, he never did. The rest was up to them.

As the day wore on, I became distracted with preparations for the drive back to New Jersey. I left the two dogs in the kitchen with my mother in charge of supervision and went about the business of gathering my belongings and packing the car. After forty-five minutes or so, I returned to the kitchen. The Philadelphia Eagles were fighting for the lead on the small color television that blared from the counter next to the stove. My mother was only lending an ear to the noise while she prepared a dinner of ham steak and baked potatoes. I searched the floor for an update on the dog drama. What I found brought a smile to my face and a lump to my throat.

Ludie was curled up, sound asleep on his towel. However, he was not alone. Curled around the puppy's toasty body was Eric. And so began the thirteen-year relationship between these two wonderful dogs. Much of that time they existed as the lump under a blanket on the couch or the covers of my bed. They liked to twist their bodies into a pretzel, taking full advantage of each other's radiant body heat. Without human intervention, they had found their way to becoming best friends.

I Do...

At the beginning of my second year working for the Raquette Lake Girls Camp, I met my future!

I agreed to return a second summer to the RLGC under the condition that the riding facility underwent major improvements. Riding had become a popular activity. Young girls learned how to care for and love great big horses, an intoxicating accomplishment. As my program was growing, I was in a position to make necessary demands of the camp director. He promised a newly excavated ring with sturdy fencing, real jumping equipment, and a box stall in the barn so that my own horse could join me at camp.

In May I took a road trip to visit Grammie. Our plan was to drive up to the Girl's camp and check on the facility's progress. She and I arrived to discover that the promise had yet to be fulfilled. In fact, work had not even started! On a tour around the camp, we came across one of the maintenance guys working on a boat. I was so annoyed that I hardly noticed how good-looking he was. My grandmother would report much later that when I rolled the window down to ask him details about the ring, she felt a surge of energy between us. That energy was probably the disappointment I felt about the lack of progress at the riding stable. This poor guy took the brunt of my mood as I questioned him.

Six weeks later when I arrived at camp with two Dachshunds and Promise, the facility still looked the same as it had the year before. So much for the clout of my growing program! I refused to teach lessons until the ring was fixed. In the meantime, the girls spent their riding time grooming and caring for the horses. Occasionally, we took trail rides through the woods. Within two weeks, I was teaching lessons in a large, flat sand ring with a sturdy post and rail fence and four pairs of durable jumping standards. Life was good and about to get a whole lot better.

Remember the maintenance guy on the boat? Well, he began showing up around the barn, particularly at dusk, dressed in a clean flannel shirt and faded jeans. I began to notice his thick dark hair, his easy smile, and his friendly brown eyes. Although he seemed somewhat shy, he clearly wanted to be in my company. His easy-going personality made me feel comfortable and happy to see him. One evening we went to a local bar with two other RLGC staff members. After that evening, the maintenance guy, Rod, and I spent most of our non-working time together. Before we knew it, we fell in love. Fortunately, he took to my dogs, Eric and Ludie, immediately. He was raising his own puppy, a female husky mix named Mishka.

Roderick Phinney grew up in Ridgewood, New Jersey. However, every summer of his life had been spent at Sucker Brook Bay on Raquette Lake. Rod's mother's family had owned a boat-access-only camp called Sunny Cliff since 1904. Not only had he grown up there, but his mother, Rachel, and her three older brothers had spent their summers there as well.

On Raquette Lake, Rod and his four older sisters learned to fish, identify trees, pump water, make balsam pillows, exist without electricity, row and paddle boats, sleep under the stars, endure gnawing mosquitoes, chop wood and build campfires. During the long summer days, they water skied and hiked up West Mountain for a view of Raquette Lake. At night they placed chicken bones around the fire in hopes of baiting wild animals that they could observe from their beds in the lean-to in their open camp. Luckily, nothing more dangerous than a raccoon ever arrived to entertain them!

One evening the children took hunks of foxfire, a bioluminescent fungus, to bed with them in an attempt to read by the organic glow of its light. Their mother cooked pancakes every Sunday on "Big Bertha," the wood-burning cook stove in the rustic camp kitchen. There was no phone at Sunny Cliff, and for several years Rachel washed diapers by hand for at least two children not yet potty trained. Growing up on Raquette was a magical experience. Rod's family spent the rest of the year counting the days until they would return to camp, the one place where they all felt connected to the mountains, the lake and to each other. It is no wonder that this beloved camp is what keeps Rod united with his sisters who still visit Sunny Cliff with their own families every summer.

As the only boy at Sunny Cliff for most of the time, (his Dad came up occasionally on weekends), Rod kept busy by building and taking things apart. As a result he learned how engines and switches work. He could maintain a chain saw and make minor repairs on the motor boat. At home in Ridgewood, he was more fascinated by his bicycle when it lay on the driveway in pieces than as a vehicle on which to explore the neighborhood. The day he got in big trouble for disassembling his neighbor's tricycle is now family lore. He was unable to reassemble it without the help of his angry Dad.

After high school Rod made an attempt to major in Forestry at Paul Smith's College, but his heart was not into his studies. After one semester, he left school. For the next several years he searched for something that would allow him to prosper without an education.

Although he was motivated to work, no options seemed to scratch the itch that he felt certain was his destiny. He moved to Sarasota, Florida, where his parents were then living in retirement eight months of the year. Two of his sisters, Donna and Dodi, lived there as well, each with a husband and eventually a young family of her own. Rod spent that winter on Longboat Key, providing boat maintenance at a marina. But once summer arrived, he headed back to Raquette Lake to work providing maintenance for a private family's estate on North Point. He spent the winter there and moved to Syracuse the following spring.

Next, Rod attended community college to learn electronics and computer programming. While enrolled, he took riding lessons for a physical education requirement. After earning the credit, he signed up to work in the barn during a vacation so that he could continue to ride.

After two semesters of community college, Rod still didn't feel that he was headed in the right direction. He took a job maintaining the stores of a chain of fast food restaurants that included Arthur Treacher's and Kentucky Fried Chicken in the Syracuse area.

With the coming of summer once again, he headed back to Raquette Lake where eventually he began working on the maintenance crew at the Raquette Lake Girl's Camp. Rod also provided mechanical maintenance in the months prior to and after camp until winter when he headed back to Sarasota to work construction until the following spring. He lived frugally, saving his money. By the fall of 1984, he had saved enough for the down payment on a severely neglected camp about ten miles southwest of Raquette Lake in Inlet, NY. Although the camp was an eyesore, the land and the Sixth Lake frontage it sat on had the potential to be quite lovely. His plan was to fix up the house, landscape the property and then sell it within the next four or five years. Little did Rod know that close to twenty years would pass before he moved out of his first house.

The summer I met Rod, he had already spent one winter remodeling his lake house. By the time I saw it for the first time, it was well on its way to becoming a cozy little cottage with close to 200 feet of private lake frontage.

Rod loved animals too. Earlier in the summer of 1983, his sister Karen had arrived for her annual visit to Sunny Cliff with an eight-week-old ball of fluff. Mishka was a mixture of several breeds, including Malamute, Husky and Samoyed. Karen and her husband Dave bred these dogs from two beautiful females that they owned. Rod had expressed an interest in taking one of the future puppies after visiting his sister in Virginia over the winter. July was perfect timing to wean the pup and deliver her to her new master. As much as Rod loved Mishka and enjoyed watching her grow up at Sunny Cliff, his job prevented him from spending lots of quality time with her while she was small. The task of raising the puppy fell to his mother Rachel, who gladly accepted the responsibility. It is not surprising that Mishka and Rachel developed a strong bond.

Rod's mother was in her early sixties when I first met her. Tall and lean, Rachel epitomized the typical Adirondack retiree. Her permanently tan complexion complimented closely cropped steel gray hair framing her sturdy face. Her smiling blue eyes crinkled with wisdom and appreciation gleaned from having spent every summer at her family's camp on Raquette Lake. When I first knew her, Rachel traversed the woods that surrounded Sunny Cliff despite stiffness from crippling arthritis. She bathed in the lake, fished from her guide boat and prepared meals with the bounty from her husband's garden. In later years, her family purchased a golf cart so that she could still visit the landscapes of her childhood around camp.

Rachel had a trained soprano singing voice that trilled across the lake when the mood struck. She was a gifted woodcarver, creating exquisite wildlife from blocks of soft pine. She enjoyed cooking, reading, but most of all she loved spending time with her five children and their families, particularly at Sunny Cliff.

Rachel was a consummate animal lover, particularly of wild animals and birds. She grew up between two worlds. In summer she lived a primitive life at Sunny Cliff where she learned to appreciate the simplicity and beauty of nature. In winter, she joined the prosperous family who migrated from Montclair, New Jersey, to wait out the cold weather in Sarasota before returning to Montclair in the spring. She, along with her three older brothers, switched schools, back and forth, in late fall and again in late spring. Through this combination of lifestyles, Rachel developed into a lively, adaptable woman who attended fancy parties with the same ease with which she baited a fishhook, built a campfire and rowed a guide boat.

Rachel and Mishka became inseparable during the carefree summer months at Sunny Cliff. If Rachel was wood carving on the sagging porch of the old house with her power tools close at hand, Mishka was lying lazily on the lawn, chewing on a dog toy or napping in the shade of the tall white pine trees that protected the house from wind. If Rachel was reading a book on the dock in the sun of a glorious afternoon, Mishka was plucking blueberries from the side of the hill between the house and the lake. This relationship worried us as we wondered how Mishka would react when Big Rod and Rachel headed to Florida for the winter and she was left with young Rod, her intended master.

At the end of the summer of 1985, Promise, the dogs and I made our way back to New Jersey, wondering if my relationship with Rod would survive long distance through the coming winter. It did. The following year on June 7th, (Promise's 13th birthday), Rod and I were married.

The winter was a flurry of wedding plans with many decisions and arrangements to make. Rod and I visited each other just about every other weekend. I taught a second year at Centenary while he diligently remodeled the house in Inlet. By spring we had decided to settle in Inlet after our wedding and make a go of life together in the Adirondacks. On June 7, 1986, we were married at Grace Presbyterian Church in Jenkintown. Rod wore a morning suit. I wore my mother's ivory satin wedding gown. Its long train from the 1950s was fashioned into 1980s style puffy sleeves. However, the tiny buttons that ran down the back of the gorgeous dress remained the focal point. We exchanged vows while one hundred of our closest friends and family witnessed. Afterwards we celebrated with champagne and sat down to dine under a tent in my family's backyard. Lori caught the bouquet. It was quite late when Rod and I finally left the dance floor and exited the party. After a week in Bermuda, Eric, Ludie, and I moved into the house on Sixth Lake with Rod and Mishka. Almost immediately, plans to include horses on the small acreage began to take shape.

LIVING WITH HORSES...

Rod and I spent our first married summer together at the RLGC, living in a little cottage next to the riding stable. Promise was shipped up from New Jersey, but this time no return arrangements were necessary. The other leased horses arrived shortly before camp began. Several days into the new camp season, Billy developed an abscess on one of his hind legs that prevented him from being ridden. The horse dealer agreed to replace him; within a few days the swap was made.

A skinny chestnut Quarter Horse gelding emerged from the trailer. Only three years old, he was fairly well started, but not necessarily a good mount for beginners. In fact, he was too young and too green to instill confidence in children who were just beginning to get used to the bounciness of the trot. Therefore, I began riding Windy to school some brakes into him. Naturally, I developed an emotional attachment to the gangly youngster. As the summer progressed, it began to occur to me that Windy might be a good companion for Promise once camp ended and the camp horses left her all alone.

In mid-August, Rod and I moved back to our lake house in Inlet. As the summer days shortened into fall, we planned to move Promise to our property. First Rod had to clear a wooded area and build a paddock that would hold a horse until a barn and other paddocks could follow. We moved Promise to the local hack stable just down the road where she remained during the month of September.

Meanwhile, discussion about the purchase of Windy began to take a more serious tone. Promise had demonstrated her feelings about living as an only horse. In fact, she had never lived alone. Horses are herd animals; they depend on the herd for emotional health. Before camp started, Promise had spent one night alone before the camp horses arrived the next day. She could hear other horses up the road at a neighbor's barn in Raquette. I remember her leaping over the four-foot door of her new box stall and ripping it off of the hinges as she caught a hind toe. Unhurt, she raced out of camp in the direction of the neighboring horses. This incident made Rod and me realize that she would need companionship when we moved her to our home.

We made arrangements to purchase Windy at the end of October and bring him to the boarding stable where Promise was awaiting the completion of our new barn. On November 1, 1986, I walked Promise and Windy two miles from the hack stable to our house and waited with them on lead ropes as Rod finished installing the last few rails of their paddock. On that day I realized my life-long dream of living with horses on my own property! While I waited, I allowed the two chestnuts to graze on the sparse lawn next to the house.

They appeared content to stand there and eat. At noon, I decided to unclip their lead ropes and leave them while Rod and I headed indoors for lunch. Big mistake! All was peaceful for a time as I checked on them often. We even took our lunch outdoors to keep an eye on them. Suddenly,

Finding My Way to Mountain View Farm

Promise lifted her head, realizing that she was in a strange place with no fence. She stopped chewing for a few seconds as her brain made the decision to head for the only home she knew, two miles away! Off she went with Windy in tow, all the way back to the hack stable. Luckily, they were not hit by traffic. Once again I walked the two of them back to their new home where Rod secured the new paddock with several nails since the gate had yet to be installed. And so our horse-keeping experience began.

For weeks, Rod worked diligently through November and December constructing the perfect horse home, a two-stall pole barn with a wash stall, huge feed bin and a small area for tack. The hayloft could hold up to 150 bales of hay, enough to keep two horses satisfied for months. That first winter I pinched myself every day as I cared for my horses at home while snow blanketed the Adirondacks from mid-November until late April.

Promise and Windy moved into their stalls on Christmas Eve. My mother and father were visiting with us when we tucked them into their stalls and began the tradition of "Bedtime Carrots," a ritual that has carried on nightly ever since.

As the pieces of life with horses began to fit into place that first married winter, I began to plan my career as a riding instructor in the Adirondacks. The local hack stable where Promise and Windy had spent the month of October did have a fenced in ring of sorts. In exchange for caring for all of their horses while the owners were on vacation that spring, I was offered free use of the ring during the coming summer. Two girls who worked at the hack barn signed on to take lessons along with a few local children, two of whom had horses of their own. I was officially in business.

The summer routine began each morning with me leading Promise and Windy two miles up the road to teach at the riding stable. The problem with this situation arose when a thunderstorm would catch us on the way in either direction. Although I was grateful for the use of the facility, I was eager to teach in my own backyard.

Rod and I began to study our property that consisted of a large wooded area across from the barn and paddock. After much planning, both financial and aesthetic, we made the decision to clear and fill an area for a 180-by-80 foot fenced-in ring. By the beginning of summer 1988, the fence was in place, and Promise and Windy had a larger turnout paddock in which to kick up their heels. Riding in the new ring was liberating. Finally I not only had a barn in my backyard but an area to train in as well. I thought life couldn't get any better than this. But it did.

Once the outdoor ring was excavated and fenced in, I advertised my services as a riding instructor. With Windy and Promise, I ran quite an efficient lesson program that carefully and creatively used the talents of my two horses. Three of my students had their own horses, which alleviated the pressure on mine. I rarely used Promise and Windy for more than one lesson a day unless one of the students was a rank beginner who didn't require much of the horse's energy as she focused mostly on steering and applying the brakes. Both horses had at least one day off during the week. My own riding suffered as there just wasn't enough time for me to ride and give all the lessons. Occasionally I hopped on Windy, who was still fairly green and inexperienced, to refresh some of the lessons that he had been taught over the last year.

Owning horses is expensive, and teaching riding is not necessarily a lucrative way to cover the monthly expenses associated with their upkeep. Rod was working full time for a local contractor and taking in approximately $300 per week. Our monthly mortgage was $316 and once we paid electricity and food, there was little left to hoard in our savings. My college degree in Animal Science was essentially worthless in Inlet. Although I was using it to care for my horses, it wasn't generating a single dollar of profit. To supplement my income, I worked part-time at the local convenience store and cleaned rental cottages on Saturdays or change-over days at a local resort. Both of these jobs were opportunities offered by parents of my riding students, and I appreciated the income.

With only two horses, my lesson schedule was as full as it could possibly be during the summer months. I really couldn't afford to add another horse. Besides, I only had two stalls in my barn. Once summer was over, I worked more hours at the E-Z Mart. Frequently I worked the 4:00 p.m. to midnight closing shift. While I made sandwiches for local contractors who would be in early the next morning and stocked beer in the cooler, it occurred to me that I really needed to use my academic credentials.

Working in the store provided me with the chance to meet the Inlet locals. The morning shift, my favorite, began at 6:00 a.m. as the local working men gathered for a healthy exchange of town gossip over coffee before heading off to work. While I fried donuts behind the counter, they discussed the latest building code changes, APA, (Adirondack Park Agency), restrictions on their building sites, and general gossip. Working at the store provided me with an accelerated history lesson on Inlet residents and town politics.

For the first four years of our marriage, I watched the seasons change through the large picture window behind the counter at E-Z Mart. I knew I needed more stimulation in terms of income and brain exercise. At least my riding lesson program in the good weather months fed my passion. I loved working with my students, instilling a love and respect for horses that I hoped would transfer to other animals and perhaps to people as well. I began to recognize different learning styles among my young riders as some progressed faster by listening to my explanations and others learned faster when I showed them various techniques. I reveled in every "aha" moment I witnessed.

"It's going to be very bumpy when he starts to trot, so I want you to try to stand up and sit down in rhythm with the bumps. Like this; up, down, up, down, up, down," I instructed beginners as they prepared to trot for the first time on a horse.

This moment is so significant in a rider's education because the horse is just about to take over control of the ride, and the rider is most vulnerable at that time. But when the rider's brain forces the body to find the rhythm of rising and sitting with each beat, the rider assumes control. It's a powerful sensation.

"Reach down and rub his neck with your palm," I encouraged after the horse jumped a cross-rail effortlessly so that the rider felt the correct position of her body. "Tell him he is a good boy."

"Pretend your legs are two pieces of cooked spaghetti hanging off each side of the saddle." I use this visual image to convey the feeling of balance rather than grip necessary to trot without stirrups for long periods of time. There is no better exercise for developing the rider's position.

During the summer of 1988, I purchased a three-year-old Appendix Quarter Horse from the same dealer who sold Windy to me. Rod built an addition of two stalls onto the existing barn to accommodate the new herd member. Spy Hopes was a handsome chestnut gelding who had raced, winning twice as a two-year-old in Oklahoma the previous summer. His laid back personality fit nicely into my riding program, while his athletic abilities were fun for me to develop. Spy and Windy developed a tight bond almost immediately. I could never have predicted the incredible loyalty and devotion that they would demonstrate eighteen years later.

"If only I could make a substantial living teaching riding," I thought often. Unfortunately, the logistics were not realistic. I would require a larger barn and more horses, and then I would be dependent on my horses to make a living. I would require a revolving door of horse flesh because it is never financially realistic to keep horses for sentimental reasons once they have outlived their usefulness in a lesson program. This last fact always brought me to my senses. Still, I never gave up the vision of me as some kind of instructor. Perhaps my destiny did include teaching after all.

In Addition to Horses...

DOG DAYS

Although my life has been consumed by the care and management of horses, I have never lost sight of my childhood dream to live with other animals as well. Maturity, thankfully, has discouraged me from seeking to own a lion or a giraffe, but fate has connected me with a long list of creatures that have come in and out of my life over the past thirty years. At the top of the list are our dogs. Unlike the horses, dogs reside in the house with us, providing constant comfort and companionship when Rod and I are at leisure.

Mishka, Eric and Luther comprised what we refer to as the first generation of dogs that Rod and I shared. All of them lived long lives, well into their teens. Unfortunately, Mishka's husky genes encouraged her to run. Managing her outdoors required that she be tethered at all times. It is legal to shoot any dog caught chasing deer in the Adirondacks. The risk of losing her that way was out of the question. We also feared that she might be hit by a car or fall through the ice on the lake. Neither Rod nor I was raised with a dog chained in our backyard, but Mishka's sheer will and determination gave us no choice. Still, her lack of freedom gnawed at us. Eventually, we were able to provide her with some of the freedom she craved.

From late May until the end of September, Mishka went off to summer camp with the enthusiasm of a young child! At Sunny Cliff she was free to roam in the woods without the threat of cars or humans who might misinterpret her intentions. At Sunny Cliff she also had Rachel. Like a doting grandmother, Rachel fussed over Mishka, providing her with all the comfort that a dog needed. As a result of constant freedom and her devotion to Rachel, Mishka never strayed very far from the house. Occasionally, she visited Big Rod as he toiled behind the house in his meticulously weeded garden.

My Rod and I visited Sunny Cliff often, including every Sunday and at least one other day of the work week during the summer months. With Eric and Luther wrapped up in a blanket, we made the trip across the lake in Rod's party barge. Our visits always included a long walk out to the "Falls" up Sucker Brook just beyond the trail to West Mountain. Mishka trotted along, especially if Rachel joined us. Upon returning to the house, the two little dogs curled up together on the couch for a snooze, but Mishka escaped from the summer heat by crawling underneath the deck in front of the house. There, with her collection of chew toys accumulated over the years, she napped until dusk. Meanwhile, Rod and I enjoyed a delicious meal with Big Rod, Rachel and the extended family members who visited throughout the summer months. Those were wonderful times for all of our dogs and us.

All too soon, the leaves began to change color and a chill crept into the air, a signal that Big Rod and Rachel would be leaving soon. Mishka never fretted over their packed boxes or the trips they made across the lake to pack the car. Once they were gone, she returned to Inlet, accepting her circumstances with a weary sigh.

Rod frequently took her back to Sunny Cliff with him on the days he spent moving docks and closing up camps for the coming winter. Sensing

Rachel's absence, Mishka remained on Rod's party barge throughout the day. Even after Rod called her to join him up at the house, she returned to the boat, preferring to wait for him there instead.

She resigned herself to life in Inlet, accepting it with grace and dignity. But once the sun began to heat up the Adirondacks the following spring, Mishka became restless. By May she stood alert in the yard and concentrated on every car that came down the driveway. When the car did not turn out to be who she was hoping for, she relaxed her vigil and ignored the guest. Not long after Memorial Day, the car she had been awaiting finally appeared. Her entire body twisted and wiggled with excitement once she identified the driver and passenger who emerged from the car. Then she released a howl and cry with short barks that she never uttered except on this occasion. As Big Rod and Rachel fussed over her, she pranced in front of the car door. When it was opened, she leapt right in and sat down quietly in the space that had been reserved just for her.

Then Rod and I stuck our heads in to say goodbye. With an air of impatience, she turned her head away from us, refusing to make eye contact for fear we might make her get out of the car and stay behind. With a hug and a smile, we sent her off for her long awaited four months at camp with Grandma and Grandpa. After all the car doors were secured, the station wagon made its way up the driveway, back to Raquette Lake and Sunny Cliff for one more summer. This routine continued unaltered for thirteen happy years.

THE GOATIE DANCE

Three days before our second married Christmas, two Toggenburg goats, a mother and her young son, arrived at our barn unexpectedly. The goats were a gift from the couple who owned E-Z Mart. Apparently, they felt that this was the most appropriate gift to give to somebody who had admired the goat that lived with their own horses. The goats were given to me as a joke more or less, but I loved them immediately as they reminded me of poor misunderstood Pierre. We named them Noel and Gideon, a reference to the time of year that they arrived on the farm.

The fully intact little male goat entered the barn and promptly sprayed urine everywhere he could possibly aim. Within forty eight hours, we arranged for the surgery that changed Gideon from a buck to a wether and eventually cured him of that dirty habit. Unfortunately, the vet couldn't remove his well-established horns. They should have been burned off when he was a kid for once the large blood vessels develop within growing horns, cutting them off will likely cause the goat to bleed to death. For his entire life, Gideon wielded them like weapons, thrusting them against anybody or anything he found objectionable.

Noel was a dear and docile goat who appeared grateful to have ended up on our farm. Her friendly good nature allowed me to relax in her presence. And so, in addition to horses and dogs, we now added goats to our menagerie. Eventually, we rescued another horned goat, Helen, who also thrust her abusive crown from time to time.

Living with our three goats gave me insight into the unique temperament and behavior of caprines in general. Goats were the first animals to be domesticated, having provided humans with meat, fiber and milk for thousands of years. A goat's personality is rather extroverted although aloof at times. Nothing demonstrates the sheer exuberance of the goatie spirit than the crazy, jaunty dance they perform when their mood is high. One can't help but feel uplifted, (or better yet, tempted to join in), while watching goats bounce up off of all four legs only to land in a spastic twisted heap before taking flight again. The agility of the goat is particularly impressive when the animal races down a steep hill performing the "goatie dance." The first sunny days of spring or crisp fall days after a hot summer inspire the goats to dance.

Five months after Helen visited briefly with a buck on a breeding farm two hours away, she gave birth to two little does whom we named Rachel and Hannah. Many anticipated their birth, including Mom, Sue and Grammie, who all arrived just hours before their birth. Even Amy, only five years old at the time, was present to see these tiny miracles.

With the arrival of Rachel and Hannah, we were officially in the milking goat business. For the next six months, I milked Helen twice a day. Rod dutifully poured the milk on his cereal despite the pungent aroma that reminded us of old Band-aids. The large quantities of milk that Helen provided forced me to become creative. I dabbled in cheese making and used the whey that was separated from the curds to bake bread. Big Rod sent me many articles and books to fuel my endeavor.

Five months after a second visit with the same breeding buck, Helen gave birth to an enormous male kid that we named Jordan. His striking markings included two black and white stripes on either side of his face against a honey colored background. From the beginning, he exuded great confidence by leaving his mother's side and curling up in my lap for a goat nap. Even as he grew bigger, he still tried to cuddle in my lap. Eventually, we had to come up with an alternate arrangement. By lying down close to my side, he could stretch his head into my lap where I could scratch, rub and kiss him.

Jordan and I shared a special bond. I didn't love him more than the other goats, but I felt he and I communicated on a more intimate level. Therefore, the decision to have him euthanized when he was only four years old was that much more devastating for me than the inevitably sad decision that is made when an elderly animal clearly communicates that the time has come.

In late spring of that year, Jordan began to strain when urinating. After many visits, our vet Meg Brooker determined that Jordan was suffering from urinary calculi or bladder stones. The male goat's urethra is a long convoluted tube with a small diameter. He is prone to developing stones when fed high protein concentrated feed. This combination of factors produced a poor prognosis for Jordan. Even an experimental surgery, (similar to the one performed on cats with the same condition), which Dr. Brooker agreed to try as a last resort was not able to cure the condition. By the end of July, it was clear that Jordan was suffering as his kidneys produced urine that his bladder could not eliminate. With a crumbling heart, I held Jordan's head in my lap one more time. Our vet performed the ritual that took his pain away and brought him final peace.

Finding My Way to Mountain View Farm

The rest of the goats lived long into their teens. Eventually, we were left with Hannah all alone after the death of her mother Helen. Her sadness cast a cloud over Lakeview Farm for two weeks until Rod and I made arrangements to purchase a young doe to keep her company. In the meantime, Hannah cried constantly and camped out on our deck at the patio doors where she waited and bleated for us to come out and be with her. Finally, we arrived home with Lacey, a small Nubian Pygmy cross who established herself as Hannah's companion for the next two years.

I have often wondered over the years whatever became of Pierre. His memory is vivid in every goat encounter that I experience. Hopefully, owning goats is a way in which to honor him. Our guests often ask me why I keep goats as pets considering how pushy they can be. With a smile I always offer the same reply.

"Somebody has to be in charge of the barn."

FEATHERED FRIENDS

Perhaps what attracted me most to Rod when I first met him was his love of animals. He had grown up with a family dog named Taffy and an interesting collection of wildlife that strolled into the family from time to time. A baby skunk named Flower is fondly remembered for releasing his musk right in Rachel's hand while crossing Raquette Lake in a boat. There was also an orphaned Mallard duckling who lived comfortably at Sunny Cliff one summer until he was old enough to take care of himself.

Rod can identify every species of bird that inhabits our yard by song or plumage. As the lake house entered its final stage of construction in the early 1990s, he began to think seriously about building a chicken coop and raising a flock for eggs and perhaps meat. This idea occurred early in our marriage when we practiced some homesteading skills. I was milking the goat and making cheese. We spent one spring tapping trees and boiling maple sugar in our yard. Rod also created a garden and enclosed it with a high fence to keep the deer and goats out.

Although I knew nothing about chickens, I had had a pet Rhode Island Red hen years ago. She had appeared out of nowhere one day at the barn where Promise was boarded. The only explanation for her sudden arrival was that she must have fallen off of one of the large trucks that raced up busy highway Rt. 309 that ran parallel to the barn. "Chicken" spent the first week in the basement of my house recovering from her ordeal. Eventually, my father found out about her and suggested that she move out to live with the other farm animals. From then on she took up residence in Promise's stall and eventually could be counted on to produce an egg a day in a nest that she made in the corner. Being an only chicken, she became quite friendly and followed me around the barn. She sat in my lap on those summer afternoons when I sought refuge from the heat and bugs in Promise's stall. Sadly, that fall, Chicken disappeared as suddenly as she had appeared. I searched for her for days, hoping she would reappear in the barn yard. Years later Lori confessed to me that Chicken had been killed by two Dobermans who visited the property from time to time.

Rod built a coop and a pen for his Araucana chickens. Chickens are a magnet for predators, so half the challenge of raising them is building a fortress that will protect them from the most diligent foes. Raccoons, weasels and foxes are determined to decimate a whole flock. Once they discover how to break through security, these predators will return again and again until the last bird is killed. For over ten years, Rod succeeded in keeping his birds safe. Unfortunately, they outlived their egg production ability by more than half of those years and spent the majority of their lives more or less as pets. We were too attached to them by then to butcher them for meat.

In the early days of the flock, we discovered that two of the chickens were roosters. Our small flock could only handle a single rooster so Rod decided that we should eat one of them. It was a time consuming and unpleasant experience for Rod. Each phase from killing to serving it on a plate was difficult for him emotionally. Both of us have tremendous respect for how meat is produced and conveniently sold in cellophane so that we don't have to identify it with the animal who sacrificed itself for us. Perhaps this is hypocritical thinking but I prefer to think of it as gratitude.

BACK TO SCHOOL...

In December, 1988, I received a phone call from the Superintendent of the Town of Webb School, the local public school in Old Forge, just ten miles south and west of Inlet. He wondered if I was interested in taking on a long term substitute teacher position in Science for the third quarter of the year. The Chemistry teacher was expecting her first baby then and planned to take ten weeks of maternity leave.

"No, thank you," I replied as images of my struggle through high school chemistry surfaced from only a decade ago. I was a bit more successful in college chemistry, but the thought of teaching the concepts was too traumatizing to even consider. A week later he called back.

Two years prior to the phone calls, I had submitted my resume for substitute teaching to several schools in the area. The elementary schools in Inlet and Raquette Lake had called as often as they needed to hire subs for their small number of teachers. Raquette Lake School boasted itself as the smallest district in New York State, with only two teachers to cover the entire curriculum for students Kindergarten through sixth grade. The total student population fluctuated between fewer than ten and just over twenty on any given year. The Town of Webb School administrators had never called me until they realized that my science degree just might make me a candidate to teach Chemistry.

"Please give this request some consideration before you flat out refuse," begged Superintendent Bill Gilbert. This time he sounded a bit desperate as the clock ticked ever closer to Mrs. Smith's long term absence from her Regents Chemistry class.

"Perhaps if you stop in to talk to Mrs. Smith and look through the textbook, you could get a feel for what is expected," he urged.

Just before the Christmas break, I walked into the Town of Webb School for the first time. After a brief interview with Mr. Gilbert, I found Sue Smith busy in her science classroom. Her big smile and welcoming attitude put me at ease immediately. The large textbook that she hauled off her desk produced a look of panic on my face. Sensing my anxiety,

Sue assured me that I would have no trouble with my scientific background. She was right!

In order to teach a subject, the teacher has to know the material backwards and forwards, inside and out. There is no faking it if you expect your students to learn it correctly. The class was covering the levels and sublevels of atomic models. While vividly recalling the days at Abington Friend's School as a tortured Chemistry student, I began to scan the large textbook. With a bit of time, it all began to make perfect black-and-white sense, almost like a multiple step math problem. Suddenly there was a spark in my confidence.

"I can do this," I affirmed strongly, denying my doubts.

And I did.

Early in the morning of a late frosty January day, I received the call that Sue had gone into labor, and my career with the Town of Webb School officially began.

For ten weeks I taught Chemistry, Environmental Science, and two sections of Earth Science. I loved every minute of it. The biggest challenges came from managing the adolescent and teenage students in my classroom. Luckily, the principal supported every discipline referral that I made. Most of the students were well behaved and generally interested in doing well. The time flew by; in no time the snow had melted and spring was on its way back to the Adirondacks. Mrs. Smith was also on her way back to the classroom. When my services were no longer needed, I left the classroom with a sense of loss and foreboding. I had enjoyed the routine of teaching and the interactions with educated adults and other co-workers. I wanted to feel that way again but wasn't quite sure how to go about it.

For the rest of the school year, I continued to sub often at Town of Webb. One day I would cover a second grade classroom, the next day classes in high school social studies. After one or two days of not being called in, three days in a row might find me bouncing from science to math to Kindergarten. I loved the contrast, and my experience teaching college students gave me the confidence to walk into a classroom and take over whatever content required covering.

Finding My Way to Mountain View Farm

As luck would have it, there was a shift among the teachers the following school year. I was hired to fill a teacher's aide position. This full-time position placed me in the school library where I inventoried all forms of media while cataloguing books. At various times of the day, I worked with elementary students one on one, providing extra practice in math and reading skills. In addition I spent an hour a day supervising the cafeteria while the elementary school students ate lunch. The job was stimulating, diverse and paid our health insurance. As much as I loved the job, I couldn't help feeling that, with my education, I should be aspiring to teach rather than settling for the aide position.

By June of the following year, I had enrolled at Goddard College in Plainfield, Vermont, to pursue a Master's Degree in education. At the time the Town of Webb was expanding and adding teachers every year. Therefore, I planned to earn my degree and certification in elementary education, middle school science and biology. That way I would be qualified for a number of positions if the need arose.

Goddard's program offered correspondence courses in which the student worked independently on curriculum and submitted term papers, periodically to an assigned adviser. However, a one-week, on-campus, residency was required at the beginning of each semester, a small price to pay to avoid a commute to attend classes in Utica or Albany.

While at Goddard I met and became friends with many interesting professional people. One was an art teacher from Cape Cod named Cathy who spent her summers documenting whale behavior on a whale watching boat. She was fun to be with and shared my sense of humor. During the last required residency in which we presented our theses, Cathy brought with her one of her best friends from home. Spending time with them that weekend was pure joy. Their camaraderie based on the longevity of their friendship reminded me of my bond with Lori, Lisa, Missy and May. They made me realize that although I had acquaintances in Inlet, what I was lacking were a couple of good girlfriends who loved me at my worst as well as at my best. Friends who listened when I needed to vent and offered advice with no strings attached. And most of all, I needed friends who loved horses.

A Promise Kept...

By the spring of 1990, Promise was having severe respiratory issues. She was only seventeen, but years of exposure to dusty barns and hay had wreaked havoc on her lungs. The first attack of heaves had occurred shortly after she returned to Centenary in August of her first summer at RLGC. Systemic steroids and twenty-four/seven turnout had brought it under control, but from that first episode she became very sensitive to the quality of air in her environment. From then on, I paid close attention to her breathing, always providing her with wet hay and keeping the barn doors open, even through the winter.

That spring she seemed to be suffering more; unfortunately, the steroids were having little effect in relieving her discomfort. The hot, dry summer didn't help, and I worried about what to do. She seemed too young to euthanize, and I wasn't ready to let her go. Eventually, she took care of the matter herself.

It was Monday, August 13th. My mother and Sue were visiting along with Amy and her little brother John. The horses were turned out in the ring for the morning hours. My plan was to leave them there as long as the flies remained at bay. Once they arrived the horses would start racing around the paddock, frantically trying to escape the stinging bites.

At noon I began to make sandwiches for my family. The horses were still calm when I glanced out the window. In the middle of my preparation, I noticed that Windy and Spy had begun to trot around in the ring as the first flies of the day began to pester. I just needed to finish making lunch before I headed out to the paddock to rescue the horses. Within five minutes, I was on my way out the door and up the driveway to complete my mission before sitting down to enjoy lunch with my family.

Halfway to the barn, I heard a loud crack. When I looked up into the paddock, Windy and Spy were galloping at top speed around the ring, partly in fear of the loud noise and partly to escape the nibbling flies. But Promise was not in the ring. She was nowhere to be seen from where I stood in the driveway. Eventually, my scanning eyes spied four broken rails on the far side of the paddock where the earth dropped a good eight feet into the swampy woods on the other side. There was no sound of struggle or of a horse crashing around in the woods. I began to panic as a sickening thought occurred to me. Quickly, I brought the two stressed horses into the barn and secured them in their stalls. Then I ran back up to the paddock and rushed across to the hole in the fence. My heart pounded in my chest as I prepared for what I was about to see.

She was lying very still at the bottom of the drop-off. Only her chestnut mane fluttered in the gentle breeze. Her head was twisted back toward her neck at an unnatural angle. I knew she was gone. She must have died instantly when her neck broke. At that moment a quiet surreal sense enveloped me as my mind began to comprehend that Promise was gone. To this day we do not know what happened. It is hard for me to picture her running around the paddock with Windy and Spy when the voracious flies arrived in the moments before I could rescue them. Her difficulty in breathing prevented her from engaging in such efforts. Had she collapsed while standing next to the fence, thus breaking the rails with the force of her body? We will never know. In the twenty years since, I have thought of that day often, relived it with my sister, Amy, and mother and prayed that she hadn't suffered at all.

Desperate attempts to contact Rod who was working up in Blue Mountain Lake that day failed. When he arrived home late in the afternoon, he was left with the task of arranging for a backhoe to come and bury Promise. By then it had begun to rain. The mood in the house was solemn as we watched the final preparations up in the ring. I could not bear to watch when they finally lifted her up in the bucket and lowered her into the giant hole. Six-year-old Amy watched out the kitchen window and assured me that Promise looked peaceful and comfortable resting in the big scoop.

My mother offered the most comforting words to me that day. She said, "Isn't it something that I was with you when we first laid eyes on Promise, when she arrived at the barn and became yours, and now here today when it is time to say goodbye?"

Yes, that was something. But it saddened me that I never really got to say goodbye and to tell her how much she meant to me in all the years that we were together. She followed me to the end of my childhood and into adulthood, never disappointing me along the way. I vowed on that day that I would stay with all of my animals until the very end. So far I have kept my promise and I hope I will always be able to plan that day and follow through. Although the pain of loss is immense, I owe it to each one of them to hold on tight until their last breath.

WHEELS FOR LUDIE...

Two days after Promise's untimely death, Ludie jumped out of the car in the driveway and was surprised to find that his hind legs were dragging behind him. There had been warning signs all spring and summer. Sometimes he yelped when we picked him up or squeaked while changing position in bed. Our vet at the time hoped that a combination of steroids and keeping Ludie inactive would thwart the most common condition in Dachshunds and other long backed breeds.

With this prescribed care, Ludie appeared to recover and life went on as usual. Rod and I tried to keep his jumping activity to a minimum but were not as diligent as we should have been. This time, however, his useless legs didn't seem to cause him the discomfort that he had displayed previously. Our vet recommended that we take Ludie to Cornell University's Veterinary School Hospital for a more thorough examination and more up-to-date options for treatment.

On a humid August day, Rod and I drove to Ithaca. How strange it was to return to this grand Mecca of education. This time I would be on the receiving end of the research performed there. The young veterinary intern assigned to Ludie examined him thoroughly. Most of the inspection consisted of pinching his toes and tail. The vet stood Ludie up on all fours and supported him with one hand under his chest while the other held his tail straight up. With Ludie in standing position, he released the tail and Ludie's whole hind end swayed from left to right before folding on its haunches in a heap. There was no question that Ludie had lost all control of his back legs.

Our only option, according to the young vet, was surgery to remove the protruding disks that were pinching vital nerves between Luther's vertebrae and then fuse the bones together. This procedure would stabilize the spine, but did not guarantee that the dog would gain the use of his hind legs. Rod and I were not really in a position to justify the expensive surgery. Feeling guilty, I declined the operation. Our next option was to purchase a small cart that would replace Ludie's hind legs and allow him to move freely around the house and yard. This solution was within our price range, and we returned home with Ludie and all the information necessary to get him back on four feet again.

Two weeks after we measured Ludie carefully for the perfect fit, the cart arrived via UPS. Meanwhile, I made several phone calls and inquiries about our little dog in an attempt to find other options that could help his condition. A veterinarian from New Jersey suggested that I put Ludie in the bathtub for swimming exercise. If there was any chance of recovery, I would know the instant the dog was put into the water. Dogs instinctively swim. Sure enough Luther's back legs began to paddle with uneven coordination when I held him just below the surface of the water. Three times a day, I took him out to the lake and held him for five minutes so that he could engage in this "doggie paddle" therapy.

But it was a chance encounter with a woman who just happened to be walking her Dachshund on a leash near the post office one day that allowed me to feel more optimistic. On my way in to get the mail, I started up a conversation with the woman as I bent down to pet her liver-colored Eric look-alike.

"Oh I have one who looks just like this one," I chortled more to the dog than to his owner.

"Aren't they wonderful dogs!" she exclaimed.

"Yes, but our other one is suffering from back issues at the moment and is dragging his hind end," I said with a sigh.

The woman had not missed my mood. Suddenly she began to speak enthusiastically. "Don't get discouraged. You just have to wait and you might have to wait a long time, weeks maybe, but don't give up. This dog had the same affliction and after two months, which I know is a long time, he started to regain the use of his legs."

She had my full attention as I waited to hear more.

"It took a long time, but eventually he began to use his hind legs more and more. Now, after developing strength and feeling back, he is fully recovered. You just have to be patient. Our vet wanted to do surgery on him, but we couldn't afford it and we are so glad that we just waited. Now we are very careful when he gets to jumping around."

She wished me good luck. For the first time in the weeks since Promise's death and Ludie's injury, I began to feel real hope. Her words continued to inspire me over the next several weeks as I tended to Ludie's needs.

Once he had figured out how to use the cart, Ludie's depressed mood lifted. With wheels attached, he could race around the yard and tend to his business without my hovering. Through the whole ordeal, he never lost control of his bladder; but the steroids made him thirsty and, therefore, increased his need to urinate. Sometimes he had accidents in the house.

By mid-September, Ludie still showed no signs of gaining the use of his hind legs. I tried not to get discouraged as I remembered the woman's emphasis on "a really long time." Then, on the last weekend of September, I took Windy and Spy out to Rochester to visit a friend and work with her trainer for the weekend. I was gone for three nights. It felt good to get away from all the sadness of the late summer and concentrate on the education of my two young horses. When Monday morning arrived, I was renewed and ready to return to the challenges at home. After the long trip back to Inlet, I pulled down the driveway with the horse trailer in tow and noticed a sign sitting on one of the deck chairs. On closer inspection, I noticed that the sign was attached to the little dog cart. My spirit began to soar as I read the message that had been generated on our new state-of-the-art dot matrix printer.

It read: *Cart for sale; ask for Luther!*

From that weekend on, Ludie's hind legs became stronger and stronger as feeling in them returned. Eventually, he gained full use of them, although the muscles never developed their full tone. As a result, his hind end looked bony, and he moved with a bit of a swagger. We hung the little cart in the garden shed, and Ludie went about his life on all four legs for ten more years.

PHOEBE...

As if my life wasn't full enough, I decided at one point in the early 1990s to get my wildlife rehabilitation license. I was beginning to receive many phone calls from folks who had found wild animals under stress. The license was a necessary credential in New York State, enabling one to possess and handle any form of wildlife. Word was getting around that I had a number of animals in my care and that I might be able to help in dire situations. Baby raccoons, birds of all species, a beautiful Barred owl and a Grebe all came my way in those early years. Sadly, they all succumbed to the stress of their injuries or diseases. Unfortunately, this is most common for wildlife rehabilitation. The message is that wildlife should be left in the wild, allowing nature to decide what is best for the animal. However, once in a while animals do recover successfully, and in the case of a special fawn, leave me with a most amazing experience to share.

It was one of those Decembers when the landscape freezes weeks before snow arrives, burying the Adirondacks for the next four months. Walking in the driveway is difficult because of permanent ruts left from November's mud. The residents begin to wish for a snowstorm to fill in the challenging terrain. The lakes appear to freeze instantly as temperatures remain well below freezing all day and all night. Light breaths of teaser snow swirl in the wind that will eventually deliver winter to Inlet. Without significant insulating snow, the surfaces of the lakes take on a glassy appearance that entices every would-be ice-skater to glide from one end of the lake to the other.

A retired couple living on Big Moose Lake had witnessed this spectacular phenomenon from the picture window of their camp. One morning, they were surprised to see a fawn sprawled on the frozen surface of the lake. The fawn was completely alone, lying motionless on the ice. Not sure what to do, they waited for a time to see if the fawn would make any attempt to move or if its mother would come back to rescue it.

By late morning, the couple could watch no more. Out to the ice they hurried to have a look at the situation. As they neared the form on the ice, they saw that the fawn was unable to get up as its hind legs were splayed at a ninety degree angle from its torso. The fawn appeared exhausted after perhaps hours spent struggling to stand up. It took the strength of both the man and the woman to haul the fawn to its feet and drag it to the shoreline. Fully expecting the fawn to establish its balance and bound off into the woods, they were surprised when it sank to the ground and refused to move. Eventually, they came to the conclusion that the fawn could not use its back legs at all as a result of falling on the ice.

Rehabilitating wildlife is extremely gratifying when the animal, healed from its injury, returns to its niche in the wild. Unfortunately, wild animals never arrive at a convenient time in a busy school teacher/horse trainer's life. The preparation time required to accept an injured animal is always challenged by how soon the animal needs to be delivered. The fawn was no exception. When the call came, I needed to prepare a cozy stall and sling situation for a partially grown fawn that had lost the use of its hind legs.

Thanks to my husband Rod and an old canvas wood carrier, we were able to rig up a sling that hung from the sturdy rafters of our old goat barn. The goats had moved out months ago to an empty stall in our horse barn, leaving their old shed vacant. By the time I returned from school that day, the fawn had arrived and was resting comfortably in the fresh bedding of the shed.

At first glance, I was taken by how extraordinarily beautiful the fawn was. Its large brown eyes and black nose composed the most endearing facial expression I had ever seen up close. Slowly, I entered the shed, careful not to frighten this wild animal now trapped in a small space. Its body tensed and tried to rise as I lowered myself into the straw, attempting to appear small and unthreatening. Carefully, I lifted the tail and was able to identify that the fawn was a young doe. She was very tiny, perhaps a late July or August birth. When I gently pinched her hind ankles, she reacted by pulling them up to her torso, a good sign that she did have feeling in the limbs. My guess at this point was that she had badly torn the muscles in her groin when she went down on the ice and further complicated her injury by struggling unsuccessfully to get up. Perhaps all she needed was a long rest so that the fibers of her muscles could repair and heal.

Finding My Way to Mountain View Farm

To prevent her from straining her hind limbs, I tied them loosely together with an old fleece polo wrap used to protect the legs of horses when training. That way if she did successfully rise on her own, there would be support to prevent her from re-injury. As long as I did not try to touch her, she remained calm. But when I wrapped my arms around her body to hoist her into the sling, she struggled to get free. I could feel her heart pound until I let go. The sling provided her with the support she needed to stand, a vital position for ruminants to digest food properly.

For approximately two weeks, the fawn, now named Phoebe, rested in the goat shed. Three times a day, we hoisted her into the sling so that she could practice standing and alleviate the stress on her vital organs. With her legs still bound together, she swayed quietly in the sling, seeming to accept our help. Eventually, she stopped struggling when I had to lift her. Now she was beginning to understand that I was associated with food, both hay and hot bran mash twice a day.

The snow arrived Christmas week, making up for lost time by dumping several feet over five days. School was out for vacation, so I was able to devote full time to my menagerie, including Phoebe. She was gaining strength and able to support weight on her limbs while hanging in the sling. However, she showed no interest in trying to rise on her own from the deep bed of hay. This reluctance began to concern me as I wondered about the extent of her injury.

I wondered if her spine was involved, preventing her from having the coordination to get up. If that was the case, what would I do with a paraplegic fawn? Obviously, she could never live in the wild. To care for her over the course of her life at my farm was not really an acceptable scenario either. I needn't have worried. Phoebe was just taking her own sweet time to heal and recover.

On New Year's Day, just one day before my vacation ended, I approached the goat shed early in the morning to feed Phoebe. There to greet me was the fawn with her head over the top of the lower half of the Dutch door. The rest of her body was standing, a bit wobbly, behind her. She had managed to rise to her feet in anticipation of her breakfast; for the first time, she enjoyed the steaming mash without hanging in the sling.

From this point in time, her recovery progressed quickly. She stood for most of the day and moved about her stall, thus strengthening her hind legs. I loosened the polo wrap that bound her legs, but was reluctant to remove it until she demonstrated more balance and control of her hind end. By the end of the first week of the year, I removed the wrap and began to entertain thoughts of moving her up to the goat paddock for more exercise than she could manage in the stall.

Because of her small size, I was able to carry her across the driveway and up to the paddock one day after school. It had been almost three weeks since Phoebe had arrived, and for all of that time she had only known the inside of the goat shed. Now, outdoors for the first time, she explored the paddock cautiously. With great interest, our three goats stretched their heads over the stall door that prevented them from joining Phoebe in the paddock. I had no intention of turning them out with the fawn. For now they would have to take turns using the paddock for exercise. Thus began the next two weeks' routine. The goats spent the school day in their paddock; when I returned in the afternoon, Phoebe took her turn out in the crisp fresh air.

As Phoebe's strength returned to her hind end, I began to ponder her release, always a difficult decision for a rehabilitator. There was no question that she would be released. It was a matter of when that challenged me. Now late January, the snow was several feet deep in the wooded areas of the Adirondacks. Finding food would be difficult, especially for a small weanling facing her first winter. The resident deer of Inlet were not traveling through our property, so she would be totally alone if I just opened the gate to the pen and let her go. But the longer she stayed in captivity as a juvenile, the more likely she was to imprint on humans and never stray far enough from them to keep herself safe. This dilemma weighed heavily in my thoughts until one day when Phoebe took care of the matter herself.

The goat/fawn turnout routine was steady as clockwork until the day I accidentally left the gate open while turning Phoebe out through the barn door into the paddock. Phoebe quickly caught my error and dashed through the open gate into the driveway. At first she appeared shocked by her freedom as she stood motionless, considering what to do next. Time stood still as I raced back through the barn and into the driveway, hoping to herd her back through the gate. Too late! Fully aware of my intentions to capture her, Phoebe took off up the driveway and into the deep snow of the woods. Darkness was falling quickly; and although I tried to follow her, hoping the deep snow would restrain the fawn until I could capture her, she simply disappeared.

I stood in the deep snow filled with worry. Would she be ok? Would I ever see her again? Had I just sent her to sure death by starvation, predation, or worse yet, automobile?

I decided to leave the light on and the door open in the shed just in case she found her way back. I left hay and grain for her in her stall. Despite the comfort of my domestic animals, all safe in the barn, the loss of Phoebe made for a restless, sleepless night. The next morning I felt sad as I trudged past the empty goat shed on my way to care for the animals in the barn. All day in school I wondered where she was and if she was frightened to be alone.

Two days after Phoebe's escape, the temperature plummeted to 17 degrees below zero. There happened to be a Board meeting at school in the evening that I needed to attend; it was well after 8:00 p.m. when I returned home. At the bottom of the driveway, my headlights shone on the silhouette of a small deer. Phoebe had found her way back. There was no telling how long she had been without food, but she was back! I immediately parked and jumped out of the car. She made it quite clear that she would not allow me to capture her. As I approached, she darted off into the woods out of sight once more.

Perhaps she was looking for food. Later that evening when I went out to do a barn check on the goats and horses, I decided to place hay and grain in Phoebe's stall and leave the door propped open and the heat lamp on in case she decided to come back to investigate.

All night long the lake moaned and cracked as the temperature dropped down to 22 degrees below 0. Trees popped and snapped as they adjusted to the extreme cold. Dreading my early morning barn chores, I made my way, grumbling under my breath, to the barn. I was fixated on my discomfort when a slight movement inside the shed caught my eye. Changing course, I approached to find Phoebe curled up in the hay of her stall. My icy disposition melted instantly. She had figured out how to be free and safe at the same time, making her way back to the stall for food and comfort. She stood right up as I approached, fearing that I might close the door behind her. Phoebe had come too far to risk being trapped. Respecting her wishes, I established a new routine as Phoebe demonstrated responsibility for her own freedom. Twice a day, I placed hay and grain inside the little shed. Most mornings she could be found nestled in the bedding. Eventually, I saw less and less of Phoebe but was reassured that she was doing well when the hay and grain disappeared from the stall during the day and night. The weeks went by with only occasional sightings of the fawn.

Winter appeared to be waning at the end of February, with longer hours of daylight and a strong indication of warmth from the sun. Now Phoebe visited only once or twice during the week. I was hopeful that perhaps she had joined the small herd of deer known to be living around the perimeter of Sixth Lake.

REALIZATIONS...

On Monday March 8th, 1993, the house phone rang at 6:30 in the morning as I was in the barn before school, taking care of Windy, Spy and the goats. Because I had awakened with a fever, chills and a pounding headache, I had already made arrangements to be absent for the day. I still needed to go to school early to finalize lesson plans for the substitute teacher hired to carry on in my absence.

As I was removing my coat, gloves, hat and boots in the warmth of our house, Rod greeted me with grim news.

"Your father died last night," he choked softly.

Certain I had heard him incorrectly, I scowled, searching his face for some clue that the words were a sick joke or had a different meaning.

"What?"

He repeated the same sentence and waited for me to absorb the weight of his words. My mind repeated the phrase several times as I stared blankly at him. I simply could not comprehend what it all meant. Moments later the phone rang again. My brother John, who had just delivered the news to Rod, had dutifully called back to tell me what had happened.

My mother and father had been on an extended vacation in Hilton Head, South Carolina, enjoying the fruits of my father's long career only eleven months after his retirement from Moore Products Co. Reluctant to leave his job, Dad needed time to feel comfortable in his new role as pensioner. My parents had escaped the cold of Philadelphia for one month of endless golf at Hilton Head. John and his first wife happened to be visiting and had already spent a few days with my parents at their rental cottage. On Sunday, my father had a wonderful day, relaxing and playing golf with my brother and his wife. He was, however, very tired that evening. After dozing in his chair he went to bed around 11:00 p.m. and never woke up.

My mother awakened around 2:00 a.m. when his familiar snoring was replaced by wheezing gasps. From that point on, the story included paramedics, failed resuscitation attempts, an ambulance and the final realization that all had been done in an unsuccessful attempt to save him. A massive heart attack had killed him at the age of 62. My mother left the hospital with my brother, both in a state of disbelief.

Back at the cottage, while my brother cleaned the room where my father had died, he suddenly became aware of a full moon shining brilliantly through the window. For a fleeting moment, he felt indescribable peace and clarity about the events that had taken place over the last few hours. Then he and my mother went through the motions of packing and preparing for the long drive home to Philadelphia where the family had to make funeral arrangements.

Since it would be two days before my family and my father's body arrived back in Pennsylvania, there was no urgency for Rod and me to leave until Wednesday. Off to school I went to prepare for my substitute teacher.

Once home I made my way up to our bedroom to rest and contemplate all that had occurred early that morning. The three dogs climbed the stairs with me and surrounded the bed. I lifted the two Dachshunds up with me as Mishka, with a great sigh, settled next to Rod's side of the bed. Eric and Ludie pressed loyally against me, offering support with the warmth of their little bodies. Instinctively, I wrapped my arms around them and wept while trying to remember when I had last seen my father.

It had been Labor Day weekend, six months ago, when he and my mother had planned an impromptu trip to visit us before I ran out of summer vacation and began a new part-time teaching job.

On that visit, he had come out to the barn where I was feeding Windy and Spy at the end of a warm afternoon. I stood before him as an adult surrounded by the achievement of my childhood goals.

"I want you to know how proud I am to see you living like this with your horses and all your animals. Rod has built a really beautiful place for you."

I hope I thanked him or said something profound, but the truth is I don't remember. It doesn't really matter now except I would have liked for him to know how truly happy I was living with Rod and our animals on Sixth Lake. We were truly blessed.

On Wednesday, after leaving a lengthy list of details for our house sitter, Rod and I were off to Philadelphia. We picked Grammie up in Hudson Falls along the way and continued our long trip south, hoping to arrive by late afternoon. The weather was cold and overcast, threatening to rain or snow depending on elevation. Many hours later, we were together with the whole family crying and laughing as the shock of our father's death evolved into grief.

On a drizzly, cold Thursday afternoon before calling hours, my family assembled at the Helweg Funeral Home in Jenkintown to view our father's body in the casket. At first I had declined to participate, but my childhood friend, Christine Putney, (whose family owned Tiny Tim the Chihuahua), convinced me, from her personal experience, that seeing my father one last time would help with healing and not be the creepy experience that I was anticipating. She was right.

When the lid was lifted, my father's body, dressed in a dark suit and black wingtip shoes, was revealed in the warm glow of the softly lit funeral parlor. With Rod right behind me and my mother at my side, I peered at the familiar shell that had once housed his large personality. It was a moving experience as we came to realize that he had vacated his body, leaving behind only the uncomplicated and tangible shell.

A sunny spring day provided the setting for my father's internment the next morning at the Laurel Hill Cemetery outside of Philadelphia. With only immediate family members in attendance, we said our good-byes. Next, we watched as our father's casket was prepared for burial next to his parents and infant sister, a victim of the 1919 influenza epidemic.

Over 300 people attended the memorial service later Friday afternoon. My brother George's beautiful eulogy provoked laughter as well as tears from everyone present. The staggering number of mourners offered much comfort to my family as we bade farewell to this man who had given us so much while remaining at an emotionally safe distance. Sue and I stood next to each other in the receiving line for hours, shaking many hands that belonged to people we had never met. We marveled at how each one remembered our father warmly for his great sense of humor, kidding abilities and undying support for the Philadelphia Eagles.

But what intrigued me the most was the number of people who looked from Sue to me and asked, "Now, which one of you is the horsewoman?" or "Which one of you has horses?" or "Which one of you rides horses?" "Your Dad used to talk a lot about his daughter who loved horses."

Although he had rarely shown enthusiasm for horses with me, there were people to whom he proudly bragged about his crazy kid who loved horses. This realization had a profound effect, allowing me to accept my father with adult wisdom. He was a flawed man, inept at showing his children much in terms of emotional connection. But today I have no doubt that he loved us all. Since his death, I have felt that love even more than when he was alive.

Funeral week had put my family through the roller coaster of emotional highs and lows necessary to the grieving process. My mother had fared well, appearing for the most part to be "ok" as she took control of all the necessary arrangements that turn a tragedy into a social gathering for friends and family. Caring friends delivered enormous quantities of food to provide sustenance for the mass of people who attended the memorial service. Our house filled up with aunts, uncles, cousins and many of my father's closest friends and their families. They recounted warm anecdotes of our times together always with my father as the central character.

By late Friday afternoon, the topic of conversation changed from memories of my father to a massive snowstorm that was making its way across the country. It was due to hit Philadelphia on Saturday morning and last all through Sunday. Our house sitter was committed until Sunday; but since she was also a teacher, she needed to go back to school on Monday.

People who don't have animals are free to come and go from their homes spontaneously or with little planning. Although there are moments when I envy this carefree lifestyle, I would not trade a moment of the pleasure that I derive from sharing my life with pets of different species. Therefore, I have had to accept the responsibility of providing quality care in the rare instances that we have to be away from them. Over the years, I have engaged the services of great house sitters. The most important criteria that I look for in a candidate is the desire to experience my lifestyle for a short period of time.

I have been pleasantly surprised over the years at the number of friends and acquaintances who have risen to the task. Their help has allowed Rod and me to join our family for vacations in Florida, and cruises to Bermuda and Alaska. Arriving home to dogs who are only mildly happy to see us and horses who never missed a beat in their daily routine proves the quality of the caregivers I hire. To be honest, I am happy to remain at home in the beauty of the Adirondack Mountains where the rhythms of nature and my own animal's lives are the perfect complements to my own existence. They keep me fit, physically and mentally. Most people take vacation to relieve stress through enjoyable activities. My farm provides those benefits year round.

The next morning we awoke to blizzard conditions, quite a contrast to the promising spring sunshine twenty four hours before. The forecast included a total of two feet for the Philadelphia area and increasing amounts farther north. The entire system stretched up into the Adirondacks and beyond into Canada, reaching the east coast from Maine to Maryland. It was labeled the blizzard of 1993. Although a number of major roads had been closed, Rod and I remained hopeful that we could leave on Monday morning.

All day Sunday, we watched the Weather Channel. I thought about the animals, fretting about who could take care of them if we were delayed beyond Monday. Thankfully, the phones were still working and we remained in touch with our house sitter. It was highly likely that our own school would remain closed on Monday as crews had been unable to keep roads cleared in the blizzard conditions. Finally, the storm subsided; by Monday morning bright sunshine returned. After a tearful goodbye to my mother and the rest of my family, Rod and I headed back home to the Adirondacks. Grammie chose to stay behind for several more days to provide moral support for my mother while she began her new life as a widow.

Never was I more relieved to return home. After the emotional duress of the previous week, I looked forward to the familiarity of my chosen lifestyle. I craved the smell of my horses and the bleating of my goats. I needed to shovel manure and carry heavy buckets of water. I needed to watch the melting ice on the lake as it prepared for the return of wild ducks and geese. I needed to breathe the mountain air as it warmed in the ascending sun and melted the woes of winter. Most of all, I needed to lie in bed at night supported by the warmth of my two Dachshund "bookends" while my husband slept beside me and our husky lay on the floor. With my rhythms reset to the beat of Lakeview Farm, I was able to realize peace.

The blizzard marked the end of Phoebe's rehabilitation. I never saw her again after the great storm and could only hope that she had found her way to safety with a group of local deer. I did not fret because I was confident that I had done all that I could to return her to the wild. I was convinced she was mature enough to live on her own. This time she was ready. This time she could survive. And so would I. Despite the grief of his loss, I knew I had made peace with my father. I knew he loved me. Just as Phoebe moved into the deer world on her own, I would move on as an adult, with greater maturity and understanding of my father and myself.

CHRISTOPHER...

Christopher's story began in late fall of 1993 as Fourth Lake in Inlet began to freeze. How a domesticated Pekin white duck, bred for meat, ended up living with wild ducks is still a mystery. However, he had been thriving with them for several months. The fact that Pekin ducks can't fly prevented the white duck from taking flight with his wild flock when they flew off to open water in the channel between Fourth and Fifth Lakes. Residents along the shore of Fourth Lake attempted to rescue the duck, but the ice proved too thick for a boat to pass through and too thin for a person to walk on. They watched, helplessly for a whole week, surprised each morning to discover that the duck was still alive.

On the seventh day, the residents could stand no more. Any creature who had survived that long deserved one last attempt either to be saved or put out of its misery. Equipped with a raft, ropes, life jackets, and a gun, two men crept across the ice with the moral support of an accumulating crowd on the shoreline. When the two men turned toward the shore with the duck grasped in their arms, the onlookers responded with a roar of relief.

As residents of Sixth Lake, Rod, and I were unaware of the drama unfolding on Fourth Lake. A phone call on the Sunday before Christmas increased our population of animals by one duck. Hearing the sad tale with the miraculous ending convinced us to adopt the duck who arrived at our house shortly after the call. What caught my attention first was how large he was, approximately ten to twelve pounds, and the softness of his pure white plumage. For a duck that had been starving for a week, he appeared to be in good shape. His bright orange feet stood squarely on the ground while a low vibration barely quacked from his neon orange bill. He did not resist being held as I checked him all over for evidence of his week long ordeal. He seemed healthy. There was no doubt he needed a name that hinted at his arrival during the holiday season. We named him Christopher.

Christopher spent his first several days with us in a horse trailer, which provided him time alone to recuperate and catch up on some much needed calories before being introduced to the residents of the barn. On Christmas

Eve we took him to the barn to get acquainted. His first reaction was that of a shy child new on the playground. The horses and goats paid little attention to him as he cowered in the darkest corner. Then he saw Louise.

Louise was a Rhode Island Red chicken who had hatched from an egg on our kitchen counter the year before. As a result of her imprinting on us, Louise preferred human company to that of the flock.

Christopher's shyness dissolved into curiosity as he abandoned the safety of his corner to inspect her. She was unimpressed, going about her business, scratching in the hay for tidbits. Honking softly, he followed her around the barn and out into the driveway where she continued to scratch and peck in the snow. Later, as the day faded to twilight, we found Christopher and Louise snuggled together in her thick nest of hay at the back of the barn. Thus began a relationship that lasted for years.

Through every season of the year, Christopher and Louise were together. The only time they parted was when Christopher sneaked down to the lake to behave like a duck, dunking, oiling and preening his magnificent white plumage in the water. He stayed long enough to tend to his grooming needs, and then waddled up the lawn, honking urgently to find the hen. Once he was back in her company, the honking quieted to his signature low rumbling, indicating all was well in his world.

During the deep freeze of the winter months, Christopher and Louise remained close to the barn, leaving only briefly to investigate those rare days when sunshine visits the Adirondacks. During the spring thaw, as water rushed in the lake, Christopher could be found celebrating by splashing gleefully in the runoff crevices of our driveway. Louise, always close by, scratched in the exposed mud for earthworms.

In the summer the pair left the barn at first light. They spent the long hot days browsing and napping all around our property. The twosome entertained many friends and family members who visited us in the summer. In the late evenings of those long summer days, Christopher and Louise, full from a day of gorging themselves on the lawn, were always be found snuggled in their nest, safe and sound for the night.

Autumn was a time for them to alter their habits in preparation for winter. They spent more time in the barn, not wishing to venture outside until the sun had warmed up the day. They ate voraciously as if they might never see food again. On Indian summer days, the duck and the chicken returned to their summer routine with Christopher stealing chances to bathe in the lake.

During the year, particularly the summer, I worried about predators putting an end to their bliss; but Christopher and Louise were so regimented about being home before dark, that I did not dwell on my fears. As each year passed without incident, I felt confident that the boundaries and activity on our property were enough to keep predators away. Sadly, after six years, I was proved wrong.

In April, 2000, as Christopher and Louise were tending to their annual rites of spring, tragedy struck. From outside the kitchen window, something caught my attention. In disbelief, I watched as a red fox crept across our driveway, preparing to pounce on Christopher! Out of the house I flew, screaming at the top of my lungs. Adrenalin allowed me to reach Christopher faster than the fox. In one fluid motion, I shoved him into the barn and shut the door, realizing how close he had come to death. I turned around, shocked to see the fox sitting, unfazed by my dramatic rescue. It sat surprisingly close by, looking calmly determined to take the easy prey honking loudly on the other side of the door.

Christopher's desperate quacks made me realize that he was looking for Louise. As I scanned the driveway for her, a sickening feeling spread through my body, already shaking from the rush of adrenalin. She was nowhere to be seen. I hoped that she had sought safety under one of our sheds or perhaps was laying an egg in a quiet corner behind the barn. I searched for her everywhere, hoping that she was safe. When it became apparent that she was in none of her hiding places, I knew what had happened. With the fox still keeping his vigil at the barn, I began to search farther afield.

In the woods between our property and that of our neighbors, I caught sight of her red plumage on the damp ground. Her feathers ruffled lightly in the wind; I knew she was dead. I had saved Christopher, but I was too late to save Louise.

My own grief for our beloved Louise could not begin to match Christopher's in the days and months to follow. Fearing a return visit from the fox, I kept him secure in the barn. His confinement only added to his torment as he honked desperately for Louise. He camped out at the barn door, ready to dash out whenever it was opened. His beautiful plumage began to lose its healthy sheen as he was unable to get to the lake to care for it. We provided a tub of water, but bathing in it was not the same; he often ignored it, sulking in his nest instead.

During Christopher's imprisonment in the barn, the fox returned often. My stress level was high as I remained conflicted between keeping Christopher unhappily safe in the barn and allowing him to roam the property freely, certain to meet the same fate as Louise. Meanwhile, Christopher's lonely unhappiness clouded the springtime activities around the barn.

Apparently, this fox was a nuisance all over the community. We surmised that he had been reared by his mother too close to people and, therefore, never learned to fear them. In fact, he was attracted to people. Area residents were concerned when they found the fox curled up on a porch or playing a game of fetch with golfers on the golf course. As a result of his tame behavior, the conservation authorities took matters into their own hands and destroyed the fox. Believe it or not, I actually felt sorry for the fox, for he was only acting as foxes do; he was the victim of human encroachment. For Christopher, however, I was elated. Now he could resume some of his normal activities without being confined to the barn. Little did I know that his freedom would drive him away, risking his life once more.

As spring warmed into summer, Christopher spent more and more time on the lake in the company of the wild ducks. For all the years that he was at Louise's side, he showed little, if any, interest in them. But now he gravitated toward the ducks and was spotted all over Sixth and Seventh Lakes with his wild cousins. At first he spent the days with them and returned to the barn before dark. As the days got longer, however, he stayed out with them later and later until mid-July when he stopped coming home altogether. There was nothing I could do to lure him back to the safety of the barn at night. Sadly, I stopped trying.

As summer stretched on, Christopher became a respected member of the wild flock of ducks on our lake. It was quite a sight to see the smaller wild ducks with their dull plumage traveling in a great mass across the lake with one bright white beacon in their midst. They spent the day visiting residents along the shore who were usually good for a handout of bread or corn. Christopher became a celebrity of sorts that summer. With many people reporting his whereabouts to me, I was able to relax and take comfort in the fact that he was happy. I checked on him daily and went about my own life, relieved to see him healthy and sound. At the back of my mind, I wondered what would happen in the late fall when the wild flock took flight and ice seized the lake. Once again, Christopher would be left vulnerable to predators and starvation. These threats were unthinkable, yet still several months away. I had time to plan for his future.

Summer blazed into fall, and Christopher thrived in the company of his wild companions. As the residents of Sixth Lake boarded up and abandoned their camps, the ducks were forced to forage for themselves. I fed them routinely so that I could check on Christopher every day. My plan was to keep feeding them and eventually capture him right on our property. Easier said than done! Several attempts to capture him failed. Although he visited every day, he always managed to elude my feeble attempts to grab him. As November turned to December, the warm weather trend of that year continued. I knew it would not last forever. I needed to capture Christopher soon.

Capturing him, however, was only the first challenge. On top of that, I needed to find a way to keep him happy in captivity. I could not bear the thought of keeping him a prisoner in the barn for the long months of winter. I had to find a solution to his loneliness. I found an answer just two weeks before the deep freeze took hold.

Only four days before Christmas, while Christopher was still living as a wild duck, the extended fall weather was sent packing by a cold front that dropped the temperature into the single digits at night. The ice on the lake began to stretch from the shoreline to the middle of the

Finding My Way to Mountain View Farm

lake, making it impossible for the ducks to browse in shallow water. They took flight to the open channel miles away and left Christopher alone, disabled by his inability to fly. When we found him, he was trying to mingle among a flock of Canada geese resting in the lake on their way south for the winter. He still resisted our efforts to catch him. Rod and I both knew that this would be our last chance. The ice was not going to sustain our weight when it reached the middle of the lake. We lured him to the shore with food only to send him scurrying back to the open water when we attempted to catch him. After several unsuccessful attempts, my emotions got the best of me.

Rod sent me away from the scene. From afar, I watched as my patient husband offered handfuls of cracked corn to Christopher, who ate greedily. After twenty minutes Christopher appeared more relaxed, totally focused on the delicious food.

All of a sudden, Rod launched his entire body onto Christopher. The duck, surprised to find himself pinned under the weight of a human, was finally captured! I rushed to the scene and embraced them both. It felt so good to hold Christopher and feel those soft dense feathers in my fingers. We carried him to the car and took him home where a Christmas surprise was waiting.

Filled with joyful anticipation, we carried Christopher to the barn. When the door opened, his gift greeted him. Quacking softly from the nest in the farthest corner waited a female Black duck. We named her Holly.

KINDRED SPIRITS...

In June 1993, I was hired for a full-time position teaching sixth grade at the Town of Webb School in Old Forge. After a summer full of riding horses and visits from family, I arrived at school to prepare my new classroom. Across the hall I found Jean Risley, an ageless blonde beauty with a welcoming smile. Jean was the other sixth grade teacher and my assigned mentor. She too was preparing her classroom for the new school year. Although I knew who Jean was from brief interactions during my two years as a teacher's aide, I didn't really know anything about her. We exchanged pleasantries, and Jean offered to help me in any way as I began to establish myself in the classroom. I was touched by her sensitivity; without seeming pushy, she offered to provide help only if I asked.

Jean and I spent many afternoons in our classrooms that week. We assembled bulletin boards, wrote lesson plans and inventoried textbooks, time-consuming necessities that require total focus. During breaks, we continued our "getting to know each other" conversations.

During one such encounter, we began to talk about horses. It turned out that Jean loved horses too, but had little experience with them. As a young teenager, she and her boyfriend (now husband) Bob, had ridden the Moss Lake Camp horses after camp ended and before the horses were returned to their winter headquarters. Jean had spent two of her teenage summers living next door to the camp at Darts, an Adirondack resort, now Camp Gorham, run by the YMCA. Jean and Bob attended school at the Town of Webb.

During their college years they married and shortly after graduation moved to Wappinger Falls, New York where Bob taught physical education and coached basketball. Jean attended to their three children and taught music at various schools in the area. After much soul-searching and wishing for their children to grow up in a smaller town, Jean and Bob returned to the Adirondacks; settling in Old Forge to raise their family and resume teaching careers. The children were all married with children of their own by the time Jean and I became friends.

After hearing the story about the horses at Moss Lake, I asked Jean a casual question. "Would you like to come up and ride with me, sometime?"

"Yes, I think I would," she said confidently.

The rest is history. Jean not only came and rode one day at the end of that summer, she also came almost every day after that, unless she and Bob were out of town visiting their children. To this day, almost twenty years later, Jean is a fixture in my barn. With the help of Windy, Spy and a little horse named Sandi, she has become a competent rider. Moreover, she has become one of my dearest friends. Since that first ride, she has been a pillar of support when all is well and when there is turmoil at the barn. I can count on her to help in any way because she loves the horses as much as I do. Her strength and wisdom have seen me through a few low spots in the years since we met. I am ever grateful for this kindred spirit.

Michele deCamp is another friend with whom I share my horses. Unlike, Jean, Michele grew up with a barn full of horses in Eagle Bay, a small village between Inlet and Old Forge. At ten years old, Michele ran her own "hack line" managing nearly ten horses by herself behind her parent's restaurant, Kopp's Last Stand. Michele had no brothers or sisters to share this enterprise. Her father provided maintenance and made the decisions that only grown-ups can make. In all the years that Michele owned horses, she doesn't remember a visit from either a veterinarian or a blacksmith. Many of her horses lived into their twenty's before they either died of natural causes or needed to be euthanized with help from the state police. Her stories include carcasses being dragged by a truck to feed the neighbor's sled dogs and a feeble attempt to bury a horse under the most impossible winter conditions only to find its legs fully exposed after the winter thaw.

The stories about her riding stable are equally eyebrow-raising. She tells tales of trail rides with as many as ten horses that ambled peacefully along Trail 5, the old railroad bed along Rt. 28. Sometimes chaos erupted after one of the horses successfully dismounted his rider and fled back to the barn. Naturally, all of the horses followed suit, leaving Michele behind with her lead horse and nine patrons who, thankfully unhurt, walked back to the barn.

Aside from her history with horses, Michele is living proof that hard work and perseverance through economic hard times in the Adirondacks during the 1960s and 1970s build character and enduring spirit. She met her future husband at the Town of Webb School and followed him to New Hampshire where they both attended college. Scott and Michele married before their college graduations and returned to the Adirondacks afterwards to live and prosper in Old Forge. Michele became a fourth grade teacher at the Town of Webb School after teaching for three years in Inlet. Scott ran his own tavern, The Tow Bar Inn, in Old Forge.

I met Michele when her ten-year-old daughter Kera began to take riding lessons from me during the summer that I taught at the riding stable in Inlet. Michele wanted her daughter to experience horses with more structure than she had. Once Kera had graduated from college, Michele too became a fixture at my barn. Like Jean, Michele cares for the horses as if they are her own. She has been present for moments of celebration in the barn as well as moments of sorrow, always lending her love and support in any way needed.

Cindy Hunter, (now Diver), the mother of two little children and the wife of a local contractor, became a regular at the barn as well. She had grown up in Old Forge; in fact she is Michele's sister-in-law, (Scott's sister). Whereas my childhood had been conventional, Cindy's had been chaotic and unpredictable. She had moved frequently in her early years from Long Island to Philadelphia. Eventually, she ended up in Chicago where her father died at his desk suddenly and unexpectedly from a heart attack when Cindy was only fourteen. Cindy's mother was devastated by the loss. Therefore, Cindy sought comfort in the company of her teenage companions who rebelled against everything that their parents stood for. Before Cindy became totally lost, she discovered horses. They in turn awakened the addiction in her that would eventually place her on the list of my closest friends.

While Cindy was in high school, her brother Scott arrived in Chicago to rescue her from imminent failure. He brought her back to Old Forge with him to live with Michele and their four-year old daughter, Kera. In Old Forge she was expected to finish high school and gain control of her life. They arranged for Cindy to have a horse, an Appaloosa gelding named Chief, whose job was to keep her out of trouble while she finished school.

Sadly, Chief developed colic. Cindy watched helplessly as the adults in her life made decisions. She remembers that her sister, an avid horseman from Vernon, New York, arrived with a horse trailer and took the gelding away. To this day Cindy does not know what became of him and nobody in the family seems to remember.

When Cindy became a fixture in my barn, she was out to capture and relive the one small piece of her childhood that had brought her comfort and a sense of wellbeing. Some days Cindy just liked to come to my barn and be in the presence of the horses with no expectations of riding. Instead,

 Finding My Way to Mountain View Farm

she wanted to clean stalls, groom Windy and Spy and take on any other chores that enhanced the comfort of the horses. She reminded me that, although riding is a wonderful part of horse ownership, our interactions with them out of the saddle can be even more meaningful.

So finally, my wish to have women with whom I could share my horses had been realized. Despite the common theme that brought them to me, the foundation of our friendships has broadened beyond horses to include their children, siblings, even grandchildren. I count them all among my blessings.

ANIMALS IN THE CLASSROOM...

Good teachers find a way to infuse their passions into the school day. Michele and another teacher friend Ellen teach their students to knit and to read patterns so that they can actually knit hats or scarves or Christmas stockings. Several teachers I know inspire their students by sharing their love of books. It was only natural that I wanted to incorporate animals into my classroom to complement the integrated curriculum I was responsible for teaching.

I decided to select animals that are not considered cute and cuddly. I wanted students to learn to respect strange creatures despite their creepy reputations. One of the first animals I considered was a tarantula. When I looked at them in their sealed terrarium at the pet store, I must admit that the hair stood up on my neck and a chill shuddered down my spine. With all due respect to tarantulas, even I had limits about what I felt comfortable handling in my classroom.

Shortly after the school year started, one of my students arrived with a juvenile green iguana. His mother had bought the lizard along with a small tank and a few florets of broccoli. The child assured me that the iguana was easy to care for and that it could live on nothing but green vegetables. After doing some research, we learned that green iguanas are indeed vegetarians but require a variety of different foods to address specific vitamin deficiencies that they are prone to in captivity. We also learned that the presence of several large holes or pores along the thighs indicated that our young iguana was a male. He might grow to be over four feet long from the tip of his snout to the end of his tail. At the moment he was only six inches long and vibrant neon green in color. After a democratic vote among the students, he was christened Spike, (I wanted to name him Mozart), a unanimous decision among the eight boys who comprised half of my class.

Spike was an instant hit. The students loved caring for him by monitoring his tank thermometer and making sure it always read above 80 degrees. We handled Spike quite a bit; as a result he was friendly and never objected to being fussed over. We let him wander around the classroom for exercise. By repeatedly placing him on a discarded cafeteria tray, we taught him to relieve himself there, making cleanup much easier on all of us.

The students were diligent about washing their hands after handling Spike and making sure that his tank was clean, with fresh food and water available at all times. One of their favorite interactions with our lizard occurred when they walked him on a leash up and down the hallway outside of the classroom. Out there they were sure to encounter faculty and other students who stopped to engage them in conversation about Spike. The students were very proud of him, and all of us loved him dearly.

Shortly after Spike's arrival, I acquired a black-and-white hooded rat for our classroom. Another democratic vote named the young rat Sunshine, and she too became a cherished member of our classroom family. The children learned to take turns holding her and to "parent" her cooperatively. Although Sunshine had a cage, we left the top of it off during the day and allowed her to investigate the chalkboard and windowsill. Rats are very clean and choose to relieve themselves in one location if given the opportunity to designate it themselves.

In the spring, we acquired a male rat, Shadow, and allowed him to breed with Sunshine. Oh, the lessons learned from all of these wonderful encounters with the animals. The students waited with great anticipation through the twenty-one days of gestation and glowed like proud grandparents when Sunshine presented them with seventeen pink "erasers" that she cared for meticulously. A week later, the babies began to grow hair that divulged the secrets of their individual coat patterns. The children

Finding My Way to Mountain View Farm

identified each baby by a spot on his tummy, a dot on her chest, or a patch next to its tail.

One of their favorite games to play was "What gender is it?" I handed each student a baby rat chosen at random; they had to identify a boy or a girl by comparing the back end to a simple diagram on the board; a boy has one opening under the tail and a girl has two. There were no snickers or dirty remarks because the students were learning that animals live in a world of survival and purpose. Sex is for perpetuating the species. Babies are the adorable result. Knowing the physical difference between males and females is important. It is as simple as that.

The next year we acquired a young female iguana named Rosemary. She and Spike paid little attention to each other until the breeding season began in November, another lesson to be learned through observation rather than textbook. One morning as the students were putting coats away and organizing books for their morning subjects, Spike mounted Rosemary right in the middle of the floor! The entire room became silent; the students instinctively knew they were witnessing a special event. For fifteen minutes, we watched as Spike bit down on Rosemary's neck and held her in position. When the mating was over, Spike let Rosemary go, allowing her to scramble away to recover from his amorous behavior.

Needless to say, the students had lots of questions. Luckily, the iguanas' mating ritual had answered most of them. I tried not to make a big deal about the episode and was so proud of my student's level of maturity when the topic quickly changed to "How long until we have baby iguanas?"

For the next two weeks, Spike and Rosemary repeated their amorous trysts, first thing in the morning, right in the middle of the floor. The students eventually lost interest in watching but always remained respectful and quiet during the deed. Eventually, the mating behavior diminished and by late December disappeared completely. For the next six months, we waited and wondered if Rosemary was gravid, (with eggs). Her body kept the answer a secret for the next four months. Just in case, we bolstered her protein consumption by adding scrambled eggs and tofu to her diet.

In April, we began to notice that Rosemary's body was becoming thick and inflexible. She had a difficult time maneuvering around the classroom and on her leash. She needed to rest frequently and appeared to have a difficult time finding a comfortable spot. As the weeks continued onward toward May and June, I began to worry that she was egg-bound, a condition in which the eggs literally become stuck in the iguana's body, eventually causing the animal a painful death. We decided to allow our veterinarian, Dr. Brooker, to x-ray Rosemary's torso to see what was going on inside. The resulting images shocked us.

Rosemary's entire torso was packed with over sixty eggs, each just slightly smaller than a golf ball. No wonder she could barely move! According to Dr. Brooker, Rosemary, although uncomfortable, was perfectly healthy and just needed a couple more weeks until it was time to lay the eggs. In the meantime, the students and I needed to prepare a place for her to lay her clutch. We placed clean moist sand in the bottom of the cabinet that supported the large tank in which Rosemary and Spike lived. We hung a light inside to provide heat and waited with worry and anticipation for two more weeks.

As the days passed, Rosemary became more and more uncomfortable. She began to wander about the room and climb up the legs and into the laps of students seated at their desks. After a brief attempt to seek comfort, she crawled back down to the floor and sought another student's leg to climb. No matter how much the students tried to hold her, stroke her and soothe her, she could not be comforted.

In early June, my students prepared to take the battery of standardized tests that would determine their academic growth from the preceding year. On the morning when Part I of the Math test was to be given, Rosemary appeared to be more agitated than usual. She could not sit still, crawling around the room aimlessly with eyes bugged out of her head. Her tail thrashed at anybody who tried to pick her up. Eventually, we were able to secure her in the warm sand of her "nursery" cabinet. Once she was inside her instincts kicked in, and she spent an hour digging and scratching about in the sand pile. I pleaded with my students to ignore her as I read through the directions of the test. Eventually, they all got down to business.

Danielle, one of my top students who had finished the test early, (and with 100% accuracy I might add), was reading a book quietly, waiting for the rest of the class to finish. Her desk just happened to be located right next to Rosemary's cabinet. Unable to resist, Danielle peeked into the cabinet without disturbing the rest of the class. I can still see the look on her face as she squirmed in her seat trying to get my attention without distracting her classmates. Eventually, I noticed her and we both looked into the cabinet together. In a glance, I saw Rosie pushing a large white squishy ball out from under her tail. All around her were several other white squishy balls, perhaps as many as twenty. My eyes pleaded with Danielle to contain herself until the others had finished the test.

Finally, the fifty minutes were up. I instructed my students to put down their pencils. After I collected tests, pencils, and answer sheets and secured them on my desk, Danielle broke the news. Rosemary continued to lay eggs for the next five days. In total she produced a whopping sixty two eggs! Her body completely deflated and her appetite returned with vigor. For the next two weeks, we stuffed her with green beans, zucchini, scrambled eggs and tofu. Reptile metabolism is quite slow, so Rosie's body took months to puff up; but her docile amicable mood returned within days of her great effort.

As for the eggs, I tried to incubate them over the summer months. They required over one hundred days in the incubator. Several power outages and inconsistent levels of humidity in the incubator caused the eggs eventually to rot. Honestly, I really didn't want more baby iguanas. Spike and Rosemary were enough to manage in the classroom. The next year Rosie didn't even bother with her sand pile. Instead she laid about fifty eggs, which I discarded in the garbage can. Eventually, Spike became a nuisance to her year round, so we had to separate them. Rosemary continued to produce a clutch of eggs each spring for several more years but the number diminished to fewer than ten. Like chicken eggs without a rooster, they could not possibly have been fertilized.

At the end of the school year, my sixth graders bade a tearful goodbye to the classroom creatures, their pets who had taught them more than academic textbook lessons in biology. The animals had provided opportunities to work together cooperatively, to write interesting stories, to observe closely, to research with purpose, and to promote incentives to do one's best. But mostly the animals had forged a common bond for all of us to share and beings for all of us to love. That is a lesson that I have yet to find in a textbook. For six years, the animals in my classroom provided that extra ingredient that every teacher wishes she had to reach out to and inspire each individual in her class. Rosemary and Spike were inspiring teachers.

The rats, with only a two-year life span, taught lessons in loss and grief as well. Several times over the years, we made the sad decision for Dr. Brooker to end the life of a geriatric rat. After arrangements were made, we chose two students to accompany the rat and stand close by until the end. Not every student was up for the task, but those who were brought a signed note from home. After a tearful goodbye from the whole class, the two selected student volunteers walked up Park Avenue to the vet clinic where Dr. Brooker graciously and lovingly ended our pet's suffering. Then the students walked back to school with the little body wrapped in a towel and a story to share with the rest of us, now eager to know every detail. For those sorrowful and important lessons, I owe the rats, with their gregarious personalities, a debt of gratitude.

Over the six-year reign of animals in the classroom, several other species joined the family. A mother and baby hedgehog named Cactus and Tumbleweed arrived. The hedgehog face is adorable with its turned up twitchy nose, black button eyes and tiny ears. Nocturnal by nature, they spent most of the day curled up asleep with their pointy quills on guard. The students wore thick gloves when holding them because, at the slightest alarm, the hedgehogs erected their quills in defense. The extent of their interactions was snacking on mealworms that the students offered. We learned to respect them on their own terms and never forced ourselves upon them.

Another interesting addition to the classroom was a Veiled chameleon. He was a fascinating creature with bulging eyes that swiveled in opposite directions as he surveyed his surroundings. His diet required an unlimited number of live crickets who also took up residence in the classroom. Their occasional chirping prompted many giggles. The chameleon's base color

Finding My Way to Mountain View Farm

was a variegated mossy green. With changes of mood and temperature, he could blush in shades of aqua and teal or darken to olive green and brown. In tribute to his vivid body pallet, I named him Hue.

With time Hue grew used to us handling him so that we could look closely at his interesting physique that included "mittened" feet and a "paper doll" thin body that seemed to disappear when viewed head on. His prehensile tail enabled him to cling tight to the branches in his tank while he appeared to "cha-cha" in search of crickets. Once his eyes locked onto prey, his tongue rapidly extended from his mouth (sometimes as long as four inches) and snagged the cricket before snapping back into his mouth. This action was followed by a deliberate gulping motion to swallow the cricket, no doubt still wiggling, whole.

The lessons that the animals provided continued for six years with learning objectives that I could never have predicted in my plan book. The sixth graders took tremendous pride in their pets. Frequently, the animals visited other classrooms where my students educated younger children with the flare and polish of a Jack Hannah segment on the Today Show.

The second Thursday evening of the new school year is traditionally Open House when parents and students have the opportunity to visit with their new teacher. In my classroom during the animal years, it was also an opportunity for alumni and their families to visit with the pets they knew so well from the year before. The room was filled with parents and children engaged in the exchange of warm tales from days gone by. I always marveled at the endearing confidence that the alumni families brought back to the classroom while cooing at the rats or stroking Rosemary and Spike under the chin. The new parents, not yet fully acquainted with the daily tales of animal activity that would soon entertain them at the dinner table, watched with trepidation from the sidelines. A year later these same parents would be the ones returning eagerly to visit the animals they now knew so well.

It was a magical time. In my naiveté, I assumed it would last until the day I retired. The animals provided me with a vehicle with which to connect all of the living beings in my classroom. Little did I know in the years to come, that not everybody felt the animals were an asset to the classroom.

PIG RESCUE...

"Carl Klossner came to see me today and told me that Deb, [his wife], has an eleven week old Potbelly piglet that she wants to find a home for," I said casually as Rod and I were catching up with each other at the end of an early December day.

He stared at me, waiting for the inevitable question.

"Do we?...want one..a piglet, I mean? Do we want this piglet?"

We had spoken many times about acquiring a miniature Vietnamese Potbelly pig; but since there appeared to be a glut of them we agreed that a rescue pig would make us more responsible owners. Unfortunately, these small pigs were all the rage in the exotic pet trade. A baby pig is one of the cutest, most irresistible creatures on earth. Like puppies, they grow up and like pigs they may become a large formidable beasts. Many sanctuaries exist for unwanted pigs who were once adorable piglets.

"I guess," he said hesitantly, as it occurred to him that this luckless little fellow fit our pig requirements.

I called Deb later that evening. She and Carl had a "house" pig of their own named Zeppelin, who was a dear and charismatic creature. As a pig sympathizer, Deb agreed to take the piglet, thus removing it immediately from its current situation. However, she was not interested in keeping two pigs and hoped that she could find a home for the youngster.

Apparently, the baby boar had been given to a family as a house pet. The new family had no idea how to raise a piglet, and for a week or two the little one spent most of his day inside a small cage. Eventually, the family lost interest in their new baby and relinquished him to Deb. After calling Deb to ask more questions I told her that we would love to take the piglet.

The next day I arrived at Dr. Brooker's office to collect our new addition after his castration surgery. A boar is a formidable and smelly beast; since this little guy was going to live in our house, he had to be neutered.

The piglet was still a bit groggy from his surgery when I saw him for the first time. He was tiny, only about fourteen inches long from end to end with big liquid brown eyes. The little snout above his mouth pumped up and down, trying to recognize my scent. Reaching into the cage to stroke his little pointy ears, I fell in love with him right away. As Meg placed him in my arms, another extraordinary chapter of my life with animals began.

I brought him home in a dog crate and left him in the powder room to take in his new surroundings without having to deal with our dogs. Eventually I let him out to investigate the kitchen and the area around the woodstove while Rod kept the dogs occupied outside. He seemed overwhelmed as his little hooves tapped across the parquet floor. At one point I went into the powder room to blow my nose and laughed at the piglet's reaction.

"Neort, neort, umph, umph," he replied enthusiastically.

I loved holding him and resting my cheek on his bristles. He was not cuddly soft for those bristles poked through my sweater and into my skin. In my arms, he grunted softly through little puffs of breath. His shiny black skin was naturally clean, with no offensive odor.

Rod named him Noah, hoping that if the ancient Noah was the last one on the Ark before the doors were closed, this little piglet might be the last animal on our "Ark." In addition to all of the classroom pets, we now had three horses, three dogs, five goats and a piglet. The Ark was definitely full!

People often ask me if pigs are smarter than dogs or if they make good pets. To answer these questions requires a long explanation. In a nutshell, pigs are very different from dogs. Therefore, I am not comfortable comparing them. No doubt, pigs are very smart when it comes to getting their needs met, which usually involves obtaining food. Whether or not they make good pets has a lot to do with what a person expects a pet to be. Pigs are clean and can be housebroken, but they wreak havoc around the house when they scratch their itchy bristly bodies on the furniture or tear up the laundry for their bedding.

Raising Noah required unique training skills. Since my only experience with housebreaking was training puppies, I tried to employ the same basics with the piglet. It didn't take me long to understand that Noah didn't think like a puppy who tries to please his master. He was more of a strategist. Despite his tiny size, he was a brilliant negotiator and the currency he dabbled in was food! Noah would do just about anything for it; if food wasn't the reward, it was difficult to motivate him.

My research recommended that we teach him to use a litter box. Because he had arrived in December, the weather was not always conducive to encouraging him to go outside. We placed a large pan filled with wood shavings under our kitchen counter. I put Noah in the pan and rewarded him with a tiny dog biscuit just for standing in it. All day long, I frequently placed him in the pan and rewarded him. Eventually, he got the idea that standing in the pan paid huge dividends, so I frequently found him standing in the pan, grunting for my attention. He wasn't making a connection between the pan and relieving himself, but I was beginning to understand how pig intelligence is wired.

Pigs are among the most successful animals on the planet, able to survive in a variety of regions and climates. Their intelligence has served them well, allowing them to adapt and survive just about anywhere in the world. Feral pigs can quickly overpopulate an area, making it necessary to hunt them as they compete with native wildlife for limited resources and upset the natural balance. This fact does not surprise me after living with Noah for ten years.

Eventually, we abandoned the litter box. We successfully house trained Noah by establishing a strict daily routine of scheduled outside visits that were aligned to his bathroom habits. Every morning he accompanied me out to the barn no matter what the weather conditions were. He was always rewarded once he arrived in the barn; although I praised him with my voice, the tidbits of food were actually more encouraging. The reward didn't need to be large; a single kernel of corn or broken piece of dog biscuit was enough to let him know he had done the right thing. During these visits he went outside into the goat paddock to poop and pee. Such a good boy!

While Rod and I were at our jobs, Noah spent the day crated in the sunroom at the front of our house. After I arrived home from school, he spent the remainder of the afternoon outside with me in the barn or foraging around the property on his own. When spring came, he engaged in one of his many destructive activities by rooting up the lawn in various locations around the yard.

After many busy hours outside, he spent the evening cuddled in my arms with his little snout resting under my chin. There I sat on the couch basking in contentment while Eric and Luther slept twisted together under their blanket next to Noah and me. At bedtime we placed the piglet in his crate where he slept soundly until dawn.

Urgent grunts coming from downstairs were difficult to ignore in the early hour before our alarm clock was set to go off. Once I heard Noah stir, I ran downstairs, lifted him out of his crate and carried him up to our bed before I fully woke up. Once under the covers, he settled right back to sleep.

In the summer, we included Noah on our visits to Sunny Cliff. For the first two years of his life, he grew slowly. Although he was getting heavier, I was still able to carry him short distances. On the party barge, Noah appreciated being covered with a blanket if the air was cool on the ride across the lake. At Sunny Cliff, he followed us through the fields on our walks with the dogs. From Mishka he learned where blueberry bushes grew and frequently joined her to sample the fruit.

After the long walk, he ate his dinner, then curled up on the couch near the dogs where he fell into a deep sleep. When it was time to go home, Noah was not happy to be disturbed. Like a child, he became cross after being awakened. He grunted and squealed his complaints all the way home until he was finally put to bed in his crate. By the next morning, the foul mood had passed and he slipped right back into his amicable daily routine.

Noah frequently visited school. On one occasion, he joined my students as they watched the movie Babe, about an extraordinary sheep herding pig. Each child took a turn holding Noah on his or her lap while watching the movie. I also took him on road trips with me to visit my mother and Grammie who was now living in a retirement community near my mother in Lansdale, Pennsylvania. Noah entertained the residents in the nursing home wing, stimulating smiles and happy memories of pets from long ago.

Unfortunately, Noah was not always friendly. As he aged and grew larger, topping out at over two hundred pounds, he began to express his displeasure at guests in the house. Noah lived by the adage that guests and fish go bad after three days. By day three of any guest's visit, he began to stalk under the dining room table when we ate a meal. Suddenly, he charged a pair of legs that did not belong to Rod or me, bumping them with the full force of his snout or swiping with the large tusks that grew out the side of his mouth.

His potential to do harm combined with his large size made him difficult to manage in his later years. The tusks required maintenance several times a year to keep them a safer and duller length. Cindy's husband, Perry was always up for the task. He and Rod had developed a technique that required Perry to tackle Noah while Rod used the dremel tool to saw off a good length of the offending teeth. Rod and Perry needed ear protection as Noah squealed his objections in blood curdling screams. Once Perry released his hold on the pig, Noah stood up and went about his business with no hard feelings.

Noah's routine life continued for years with only one alteration. When he grew too big for the dog crate, he changed his sleeping arrangements by climbing the stairs to our bedroom and flopping down on the floor by my side of the bed. At 7:00 p.m., he would stop whatever he was doing and go to bed. It was a self-directed adjustment in the schedule; as long as he still fit in the space, we were agreeable to the change. Once upstairs, however, he searched for bedding material. Laundry on the floor was fair game to be dragged into Noah's nest. Rod unwillingly sacrificed many shirts and pairs of jeans that wound up as padding for the pig's bed.

Despite blending in well with our other animals, Noah preferred a solitary existence. He was more than content to stroll about the lawn alone, foraging for tidbits. The damp sand on our little beach provided a great place to wallow on hot buggy days. During the summer, he spent the whole day outside. In the winter, he was content to stay indoors and sleep the day away.

One way that we encouraged him to get exercise was by filling a plastic jar with oatmeal. We pierced small holes in the bottle to allow the oatmeal to sift out in small quantities. Noah spent hours pushing the little jar around in the dining room, kitchen and living room. It provided him with all the benefits of a swine treadmill.

Life with Noah was both challenging and delightful. We had given him a forever home and in return he fit right in among the members of our animal family. He displayed loyalty and love to Rod and me, his closest people, and remains one of our most interesting pets.

A Timely Reunion...

The summer of 1997 witnessed real progress in my Dressage training with Zambezi. As a result, I became even more enthralled with the discipline and actively sought opportunities to watch higher level rides, particularly the Grand Prix Freestyle. With the advent of the new school year, I began to consider attending Dressage at Devon, which is held at the end of September every year. My plan was to visit my sister Sue who lives nearby the iconic Devon show grounds. But, in the week prior to the show, I had flip-flopped back and forth several times between going and staying home. Ultimately, I decided to go; on Friday afternoon, I was on my way to Philadelphia. This final decision proved to be serendipitous as I was about to rekindle one of the most important relationships of my childhood and all of the answers to my wonderings about whatever happened to my friend would finally have answers.

The evening of the Grand Prix Freestyle at Devon was cold and crisp as Sue, Amy and I browsed the shops and exhibits on the show grounds. We were so cold that we had to wear the sweatshirts I had purchased as gifts just to survive the evening competition. As we shivered in the setting sun, the lights came on to illuminate the ring that displayed some of our country's best Dressage horse and rider combinations. The performances were stunning as ride after ride displayed the beauty and magic that horses ridden to music provoke. But I remember the evening more because of a fateful encounter. Constantly, I kept bumping into acquaintances from my days at Centenary College and Michael Matz's barn. It had been more than ten years since I had seen most of them so it felt good to stop briefly and catch up. At one point, I turned around to address my sister when who should come walking up behind her but a dear old friend.

"And that is Diane Williams?" I asked in an effort to draw Diane's attention. It took a split second for her to recognize me; but when she did, her face split into a big grin. In that moment I felt instant warmth despite the cold. She hadn't aged a bit in the twenty years since I had seen her last. Her dirty blond hair and dark button eyes took me back to happy times at Was-A-Farm.

We caught up briefly before it became necessary to get teeth-chattering Sue out of the cold. As we exchanged contact information, I felt as if my mission to get to Devon that year had been completed. This was my chance to reconnect and move into the future with one of my dearest horse connections. I was going to be able to mend fences and show my appreciation for all that she had given to me so many years ago.

I returned to the Adirondacks the next day, committed to keep Diane and her partner, Linda, in my life. I wrote a letter inviting them to join Rod and me for Thanksgiving. They accepted graciously. In the weeks leading up to their visit, my anticipation helped me through a very tough decision.

A week before Thanksgiving, Eric was making it very clear to me that he was ready to be euthanized. Such a decision is never easy. Because he was my first dog needing to be put down, I wasn't paying as close attention as I should have. Call it denial, but I couldn't bring myself to see him as he truly appeared—decrepit, incontinent and blind. The only thing he seemed still to enjoy was eating; I held onto his hunger as the most definitive sign that the time had not yet come.

Anticipating Diane's and Linda's visit, I allowed the thought of ending Eric's life to creep into my brain early in November. His maintenance had become a constant vigil to get him outside in time before he peed on our bed sheets or the sofa. One week before Thanksgiving, on a late snowy afternoon, our vet arrived at the house. While I sat on the couch with Eric in my arms, she ended his life.

"I believe that taking their pain away and making it our own is the greatest gesture of love we can ever give them," Meg preached through her own tears. Those words have provided me with the strength necessary to make such a final decision ever since. This is the responsibility I must accept in order to keep animals in my life.

A week later Rod and I anxiously awaited the arrival of our guests. I never expected how wonderful the cathartic events of the long holiday weekend would be. With the aroma of roasted turkey and fixings wafting through our warm house, Diane and Linda arrived as darkness blanketed the snowy Adirondacks.

For three days we talked non-stop. The conversation danced back and forth between our common history and all of the years between then and now. During these long, thoughtful conversations, I learned about the Diane's difficult childhood and how her teenage independence had been a survival tactic. Luckily, she found Linda, her life partner, along the way. Together they live in a lovely antique house on three acres with two dogs and two cats not too far from the Devon show grounds. Diane owned a young accident-prone warmblood gelding, Bayberry, whom she was in the process of training on her own. Working as a recreational therapist with brain injured men was a challenging occupation for Diane. Linda was close to retiring from her high school teaching position.

Our conversations continued among the most picturesque landscapes of the Adirondacks, including a hike around Moss Lake. By the end of the weekend, Diane, Linda and I had caught up to the present goings on in our lives. Without an open declaration, we knew that after this weekend we would never lose track of each other again. Diane and Linda now visit us often in the Adirondacks, and once a year I make my annual pilgrimage to Dressage at Devon to attend the Mecca of our common interest with them.

OLIVIA...

For days, my friend Cindy had been telling me about a female Canada goose with three goslings seen frequently on the beach outside her office window in early June, 1999. Cindy worked for Lynn University during the years when it maintained a campus in the Adirondacks as a satellite to the Boca Raton, Florida main campus.

"The babies are so ugly that they are actually cute." she declared. "They have thin, wispy feathers and long thick legs. It is hard to believe that they are ever going to look like their beautiful black and white mother." she added.

Cindy kept me informed of the adventures of the mother and babies as they endeared themselves to the students and staff at Lynn University. Then one day Cindy arrived at my house with one of the babies in her arms. The lighthearted tales had turned horrific when a menacing fox was reported to have killed the mother and two of the babies. How this one gosling escaped death is still a mystery, but one thing was clear. It could not survive on its own.

What first struck me about the gosling was its large size. Standing over eighteen inches tall, it hardly looked like a baby anything. The frizzy, drab feathers of youth were the only indication that it was a juvenile. Geese are a precocial species, so the babies are able to eat and move about on their own from the moment they hatch. However, they still need their mother to protect them from predators and cold temperatures.

There was no question that Cindy was leaving the gosling at our Lakeview Farm. She was hopeful that the presence of our two ducks, Christopher and Holly, might offer it some kind of natural "bird" experience. The access to Sixth Lake was a bonus for a bird who would eventually live near water; but for now, it needed to be kept safe from predators. That meant confining it to our goat pen, which was enhanced with mesh wire to keep the goats from climbing through the rails.

And so we added the little gosling to our growing menagerie. It was never my intention to keep the goose forever. My wildlife rehabilitator training allows my head to make a distinction between pets and wild animals. Once grown up, this goose would be free to return to the wild and live the life it was supposed to live. If I could help it get to that point, then I would succeed in helping along the way. If I locked it up in a pen for the rest of its life, preventing it from its wild existence, then I was subjecting it to a long and miserable life. My heart, however, sometimes found conflict with my head.

Whether the gosling was a girl or a boy, we will never know as Canada Geese have few distinctive gender characteristics observable to the human eye. It only matters that geese can tell the difference. We did refer to it as "she" and named her Olivia. Once her name was chosen, her personality seemed to emerge. She was extremely docile and allowed us to approach and hold her in the goat pen. Her thin dusty feathers did not insulate our hands from her bony body; she felt like a plucked chicken.

For two weeks Olivia spent her days wandering around the pen with the goats her only company. For the most part they ignored her. Christopher and Holly went about their own lives outside the pen, taking notice of her only at night when they were shut in the barn together. I never saw any evidence of conflict in the morning when I opened the barn door to start the day.

As she settled into the daily routine at Lakeview Farm, Olivia's body began to go through a metamorphosis. The scraggly, gray baby feathers were gradually replaced by a new set that remained sealed in protective sheaths of skin called pin feathers. For days she looked like a pin cushion with feathers sticking out in all directions around her head. As June gave way to the lushness of summer, so did Olivia's pin feathers, beginning at the top of her head and around her eyes. When the skin casings shed, the shiny new feathers of her adult plumage bloomed and revealed the distinct pattern of the Canada goose's black, white and smoke-colored feathers. She was beautiful! Her downy under-feathers were filling in as well, which made her now feel more like a fur coat than a plucked chicken when we held her.

About this time, Olivia began showing interest in life outside of her pen. This is always a critical time for a rehabilitator. Like a human teenager, animals always begin to show interest in grown-up experiences long before they are capable of handling them. As the parent, I had to be careful not to let her go too soon, before her brain developed the skills to handle life in the wild. I had to make decisions that kept Olivia safe until she was ready to cross over into the wild. At that point I would have to let go and look the other way. It was the third week in June and I had only one more to go before school was out for summer vacation. Mid-July was my goal for Olivia's release. Olivia, however, had other plans.

One day she took the opportunity to escape through the barn door as I was entering first thing in the morning. Off she went toward the lake as if it was silently beckoning her to begin her adult life.

"Olivia, Livy, come back here," I sang uselessly.

She was gone! The clock prevented me from spending much time trying to get her back as I had to get to school. All day I worried about her, wondering how she was doing in the great big world on her first day. At lunchtime I had an idea. I called our friends Bill and Dot Stamp, a retired couple who spent the summer at their camp on Sixth Lake. They both loved animals and had visited ours many times. After sharing my desperate story of Olivia's escape, I asked Bill and Dot to keep an eye out for the lone goose. When I hung up, I somehow knew this would all work out and that Olivia would be just fine. I was right. Sure enough, when I arrived home, there was one message on my answering machine.

"Anne? Bill Stamp. Hey, we have Olivia and just need to know when you get home so that we can deliver her. No hurry, just let us know. Thanks."

Bill arrived at our dock shortly after I returned the call. In the front of his boat sat Olivia like a Labrador retriever, catching the gentle lake breezes. He relayed his goose wrangling adventure to me. Apparently, he and Dot had no trouble locating Olivia, the only Canada goose on the lake that day. They approached her with their boat, reached over the side and hauled her body up and over the edge. There was nothing to it. In fact they sensed that she was relieved to see humans after hours spent exploring the new territory. Once secure in her pen, Olivia showed no interest in leaving for the next several days.

School finally ended in late June, and I was able to spend my long summer days relaxing at Lakeview Farm with the animals. This freedom allowed me more time to plan Olivia's release. I began by taking her for short walks down to the lake so that she could bathe and preen herself. Although, she had not imprinted on me, she did follow me, especially if Christopher and Holly were in view. Eventually, I was able to leave her with the two ducks in the lake for most of the day. At twilight she followed them back to the barn and settled in safely for the night.

Finding My Way to Mountain View Farm

After a couple of weeks of this routine, Olivia stopped coming back to the barn at night. Although worried, I had to accept that her freedom was meant to be and that I should be celebrating her return to the wild where she belonged. I had, however, grown fond of her. I so wanted her to remain safe and alive in her wild world. I needn't have worried.

The next morning, she was back at the barn waiting for her breakfast when I went outside to feed the horses. There was no telling how long she had been waiting, but one thing was clear as she honked an urgent greeting. Olivia was hungry. After she gorged herself on cracked corn, she accompanied Christopher and Holly on their morning routine and returned to the lake for the rest of the day. This new routine went on for several more weeks, allowing me to adjust to the thought of Olivia being half-wild. Her appearance each day assured me that she was sensible about keeping close to the barn for safety and food. With no other Canada geese to provide security on the lake, she had figured out how to keep herself safe.

Summer is the time of year when our family members and friends plan their annual visits to the Adirondacks. Luckily, our guests are more than happy to join in the farm routines. After riding and working with the horses, we usually spent afternoons on the dock. Our guests that summer were enchanted by Olivia when she came by in the afternoon for some social interaction. She approached the dock in search of cracked corn. After gobbling her fill, she would stick close by, bobbing in the water around the perimeter of the dock. When my sister and her four young children visited, they loved to reach over and pick her up out of the water. She never resisted despite the struggle that it was to lift her large body up and onto the dock. There she would stand or squat down while we fussed over her. When she had had enough, she plunked back into the water but remained close by until we left the dock in the late afternoon.

Our friends Diane and Linda came for a long visit in mid-August during a cool spell. Instead of sitting on the dock, we spent our afternoons sitting by a campfire in front of our lean-to. Olivia did too. It was not uncommon to see her resting next to the blazing fire, adjusting her position when she got too hot.

Canada geese mature quickly due to the short summers in the North Country. Olivia looked like a mature Canada goose by the beginning of August, but she had yet to take flight. She did flap her wings while she glided around the lake, and I supposed this was her way of strengthening them for the inevitable takeoff.

Sixth Lake is a very busy place during the ten weeks of summer. Although it is rather small, its easy access to Seventh Lake makes it prone to motor boat traffic as well as kayaks and canoes. Jet skis and water skiers add to the congestion during July and August. For most of the years that we lived there, Birds Seaplane Service also used the lake to conduct scenic rides. Don and Jean Bird were good friends and neighbors. With the Birds at one end of the lake and the Stamps at the other, I received frequent updates on Olivia.

She, along with Christopher and his new mate Holly, had joined the flock of wild black ducks who spent their days touring the lake, looking for handouts from the summer residents. They didn't seem to notice or care about the enormous new member of their group. With so much activity on the lake, the ducks were used to taking flight if a boat or jet-ski got to close. Olivia did not have this advantage. Luckily, the ducks spent most of their day cruising the shoreline away from the dangerous traffic.

By late August, it was time to focus on the new school year. I was mildly concerned that Olivia had yet to fly. With the end of summer in sight, I began to wonder would happen to her come winter, only a few months away. With no other members of her species around, how would she know what to do and where to go? Once again, my worries proved to be unfounded. Olivia found her way.

When September arrived, my carefree summer schedule gave way to the clock-watching routine of the school day. By now Olivia was living on the lake full time, only appearing on our front lawn to feed with her wild duck companions. With her adult plumage now complete, she looked like a graceful bird instead of that luckless little creature of four months ago. With the fall foliage exploding into reds, yellows and oranges all around her, her striking good looks added to the dramatic changes of fall in the Adirondacks.

In mid-September, I arrived home to find another phone message about Olivia.

"Hello Anne? It's Don Bird. "Just wanted to let you know that I saw your goose fly out of the water today. She had no trouble at all and looked like she was an old pro at it. Talk to you soon."

With this milestone accomplished, the inevitable happened. I saw less and less of her. At first, days went by without goose sightings and then the absences stretched into weeks. Just when I thought I had seen her for the last time, she would appear on the lawn with the ducks as if she hadn't missed a day. In late November, a group of Canada geese set down in Sixth Lake on their way south for the winter. They stayed for a few days to replenish their strength before taking flight to their winter headquarters. After they left, I did not see Olivia again. I made myself believe that she had flown away with the wild flock of geese. Little did I know that she would return to show me that her rehabilitation had been a complete success. As winter arrived, I thought of Olivia from time to time, but I did not obsess over her. The permanent residents of my barn kept me busy. Olivia was a pleasant memory.

One early morning the next spring as I headed up to the barn to feed the horses, I heard a familiar honking sound out on the lake. I changed course and headed down to the front lawn with a can of cracked corn. Gliding toward the dock was a single Canada goose. She seemed excited when I called and swam quickly toward me, honking loudly. About ten feet from the dock, the goose refused to come any closer. I tried to tempt her by tossing handfuls of grain out into the water close to the dock but, the goose seemed reluctant to come any closer than about ten feet. Eventually, I had no choice but to leave and get on with my chores before school.

Then in the late fall of that same year, a flock of Canada geese landed in Sixth Lake and passed by the dock on a Saturday afternoon. Rod alerted me to their presence; again hopeful, I ran down to the lakefront with the three goats in tow. The geese had no interest in me. However, when I called Olivia's name in the familiar singsong way, one goose turned from the group and headed back towards our dock. As I pretended to throw corn into the lake, the goose swam more quickly toward me. As she approached, I ran to the barn to grab a container of real corn.

When I returned to the lakefront, the goose was more interested in what I had to offer than in following its companions. The other geese were still moving swiftly to the far end of the lake. The goose with me again approached within ten feet of our dock where I tossed generous handfuls of cracked corn. She would not come any closer but honked at me as I continued to sing her name. After several minutes of feeding, the goose finally turned to follow the others who, by now, had traveled far down to the other end of the lake. Sitting on the dock, I kept a vigil with my eyes until the goose became a small black speck, undistinguishable from the others in the flock.

As I watched, I remembered the summer that she came to us; for the first time I realized that her rehabilitation was complete. She had slipped out of nature's plan only temporarily to charm, endear and educate us. In return we had kept her safe so that she could grow up to return to her niche in the wild where she most definitely belonged. She had returned, briefly, to let me know that all was well with this beautiful creature that belonged to the wilderness.

CASEY BIRD GIRL...

Our ultimate bird experience began when Rod turned forty in 2000. To celebrate the milestone and to give a home to a needy animal, we agreed to purchase a three-year-old female hybrid Cockatoo named Casey. According to her history, Casey was the offspring of a Moluccan Cockatoo and an Umbrella Cockatoo. She was a large white parrot with expressive brown eyes and a beguiling personality. The family who owned her lived in a tiny gate house with barely enough room for two children let alone a large parrot cage. They were broken hearted to give her up after raising her from a tiny baby. Once Casey uttered her most endearing phrase to us, Rod and I were hopelessly hooked.

Finding My Way to Mountain View Farm

"I love you!" she chortled in a raspy voice.

Unfortunately, our philosophy of animal care was inappropriate for managing such an intelligent bird. We wanted her to have freedom from her cage, misinterpreting her needs for our own. Something about seeing an animal locked in a cage for long stretches of time makes me feel claustrophobic. Therefore, I left Casey's cage door open so that she could enter and exit at will. This freedom gave her access to a swing that hung from one of the wooden beams above her cage. It also gave her access to the couch. After a short stroll across the back of the sofa, she could easily join Rod on his reclining wing chair.

In the beginning, she captivated all of our visiting family and friends. Every niece wanted to have Casey left to them in our will since she was likely to outlive us by about twenty years! Her endearing behaviors included dancing, which really became quite animated if someone else joined her with bobbing rhythmic movements of her own. She also twirled and spun with the skill of a pole dancer on the chains that supported her swing.

In time her voice changed from a raspy garble to a sing-song tone, and "I love you" expanded into "I love you Casey bird bird bird girl." We enjoyed challenging her with a repetition of "bird" to see just how many words she could add.

All appeared to go well initially. Rod and I spent time researching about parrots, especially Cockatoos, yet we ignored what the experts strongly suggested. Cockatoos are notorious for being the most difficult parrots to manage. (Not our Casey bird.) They must be kept in a small designated area such as a cage for most of the time, especially when unsupervised. (Not our Casey bird.) Expanding their designated area promotes territorialism. (Not our Casey bird, she loves us.).

Eventually, Casey's behavior became unpredictable. By age five she was approaching sexual maturity. This development, combined with a limitless territory to patrol, put her in position to take control of us. The results were disastrous. Anybody sitting on the couch was subject to attack, especially those with whom she wasn't acquainted. That nutcracker beak with its sharp pointy vertex frequently pierced the neck or ears of unsuspecting guests. After the attack, she emitted the most blood curdling scream followed by a cackling satanic laugh. With her mouth wide open and her feet secure on the bar of her cage, she shook up and down with all of her head feathers fanned out. The trademark crest on top of her head stood erect, giving her a menacing demeanor.

Casey used her spine tingling scream to attract our attention at the most inconvenient times. At dawn's earliest light, her day officially began. During the summer, that heart-stopping scream startled us out of sleep long before we needed to be awake. The only way to console her was to get up and join her in the living room where she immediately quieted down.

After a long day alone in the house, she screamed for attention from the moment we arrived home. One day Rod ignored her tantrum while tending to urgent computer business upstairs in the office. Eventually, Casey grew tired of screaming to no avail and hopped down from her couch and out of her territory. Sensing that he was on the second floor, she climbed the stairs stealthily and continued her clandestine mission down the hall. Next, she stood soldier-still in the doorway, waiting until her presence surprised Rod at his desk. Once he discovered her there, (with a bit of a startle), she bobbed her body to and fro with the satisfaction of a football player who had just scored a touchdown. Of course he immediately picked her up and cuddled her, thus rewarding her for her effort!

Another time, Casey was suspiciously quiet downstairs while Rod was watching his daily stock report on a small TV in the office. The TV was controlled by whatever channel was tuned in on the TV downstairs. Suddenly, the small TV began changing channels rapidly on its own, like a scene in a science fiction movie. When Rod ran down to investigate the situation, he discovered that Casey had found the remote. She was perched on her swing, holding the remote dexterously with one foot while gnawing off the little rubber buttons that changed the channel with her beak.

"Casey Bad, Bad, Bird, Bird Girl."

Rod built a special bird stand for Casey that we could easily move around the house or outside to the deck. We tried to keep her near our activities in an attempt to ease her loneliness. What we were really doing was accommodating her, enabling her, spoiling her. Real "bird" people will recognize all the mistakes that we made in an attempt to provide her with our own opinion of healthy freedom.

As Casey's behavior became more erratic, we went to extremes to reform her. At one point we borrowed a recently widowed male Cockatoo from our dog groomer and parrot expert, Jimmy Ortiz. For several weeks, we kept Marco secure in his own cage near Casey and felt nothing but pity for him as he tried desperately to win Casey over. He sang to her and whistled for her attention, but she responded with terrified high pitched screams. Defeated, we returned Marco and wondered what our next option was going to be.

As Casey's negative behavior continued to escalate, our level of stress did the same. We were not prepared because our animals had always been a source of soothing calm that alleviated stress. The only relief from the turmoil inside the house was to escape to the barn, the one place where I recognized the rhythm that aligns my life with animals. Once I returned to the house, I tensed in anticipation of Casey's behavior. I can only imagine what impact she was having on the dogs and the pig who could not escape the stress. Rod seemed better able to deal with her. She was his bird, and he wanted her to bond with him. The trouble was that she liked me better. Guilt plagued my conscience. What kind of animal lover was I? Apparently, I didn't love all animals and this realization shocked and saddened me.

Amid the chaos there were moments of calm. Sometimes she sat on her swing and softly talked to herself in what appeared to be a dialogue of inflected chirps and static. I believe she was mimicking conversations she had heard between Rod and me.

Casey lived with us for three years until one final episode made it clear that she had to go. Aside from a rogue Paint gelding that we had owned briefly, Casey was the only other animal that we ever gave up on. Luckily, her new living arrangement provided her with a permanent home and a permanent mate.

One typical evening, Casey had joined Rod while he was sitting in his chair reading. She was strutting back and forth on the arm of the chair as he absentmindedly scratched under her feathers. All of a sudden, a blood curdling scream pierced the calm. This time it was not Casey exploding in a tirade. I ran from the kitchen and met Rod on his way to the bathroom with blood dripping from his hand. After washing it away, we examined the wounds that Casey's nut cracker beak had inflicted. Two of his knuckles had several deep long gashes sliced almost down to the bone. As Rod is a carpenter, his hands are of utmost importance to his trade. The writing was on the wall. With heavy hearts, we agreed that the madness had to end. We had failed this bird and the end result was dangerous.

I consulted with Jimmy. He was sure that Casey was approaching adolescence. Perhaps now she would be more receptive to a mate. It just so happened that poor Marco was still single. Since he had been such a good partner to his first mate, perhaps he could woo Casey into falling for him. Casey and Marco were carefully introduced to each other. Eventually, he moved into her cage, and to this day they are still together. They live in a cage in a large room with lots of other birds including Macaws, Cockatiels and Lovebirds. They breed often and occasionally Casey acts as if she is sitting on a nest. However, the fact that baby Cockatoos have yet to appear is probably due to the fact that Casey is a hybrid. This condition makes her a bit of a "mule" in that she is highly unlikely to produce viable eggs. That's fine, considering that there are plenty of Cockatoos to populate the world. We are just thankful to Jimmy for solving a huge problem for Casey and for us.

I have visited Casey from time to time and have sung to her, "I love you Casey Bird Bird Bird Bird Girl."

Although her voice has returned to the raspy sound that it made when she first came to live with us, her reply is still crisp and clear.

"I Love You."

Eviction Notice...

Lakeview Farm marched toward the new Millennium with three horses, three goats, one ancient dog and one pot belly pig. I had hit my stride teaching sixth grade with the help of a variety of classroom pets who provided my students with a unique environment in which to learn. I pictured myself spending the next twenty-two years teaching this way until the day

I retired. It was naïve for me to feel this way; why would I want twenty more years of the same old, same old? Where would growth come from? As I prepared to maintain my current pace, the winds of change began to stir from every corner of my life, whipping up a perfect storm of emotional frenzy.

Five weeks into the school year, I was given a directive by the school administration to remove the animals from the classroom. The reason given for the decision was based on health concerns and an opinion that the animals distracted the students from learning. I suspect that there was more to it than that. The ultimatum was given at 9:00 a.m., which meant that I had to get a grip on my composure and get through the rest of my school day.

With fifteen minutes left before my students returned from gym class, I turned to my close teacher friend, Ellen. Ellen Wilcox was the other sixth grade teacher at the time of the animal eviction notice. She and I come from completely opposite poles of the universe, yet we share a friendship that is based on mutual respect for the other's chosen lifestyle. Ellen, like my sister Sue, is a homemaker who couldn't wait to grow up and have a family of her own. She wanted babies her whole life and raised three who have all married and are now raising their own families.

As a teacher, Ellen inspired students to love reading. Outside of school she dabbled in a variety of crafts that include knitting, quilting, weaving, and making baskets. She baked cookies that appeared in a sandwich bag on my desk during the most trying days. But perhaps Ellen's most endearing quality was a sharp and poignant sense of humor that entertained me often and lifted my spirits. On this day she did not disappoint.

I spilled the whole ordeal out through a river of tears as Ellen listened. "Oh! Do you think maybe they thought the animals were doing too good a job teaching and might start to demand a paycheck?" she wondered sarcastically in an effort to help me gain control of my emotions.

When the students returned, everything changed. They were no longer allowed to handle the animals. The animals could not leave their enclosures. I was forbidden to discuss the reasons with the students. I was only able to tell them that the animals would be leaving in a few days. The ultimatum came down on a Tuesday, so we had the rest of the week to get through without animal interactions. The rats spent the remainder of the week frantically running around in their cage, unable to comprehend why they were confined while their people ignored them on the other side of the glass. The scene was heartbreaking. The children were confused. I was angry. Somehow I made it through the rest of the day. As word spread around school, many of my colleagues expressed support and condolences.

On Saturday, Rod and I drove to school and filled the pickup truck with cages, equipment and the classroom pets. In less than one hour, the classroom went from biosphere to ghost town. Come Monday, I would be a "cookie cutter" teacher with most of the year's curriculum left to cover without the help of my animal colleagues.

On Monday morning, I returned to my classroom, now empty of the animal co-teachers who had made every day an interactive experience for the whole class, particularly those students who didn't have pets at home. When the students arrived, they sadly persisted in asking why the animals were gone.

My reply was simple. "The administration decided that the animals needed to be removed from the classroom due to health concerns."

That morning was a turning point in my career as a teacher. For the first time, I questioned whether or not I wanted to teach for the next twenty years. I had lost control of the methods I knew worked with my students.

Since I was not permitted to discuss the situation with my students, they were simply expected to move on without a clear answer to why the animals were removed. The need to have the last word on the matter inspired me to write a letter to the school Board in which I spelled out the history as well as the benefits of having animals in my classroom. Supportive friends and families wrote letters to the Board. Several letters were written by older students who fondly remembered their special year with the animals. The Board listened, reconfirmed their decision and simply dropped the discussion.

Many of my colleagues stood by with verbal support at the time of the incident, but many others avoided discussing the issue with me. Their silence led me to believe that perhaps they too were uncomfortable with animals in the classroom.

At home we tended to the needs of the evicted animals, but no longer were they handled by children who had incorporated them into stories, anatomy lessons, writing exercises, listening activities, sharing opportunities and research. They survived, but they had lost their occupation and their purpose. I grieved this loss every time I had to care for them.

INTO THE DARK...

Outside of school, other situations also began to spiral out of my control. While on a trip to Australia, my mother had met a wonderful man. Now she was spending most of her time with him. Because they were not married, she was uncomfortable being around her children. To avoid this issue they simply kept away from all of us. My mother seldom called. She kept up with emails; but trying to keep her life private, she remained distant and unapproachable. I felt that I was also mourning her loss.

In addition my fortieth birthday was approaching quickly. I felt pressured to declare whether or not we were planning to have children. I felt disappointed in the decision I finally made. I wished that I wanted to have children the way that my sister and brother's wives had. Truth is I didn't. The thought of working full time and raising a family seemed daunting. Nobody in my family worked and raised children. They all chose family over careers; at this moment, I was at the dawn of my career, one I had worked hard to achieve. Rod hoped that I would change my mind. I was living my childhood dream with animals, and I was truly happy immersed in their care. With a family, something would have to give, no doubt the financial burden of maintaining the horses. In the end I wasn't willing to give the horses up. The pain of my decision added to my despair. In my thirties, I was protected by the fact that if I didn't want children now, I could have them in a few years. Now time for childbearing was running out.

As the school year progressed, I was forced to redefine my teaching methods without animals in the classroom. I would have to adjust and move on. But, it wasn't going to be that easy.

In February, 2000, Rod and I both came down with a very bad case of the flu. Since neither of us is often sick, the intensity of this illness added to my fear of the unknown and left me floundering in a sea of anxiety. The sickness kept us down and out for almost a week, and then slowly allowed us to recover. Except for a lingering bronchial infection, I returned to school feeling that I was on the mend with each passing day. Truth is I was not. As my physical strength returned, my mental strength seemed to deteriorate. Having never experienced depression, I was not prepared for this bout of intense anxiety. I became fixated on "what if" and on the possibility of death, both my own and Rod's. The late hours of the night found me wide awake, wondering what would happen to all of these animals if I ceased to exist. Even worse was wondering how I could maintain this lifestyle if anything happened to Rod.

The school day became my relief from this mental torture. At school, I fell into a routine. I felt like my old self within the perimeter of my profession. With no time to worry, I appeared to function normally. But once home in the confines of my real life, I fell apart. While cleaning the barn every afternoon, I wept uncontrollably and dwelled on all the desperate "what if" scenarios as if I expected them to crashing into reality. For the first time ever, the animals hung around my neck like a noose, forcing me to examine what I had gotten myself into by acquiring so many.

I began to wonder if Lakeview Farm was meant to house all of us until Rod and I retired at a ripe old age. These thoughts were disturbing, because I could not imagine another homestead as wonderful as our three-plus acres on Sixth Lake. Leave Lakeview Farm? Where would we go?

Then Cindy announced that she was going to leave the Adirondacks so that she could make a fresh start with her family. Cindy was coming out of a rather rough period herself. After she and her husband divorced, she found the love of her life in a charismatic Australian named Perry. Rod and I both liked him and enjoyed spending time with both Cindy and Perry. Her two children were in second and first grade when the family moved. I knew that I was not enough of a reason for Cindy to stay in Old Forge where the constant reminder of her ex-husband and father of her children stalled her ability to restart her life. This town was too small. Cindy and Perry wanted better jobs to support themselves and a variety of opportunities for the children as well. Still my heart broke at the thought of losing her.

As the days lengthened into spring, I hoped that my darken mood would begin to lighten with the first signs of returning life and lengthening daylight hours. During the April break, I went to visit Missy in Northern New Jersey for a few days. Hoping that the change of scenery would bring me out of my funk, I looked forward to our visit together.

Missy managed her own barn in an area of New Jersey that is defined by its horse farms. Everywhere we went, including the grocery store, dry cleaners, specialty boutiques, and quaint cafes, I saw women in breeches and dusty boots on their way to and from the barn. Baseball caps or visors concealed their heads; no doubt an attempt to hide helmet hair. Watching them fascinated me. I wondered what their situations were. How were horses incorporated into their busy professional and private lives?

I don't know exactly when the epiphany occurred. Suddenly I knew what Rod and I needed to do. It was time for profound change; time to leave Lakeview Farm and begin a new phase of our lives with the animals. Time to buy a larger piece of property and build a facility where I could teach horseback riding again. As clear as this revelation appeared was the lack of clarity about how to go about it. What did the new future look like and how would we go about achieving it?

I shared my epiphany with Rod when I returned home a few days later. He had always dreamed of living on a larger property. He was waiting for me to prepare myself to say goodbye to Lakeview Farm. Although he had lovingly restored and doubled the house in size, it was not his dream house. Rod had no attachment to Sixth Lake. He viewed it as an eighteen-year investment that would provide us with the capital to develop a larger piece of land. Lakeview Farm was my dream come true. It had given me what I always wanted—horses right outside my kitchen window. The darkness of my depression made me feel guilty that Sixth Lake was somehow not enough. I apparently wanted more.

With spring well underway, we set out to investigate properties that would take us into the next phase of our life. The day I opened my resume file with the intention of bringing it up to date was a bit surreal. When I started to make phone calls inquiring about potential teaching positions outside of the Adirondacks, I still couldn't imagine leaving Inlet. But the search had to start somewhere. For several weekends, we headed out of the park to find the perfect property on which to settle. Our search took us to Saratoga and all around Glens Falls. We looked at a premiere property on the Vermont border that was showcased in *Country Living Magazine*. We ventured into Albany and even checked out several possibilities between Cooperstown and Oneonta. Each time we returned to the car, exhausted by all the information we had gleaned from the realtor, Rod's reaction was always the same. "I can build it better myself," he declared.

It was a challenge to hear this claim after spending the day looking at prospective properties that could provide instant gratification. It was daunting to think of the number of years it would take for Rod to build it all himself. But in the end, the move had to gratify him as well. I wanted him to live his dream too since he had so lovingly already built mine.

In addition to exploring various properties, I spent time investigating teaching positions. The thought of leaving my secure teaching position frightened me. But onward I pressed and even went about applying for a couple of high school science teacher positions. When the school year ended in late June, Rod and I had yet to find our future, but we were committed to continue searching.

Meanwhile, Michele was becoming concerned about the prospects of our leaving the Adirondacks. Although she never mentioned a word about it, I could tell that her mind was racing for a solution that would keep us close by.

One day at school, John Leach, a colleague, suggested that I take a look at some property that his family was thinking of selling. The Leach family owns a children's camp called Adirondack Woodcraft Camp. Woodcraft is an old camp steeped in Adirondack tradition for over 60 years. The Leach family has owned it since the mid 1970s; John and his brother David are the directors of the camp. They both teach at the Town of Webb School but reside on the Woodcraft property where they have raised their families. So after school one day in early summer, John showed me around a parcel of 77 acres that were a tax burden to the camp.

The property was nothing but woods with an unused gravel-pit long ago abandoned. John and I walked the ski trails that he and his family

Finding My Way to Mountain View Farm

still maintained during the winter months. To be honest, I had no feeling about Woodcraft on that day. It was beautiful Adirondack property, but we had been looking at pasture land for so many months that I was unimpressed with this land as a site for horse keeping.

At home I described what I had seen to Rod. I had to admit that the state of land itself was impressive. Because of the receding glacier so many millions of years ago, Woodcraft had been left with two kettle lakes and a sandy base that was perfect for riding horses. As I walked with John, I could imagine training a horse on these established sand trails. There was not a rock to be found, large or small. But my brain could not grasp the enormous effort needed to clear the land and build a horse farm complete with house, barn and indoor riding arena.

Rod was not overly impressed with the land either when he had his first peek a few days later. In his mind, he pictured his dream location with a significant stream and views of surrounding landscape, much like what we had been sampling outside of the Adirondack Park. However, he was impressed with the sandy base that would facilitate construction without a lot of guess work. With no commitment, we put the Woodcraft property on hold and faced the busy summer.

Unfortunately, the bright sunny summer days did not lift me out of my low mood. Several depressing issues compounded my effort to feel mentally whole again. There was the mysterious lameness that waxed and waned in Zambi's limbs and back, preventing me from continuing his Dressage training and competing with him. Because Zambi had good days and bad days, it would be another whole year before a diagnosis of Equine Protozoal Myelitis (EPM) was made.

This was also Luther's last summer with us. He existed for most of it as a decrepit little creature, unable to hear, see or care for himself properly. I waited for him to let me know when it was time to end his life.

As another school year began in September, Rod and I had yet to find the property that would allow us to enter the next phase of our lives. We continued to take day trips on the weekends, checking out real estate beyond the Adirondack border. Nothing struck us despite the beautiful fall foliage that brightened the backdrop as we searched. Then in late October,

I received information about a huge piece of farm property in Boonville, about forty five minutes west of Inlet.

The property was huge, 217 acres with a mixture of grassy fields and young woodlands. The Victorian house was situated only 30 feet from the road to accommodate the long-ago milk route. Unfortunately, the road had evolved into a major highway with traffic that whizzed back and forth, rattling the windows of the house. But the land had so much to offer for keeping horses. With an investment in new fencing, the pasture possibilities were endless. I could envision horses living solely on grass for at least five out of twelve months of the year, cutting our hay costs almost in half. Rod envisioned building a house farther back, away from the dangerous traffic, and positioning in it such a way that it gazed out on the majestic beauty of the interior farmland.

For weeks we leaned toward the Boonville property as a compromise. The existing house and barn gave us structures to move into for the short-term while we built the dream structures for the long-term. It was a win-win situation. Rod's need to commute to the property daily during the winter months provided the reality check that we both needed. As beautiful as the land was, as farm friendly as the existing structures were, it was not meant to be ours.

But Woodcraft was. During the late fall, Rod and I returned to Wood-craft several times to walk the trails and view the land as a prospective horse farm. Suddenly our destiny became clear. The logistics of construction at Woodcraft while we remained in Inlet and I continued teaching at the Town of Webb began to make sense. We made the decision, our offer was accepted, and Rod and I never looked back. As we proceeded with our plan, we began to feel passionate about our beautiful piece of newly acquired Adirondack real estate.

Our first challenge was to convince the Adirondack Park Agency or APA that we were going to develop the property responsibly within their strict restrictions. This state agency was created to protect the "forever wild" mission of the park. It maintains strict control of all construction, particularly near lakes and other water sources. Until they granted us necessary permits, we waited in limbo. A year later after an unnecessary

Finding My Way to Mountain View Farm

struggle with the APA, Rod was able to begin visualizing how the densely wooded land could evolve into a thoughtful set-up for horses without losing its Adirondack appeal. Finally, with a home equity loan secure by February, Rod bought a backhoe and began preliminary excavation of our new location and our new life.

And Into The Light...

One of my favorite photographs hangs on the refrigerator. It's of a black-and-tan Dachshund puppy whose large head, blunt nose and almond shaped eyes never fail to touch my heart every time I enter the kitchen. When I see it, my memory races back to the first summer when Huxley came to live with us.

The previous November, we had euthanized Luther, the last member of our first generation of dogs. He had lived to the ripe old age of sixteen and could possibly have lived longer if I had not made the difficult decision to have him put down. Blind, deaf and incontinent, Luther held onto life with little dignity. Caring for him had become extremely difficult. In my heart I knew that the decision was ultimately up to me. In fact, I had made the same decision for Mishka, one year before and for Eric, two years before Luther. To cope in this extended period of "old dog stress" I sealed my feelings in a shell of emotions.

After Luther was euthanized, I quietly made a vow that I was finished with dogs. Old dogs require constant care and clean-up. Having to wake up in the middle of the night to tend to a dog's needs made me angry and miserable. Then I struggled with terrible guilt for feeling this way when the poor animal could not help himself. How could this kaleidoscope of emotions exist when I thought I loved these dogs so much? The three dogs were so close in age that they all seemed to get old at the same time and remained that way for several years until I made the inevitable decision.

During the winter that followed Luther's death, there were no dogs in our house. Life was so much easier without them. I felt a sense of freedom, being able to come and go as I pleased without considering a dog's needs, particularly the needs of a geriatric dog. I still had horses, goats and Noah to care for, but their schedules were a little more flexible. I wondered at this time if I would ever want to own a dog again. Nothing about having one appealed to me. In fact, I couldn't quite remember loving our dogs when they were alive. My mind shut out those feelings, leaving me to wonder if perhaps their deaths had been a relief. I convinced myself that we would never have another dog.

Winter melted into spring and spring warmed into summer. In June, as the school year began to wind down, I eagerly looked forward to the summer months. They stretched before me with the promise of days spent riding and connecting with my horses. The thought of having a dog again still remained numb inside of me. School ended on the last Thursday of June, marking the beginning of ten weeks of freedom.

Rod and I looked forward to spending the first Sunday afternoon of vacation at Sunny Cliff. One of the relaxing activities that I enjoyed there was reading Big Rod's collection of Sunday newspapers. I found myself in the classified section of the Syracuse *Herald American* looking at ads for Dachshund puppies. One particular ad caught my attention. The next morning, after a restless night spent dreaming of puppies, I made a tentative phone call. The only bit of bad news was that the puppies were over three hours away in Oswego, north of Syracuse. Ready to forget the whole idea, I thanked the breeder and hung up. But Michele convinced me to go with her the next day to see them. She just happened to have errands to run in the general vicinity of the breeder. "Let's go and just have a look," she suggested. "And bring your checkbook…just in case."

I loved him immediately. The heat from his tiny black body warmed my palm as he lounged like a lump of coal in it. His soft brown eyes looked right into mine. It was the beginning of my recovery. His youthful innocence reminded me that life moved forward and memories simply bookmarked the past.

Grief overwhelmed me in that moment. I wept for all three of our wonderful dogs whom I had loved dearly for so long. How had I lived without a dog all winter? Why did I think I should deprive myself of the incredible privilege that living with dogs provides? What I deemed freedom had simply been grief.

"You have big shoes to fill," I told him through my tears. "There were others before you who fulfilled so many promises in their lifetime. I hope I can love you as much as I loved them."

Michele drove the whole way back to Old Forge, giving me three hours to stare at the new puppy in my arms. By the time we arrived home, I had memorized him from head to toe. Rod was anxiously waiting in the driveway when we arrived late in the afternoon. He eagerly took our new baby into his arms so that they could get acquainted.

A whole week went by before we named our puppy, having called him "Baby Puppy" for seven days. His official name had to fit perfectly, and good suggestions such as Otto, Karl and Griffin didn't quite match. Finally, while searching online, I came across a list of names associated with literature.

There, embedded among gifted writers such as Shakespeare, O'Neil, and Hemingway, was the name of the man who wrote Brave New World. I lifted the little form napping on my lap and held him up in front of my face. With sleepy eyes he stared at me while I christened him Huxley.

Huxley helped to heal my broken heart. He reminded me that I did truly love the three dogs who came before him. He showed me that life with a dog is a necessity for me even if loss is inevitable in the years to come. And most of all he gave me no choice but to love him too.

Thus began the next generation of our beloved canines. By mid-August, Huxley was joined by a seven week old West Highland terrier puppy whom we named Niles. Niles' mother was Missy's dog, a little Westie named Xena. Watching our two puppies cavort about on the lawn continued to delight me. Two years later another Westie, (a full sister to Niles) named Nina joined our family making a total of three dogs once again.

Lakeview Farm's final chapter was slow to live. For the next three years, Rod toiled diligently so that we could live a dream larger than either of us ever imagined. Meanwhile, the dogs, horses, goats, iguanas, a pig and I had to wait patiently. Somehow, we found a way to live each day with purpose while we waited for Moose River Farm to materialize out of thick forest and endless details of paper work.

LEFT. *Rod riding Promise the summer we met.* (1985)

BELOW. *Our goat milking adventure began with the birth of Rachel and Hannah.* (1989)

  Finding My Way to Mountain View Farm

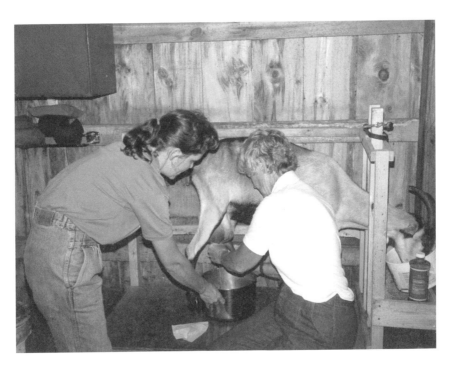

ABOVE. *Rachel trying her hand at milking Helen.* (1989)

LEFT. *The next year Helen gave birth to Jordan.* (1990)

ABOVE. *Rachel Phinney and Rod's puppy, Mishka.* (1985)

ABOVE.

Many generations of rats lived in the classroom. (1995)

RIGHT. *Rehabilitation of Phoebe the fawn.* (1992)

Finding My Way to Mountain View Farm

ABOVE. *The first of the animals in the classroom was Spike the iguana.* (1993)

BELOW. *Spike and Rosemary at the classroom Christmas party.* (1996)

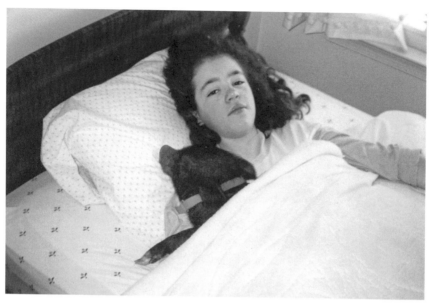

ABOVE. *My niece Amy and baby Noah.* (1996)

BELOW. *Noah wallows on the beach at Sixth Lake.* (1998)

Finding My Way to Mountain View Farm

LEFT. *Noah grew into a handsome pig.* (1997)

CENTER. *Eric, Noah and Luther.* (1996)

BOTTOM. *Noah as a baby.* (1996)

Finding My Way to Mountain View Farm

ABOVE. *Olivia the orphaned Canada goose.* (1999)

RIGHT. *After Louise's tragic death, Christopher bonded with Holly.* (1998)

OPPOSITE TOP. *Diane Williams and me at the top of Rocky Mountain.* (1999)

OPPOSITE BOTTOM. *Christopher and Louise.* (1994)

RIGHT. *A Veiled chameleon named Hue joined the classroom in 1998.*

201

ABOVE. *Rod and me with the beginning of our second generation of dogs, Huxley.* (2001)

Finding My Way to Mountain View Farm

ABOVE. *Niles, Nina and Huxley.* (2003)

LEFT. *Casey Bird the Cockatoo.* (2001)

ABOVE. *The iguanas, Spike and Rosemary*

OPPOSITE BOTTOM. *Zambezi and me.* (1999)

OPPOSITE TOP. *Diane, (right) on Spy Hopes and her partner Linda, riding Windy, visit Lakeview Farm after our timely reunion in 1987.*

OPPOSITE BOTTOM. *Rod and Rachel Phinney*

RIGHT. *Jean Risley, Michele deCamp and me.* (2002)

BELOW. *Easau, Windy, Zambi, and Spy.* (2003)

Part III
Moose River Farm

Finding My Way to Mountain View Farm

Moving to Moose River Farm...

At 6:00 in the morning on Monday, June 21, 2004, (the last week of school), I turned my car into the driveway at Moose River Farm to begin my first morning of chores. Yesterday had been long and stressful, but by 8:00 p.m., all of the horses and both goats were finally settled in their new barn. This morning, I had awakened at 5:30. After my shower, I dressed in barn clothes and packed school clothes in a canvas bag. Then I fed the dogs and packed my lunch. After I loaded the dogs in the car, we were underway. How strange it felt to drive by Lakeview's empty barn and sagging fences that never again would hold our horses.

Niles stood bracing himself on the console, straining to see where we were going. Huxley lay curled up under a blanket on the passenger seat, while Nina sprawled on the backseat. The sun shone on the lush green leaves, promising a warm summer day. Excitement competed with stress as I prepared to see horses, having survived their first night in their new home, peeking out of the stalls. And there they were; the focus of all the planning and hard work over the last four years. I couldn't have predicted the scramble of emotions I experienced during that time. At least during the low points, we never lost sight of our goal. From the beginning Rod could visualize the details for our new property in a way that I could not. It was difficult to picture the heavily wooded land excavated into a two-story home with a stable, paddocks and indoor and outdoor riding rings. Before he had felled a single tree on the densely wooded acreage, Rod knew exactly where the house would be located, at what angle it would face the rising and setting sun. He knew the barn's location, 200 feet from the house, and planned to fence the large space between the two structures for our small dogs. I couldn't see it. When we frequently visited the wooded lot during the planning stages, Rod always had to reorient my bearings.

Once the trees began to fall, I was able to imagine twelve stalls, six on either side, stretched along the aisle of the eighty-four-foot barn. Although the indoor riding ring wasn't completed until years later, its location was carefully determined in the initial phase of the plans. Behind the far end of the barn, Rod cleared and fenced an acre of land. Years later he cleared an additional acre with hopes of establishing another small pasture. The short growing season in the Adirondacks does not guarantee lush pasture. However, with careful management and prevention of over-grazing, we have been able to keep the fields green. The end result of Rod's labor, although far from complete, was finally on the horizon. Moving the horses to the new barn just before summer vacation marked the real beginning of our lives at Moose River Farm.

The first face I saw hanging over a Dutch door belonged to our goat, Lacey, curious to know who was coming to visit her in this strange new place. Windy and Spy peered over their newly stained doors as well. The other three horses' stalls were out of view on the other side of the barn. I pulled up to the barn and parked the car. All five horses whinnied to me. Their calls were signs of both hunger and relief that somebody they recognized had come back to care for them in this unfamiliar setting. Horses don't appreciate change. Life at Lakeview Farm had been predictable. Here, new stalls, new smells and completely new surroundings made them wonder what the routine was going to be. I, too, wasn't sure about the new routine. I realized on that first morning at Moose River Farm how efficient my schedule had been in Inlet. It didn't help that I had to be ready to leave for school by 7:15.

In the new barn I seemed to trip all over myself while delivering hay and grain to five horses and two goats. The brand new hardware on the wooden stall doors squeaked an unfamiliar tune as I slid the doors open and shut. In time the melody of the new barn would become comfortingly familiar to me. The Westies took off to patrol the property, while Huxley sat staring at the car door, wishing it would open so he could get back under his warm blanket on the passenger seat. Eventually, I got the stalls mucked and changed my clothes for school. I gathered the three dogs and secured them in the tack room to wait for Rod when he arrived later in the morning to work on the house. There, Huxley was delighted to find a comfortable bed and blanket waiting for him.

Finding My Way to Mountain View Farm

Back in the car and dressed for school, I sighed with relief now that I had completed my first morning of chores. Only three mornings left before summer vacation. I needed that time to organize the barn and to establish the rhythm that is so necessary for the physical and mental health of all of us living on the farm.

All morning, thoughts of the barn distracted me from teaching or whatever we teachers call trying to manage eighteen children who can smell summer vacation only a few days away. At lunch time I decided to check on the barn. With thirty minutes, including the trip in both directions, I really only had time to look at the horses. When I arrived, all was well, but the horses were still in the barn. It was a beautiful day so I decided to turn all of the horses out in the ring. After supplying buckets of water and hay and allowing the goats freedom from their stall, I took off for school, arriving back just in time to pick my students up from lunch.

The visit to the barn had assured me that everything was going well so I was able to concentrate on keeping my students busy until the end of the day. At 3:00, I hurried out to my car and took off once again for the barn. But this time when I drove in the driveway, I knew all was not well.

The horses were racing around in the paddock at a full gallop. When they saw me drive in, they ran to the gate, dancing and stomping. Their nostrils flared and sweat soaked each one from nose to tail. Blood trickled down Target's white hind legs. Immediately, I knew what was wrong. They were being tortured by the largest, most menacing horse flies I had ever seen. Once or twice in eighteen years on Lakeview farm, I had seen a couple of these monsters attacking my horses. But here there were hundreds of them ferociously draining my horses of blood and strength. The poor horses employed the only weapon they had to escape the tormentors— reckless speed.

With ears pinned and hooves flailing, each horse fought to be first out of the gate. Still wearing my school clothes, I grabbed lead ropes and began to rescue them one at a time. Once they were secure inside the barn, only a few of the giant flies continued to harass them as they huffed and puffed their exhausted lungs. Next I needed to locate the hose among all the stuff we had moved from my little barn the day before. Frustrated, I searched every possible hiding place, failing over and over to find the elusive hose. Standing hot and sweaty in the stalls, the horses were overheating, a greater threat than flies. I continued to scour boxes and bags. Eventually I found the hose packed neatly in a black garbage bag in the horse trailer and hurried to attach it to the hydrant behind the barn.

Starting with Target, I led each horse to the unfamiliar location. They hesitated, wasting more precious time. Each one finally allowed me to spray him with cold water. I scrubbed the blood off of every leg and tortured sheath between their thighs. Once they were clean and calm, I returned them to their stalls and offered flakes of hay. After the last horse was hosed and comforted, the atmosphere in the new barn calmed down. My calm lasted only seconds until I began to wonder anxiously about those flies. Was this the normal summer population of flies out here in the woods? Had I moved my horses from a more hospitable environment to be voraciously consumed by a mass of flying predators? If so they would never be able to leave the barn, be worked in the ring or enjoy a trail ride during the summer months. What had I done? We needed to go back to Inlet, right now! But of course we couldn't go back. We had come so far in the last four years that the only direction to go now was forward. Sadly it was going to get worse before it got better.

Since Jean and I had taken a ceremonial last ride in Lakeview's perfect ring the week before, I had lost my hunger to ride on the new farm. Too many other details crammed my brain. When school came to a close on Thursday afternoon, we decided to christen the new ring.

The monster horse flies only appeared to menace the horses in the middle of the hot day. By late afternoon the flies were more tolerable. Michele joined us for the inaugural ride in the new ring. After pawing through tack that still lived in the horse trailer, we found saddles and bridles for Windy, Spy and Zambi. Once our horses were tacked up, we headed out to the new ring.

Rod had just finished excavating the 80-by-170 foot space within the last ten days. It had required the removal of close to 100 trees, large and small. Each tree required the unearthing of a stump with roots that penetrated deep into the ground. Once the topsoil was scraped away, the horse-friendly sand footing underneath was exposed. The work had been long and backbreaking. But from the top of a horse, the ground looked pocked and uneven underneath the sand that had been graded flat on top.

After stretching our horses with a long walk, we began to trot. It didn't take long for all three horses to begin tripping. We tried again and again; but with each trip, the horses grew more cautious. They resisted any gait faster than a walk. My heart sank and my eyes filled with tears. Jean and Michele remained silent, not knowing what to say or do to comfort me.

Despite all of Rod's long hours clearing the ring, grading the space and erecting the fence, it wasn't good enough. The surface was too inconsistent, making it treacherous for riding. A horse might trip or stumble. Wood-craft Camp was due to open in three days. Already four campers had paid for riding lessons. The next day, Michele and I headed to Philadelphia to collect Amy and her horse Welby for a summer of riding, riding and riding. I had also arranged to borrow a gelding from Morrisville College to use as a lesson horse. And yet the perfect riding ring was back in Inlet. Had I dared to dream too big? Did I want too much? What was I to do now?

Giving in to defeat, we abandoned our workout in the ring and exited to walk out on the trails. Once we were out in the woods among the balsams and breezy maples, my head began to clear. Jean riding Windy and Michele riding Spy walked along with me, two wise women not willing to give up hope that Moose River Farm was going to work out well for people and horses. Every new change has hiccups, but every problem is solvable if one gives herself time to think it through.

"It needs time to settle," Michele assured me.

"But what about next week when lessons begin? It's not going to settle that quickly, and it could be quite dangerous for the horses and the riders," I replied, my level of anxiety rising.

"Maybe there's a machine that can press all that loose footing so it is level with the rest," Jean offered.

"Billy Martin has a bulldozer that he uses to level driveways and walkways before they are blacktopped," Michele remembered, referring to a local excavator who was a good friend of her husband Scott. "Maybe he can come and work on it before next week."

"It's worth a call," agreed Jean.

The next day Michele and I hooked up the trailer to the truck and took off for a whirlwind trip to Philadelphia. Jean stayed behind and took care of the horses. Billy Martin arrived with bulldozer while we were gone. We all crossed our fingers and hoped for the best.

After one night on my sister's farm in Chester County, we pried Welby away from his goats and his pony friend Skippy to put him on the trailer. After a slight hesitation, he loaded well; and we were on our way north to the Adirondacks. Amy followed along in her own car; the two way radios we borrowed from my sister helped us keep tabs on each other throughout the long trip. Several stops and over six hours later, we arrived at Morrisville College to pick up Murray. Lisa met us at the barn and handed the big horse to me at the end of a lead rope. He had been out of work since the middle of May and apparently had done little more than eat hay. His large hind end hung over the butt bar of my trailer as if he was wearing underwear that was too small. It felt wonderful to laugh at the contrast between big Murray and more diminutive Welby.

The two-and-half hour ride to Moose River Farm allowed plenty of time for Welby to declare Murray his best friend. By the time we arrived home and got the horses off the trailer and secure in their stalls at opposite ends of the barn, Welby was screaming to find out what had happened to his new best buddy. After spending a night in the stall next to Target, Welby decided that the white horse was now his only friend in the whole world. He screamed when Target was led away to the paddock. This intense bonding behavior prompted a game that Amy and I played all summer. After we assigned Welby to one stall for a week or so, we began to move him around the barn so that he had to break the bond with his neighbor and establish a new bond with a new neighbor. We called the game "Where's Welby?" and continued to play it until he had established a rapport with each of the geldings in the barn. That way they all were his best buddies, establishing him as one of the most amicable members of the herd.

With the arrival of Amy, Welby and Murray, summer vacation officially began. Luckily, the monster bugs we referred to as "bombers" vanished within two weeks of the horses' arrival at Moose River Farm. Billy Martin's work on the ring created footing that was more stable under hoof. The ring still needed to settle, a problem that time and a deep winter frost would solve. But for now, at least my beginner lessons could get underway.

Our house at Moose River Farm was not ready for us. We spent the first summer commuting daily from empty Lakeview Farm to lively Moose River Farm. Looking back, I don't know how I survived living between those two worlds. Perhaps it was the knowledge that commuting was temporary. I knew it would continue only into October before we made the final move.

Amy was a huge help in the barn that first summer. She worked full-time at the Old Forge Hardware Store from noon until early evening. That gave her all morning to ride and play with horses. On Monday and Tuesday, her days off, we took to the woods in search of new trails. Welby preferred being ridden in the woods to being schooled in the ring. We owed him this reward for accommodating riders who took lessons on him. In addition to Welby, Amy rode Easau and Target who presented more of a challenge to her skills. Her training for intercollegiate horse shows benefitted all of the horses on the farm.

My lesson business remained steady for ten solid weeks. I averaged two or three lessons a day and made time in the early morning for my own riding. Jean joined me every morning, schooling Windy or Spy and working on her own skills. I was exhausted from the commute, but frequently in the afternoon, I was able to curl up with the dogs on a futon we placed in the tack room. There I fell into a deep sleep. In the late afternoon, I fed the horses and tended to their needs. Once Amy arrived home from work after 7:00, we gave every horse a carrot, every goat a cookie, and kissed them all goodnight. Home we drove to Lakeview Farm for dinner and sleep.

Rosemary, Spike and Noah remained at Lakeview Farm that first summer. Noah was perfectly content to spend his days as he had when the horses and goats lived on the farm, foraging along the driveway and lawn for any molecule of food he could find. When it got too hot, he wallowed in the wet sand on the beach by the lake and took refuge from the sun in the wood shavings bin at the base of the ring.

"Neort, Neort, hmph, hmph," he greeted merrily when we arrived home in the evening.

He came right into the house to have his dinner, then ascended the stairs to his nest of torn blankets in the computer room. There he slept soundly until I rose the next morning.

One day in early August, Noah came down the stairs in his usual manner, walked over to his dish of pig pellets and for the first time in nine years refused to eat. Mildly shocked, I checked the condition of his food by smelling it and tried to doctor it up by adding grapes and green beans. Although he poked his snout in the bowl with interest, he just couldn't seem to eat. Later when we returned home, he nibbled at his dinner but didn't eat with his usual enthusiasm.

For the next few days, Noah alternated between nibbling his food and refusing to eat. He still went to the bathroom outside. He also went about his daily routine. By the middle of August, we decided it was time to move him as well. Although he had traveled in the car extensively when he was younger and smaller, he was now an enormous pig.

Cindy was visiting for the weekend and volunteered to move Noah in her minivan. It took both of us all of our strength to hoist him up onto the floor in the backseat. We got underway quickly as there was no telling what he might do with his sheer bulk if he decided riding in the car was not to his liking. We needn't have worried. He was the perfect passenger, and within twenty minutes we were pulling into the farm driveway with our live cargo.

Once out of the car, Noah seemed surprised to be in a new location. He sniffed the ground, afraid to leave the area where his four feet had landed. Eventually, I coaxed him to follow me toward the barn. Hannah and Lacey were there to greet him with head butts as his nose led him to leftover grain available in Target's stall. Pigs are very smart so I am certain that it didn't take Noah long to associate the familiar smells in the new barn with the animals now missing at Lakeview Farm.

Once Noah had moved, our plan was to keep him out of the house. Nine years of scratching his sandpaper body on the woodwork and tearing up dog beds, clothing and blankets had come to an end. The heated tack room would serve as his shelter, allowing him access to the barn where he could forage and get some exercise. Of course nobody had shared this decision with Noah. In the days to come, he discovered where the back door of the house was and frequently lay down in front of it. How sad it made me feel when I had to lead him back to the barn. He simply didn't understand why the rules had changed.

Noah still wasn't eating well. Just before we moved him from Inlet, he had begun to pee under the dining room table. Pigs urinate by the gallon! After nine years of no accidents, I couldn't figure out what caused him to change his behavior. The veterinarians had no answers. They concluded that he was an old pig at nine. Because he appeared to be healthy in all other respects, I let the matter go until alarming symptoms forced us to seek a diagnosis.

With Noah's move, all of the barn animals were in residence at Moose River Farm. Rod and I enjoyed our walks with the goats, dogs and now Noah, who followed along occasionally but lingered way behind. We always planned a route that would double back and meet up with him so that we could lead him home before he got too far into the woods alone.

Before Labor Day, Amy headed back to school; I was about to begin my new school year. The thought of commuting to the barn early in the morning before school weighed heavy on me, but at least now I had established an efficient barn routine. If I could just make it through the next six weeks until our planned move during Columbus Day weekend, all would be fine. Welby stayed behind when Amy left. At the end of September, I planned to deliver him home to my sister's farm on the way to my annual pilgrimage to Dressage at Devon.

Meanwhile, Noah made himself a comfortable nest out of the hay in the feed room until the nights got too cold for him to sleep in the barn. As the school year began, we continued to commute and let Noah choose his own locations to sleep. Every morning he was up with the sun, rooting in the vegetation that grew close to the barn. He never wandered off and always returned to his bed late in the afternoon.

At last, Rod and I moved into our house at the farm. The next morning was the first time in months that I didn't have to rush off to tend to the horses living ten miles away. The house, far from complete, was already an extraordinary display of Rod's incredible talents. In the pantry I fixed my coffee on the small granite counter that matched two larger ones in the kitchen. The polished surface gleamed in veins of black, taupe and transparent stone. Iguanas Rosemary and Spike spent their first night in the tiled animal room behind the kitchen. Years later Fiona would move into that space.

The cherry floors stretch into the living room and dining room. A huge stone fireplace reaches up to the top of the cathedral ceiling in the living room. Two large double-hung windows on either side offer impressive views of our woods. The carefully chosen earth tone colors applied to every wall blend perfectly from room to room: moss green in the dining room, beige in the kitchen and natural clay for the front hall. The cherry staircase ascends to the second floor. Three bedrooms including our own provide accommodations for the array of family and friends who visit throughout the year. Variegated carpet in hues of green and brown covers the whole second floor except for Rod's office. Almost every room in our house looks out to the barn and fenced paddocks. The combination of house, barn and land has truly taken me beyond my childhood dreams.

We were finally full-time residents. My spirit soared when, for the first time since June, I was able to visit the horses and goats late in the evening for "cookies and carrots." Although it was a rainy weekend, nothing could dampen my mood as Rod and I synchronized our new rhythm of daily life with the residents of Moose River Farm.

A Streak of Gains and Loses...

Sadly, Rod's father, Big Rod, passed away from congestive heart failure within the first week of our move. His death was not unexpected, and we were grateful for being fairly well settled before we had to travel to Florida. A good friend agreed to stay in the house and care for the farm while we were away. Her willingness made it easy for me to organize my lists of pet care and leave the following Sunday morning.

Finding My Way to Mountain View Farm

The weather in Florida was sunny and warm for the three days that we visited Sarasota. Rod's sisters had all gathered with various members of their own families to pay their respects to this generous man whose greatest sacrifice was made to his country as a bombardier during World War II. No one knows what demons haunted him after the war, but he managed to prosper and care for Rachel and his family until the very end. Of course I knew him best at Raquette Lake from June through September. For four months, he tended his bountiful garden, nurtured his apple trees and puttered about the property in a flannel shirt and an old pair of shorts or work pants.

In the earlier years of our marriage, Rod's dad played golf twice a week in Thendara and Inlet. As his breathing became compromised, he withdrew from those social activities, preferring to stay at camp. Sunny Cliff is designed for young people. As Big Rod's emphysema made it difficult for him to get around, he remained in Florida. Sadly, he never got to see Rod's masterpiece completed. He was only able to visit the farm in the early phase of construction during the first year that we owned the property.

Before Halloween, snow arrived. Although it didn't stick around for long, our first winter at Moose River Farm had begun. Rod was now spending his work days in Inlet, repairing eighteen years of wear and tear on our lake home. Damage caused by dogs, Noah and Casey Bird, not to mention general maintenance, demanded endless repairs. When I went back to help move furniture or pick up a stray load of belongings, I was saddened by Lakeview Farm's appearance. The fence rails around the ring and goat paddock sagged. The empty barn smelled of mildew and mold. The roof on the house had buckled along its shingled seams. The goat shed (where Phoebe recovered from slipping on the lake) at the side of the driveway leaned precariously to one side. But the lake in front of the house still shimmered dramatically, accentuating the one feature that eventually attracted a buyer in 2007 who planned to restore the property. Horses will never live in the barn again, but memories of them turned out in the ring, eating bedtime carrot snacks or softly nickering for breakfast every morning stay with me. As for Promise, Eric, Luther, Mishka, three goats and an assortment of chickens and rats buried at Lakeview Farm? They are sealed in my memory.

By early December, Noah's symptoms included bouts of vomiting after he gorged himself on his food. The veterinarian ordered a blood test. The results predicted the beginning of the end for Noah. He had a failing liver that meant an infection or more likely cancer. Weight loss, dry skin and patchy hair alarmed me as the temperatures began to dip below freezing. The vet suggested that we add dog food to his daily ration. Noah was examined in the garage of the vet clinic, which also served as a warehouse for the dog food they sold to clients. As the vet made the dog food recommendation, Noah was busy opening several bags of food that were stacked on the floor.

For the rest of the winter, Noah held his own, not getting better, but not seeming to get worse. We added Ensure to his diet to increase his caloric intake. The sweet flavor encouraged him to eat. He moved into the tack room when the cold weather took hold and slept peacefully in his bed on the heated floor.

In February I received a letter from a woman who lived up the road in Eagle Bay. Irene had purchased a Quarter Horse gelding when he was eighteen months old. She was forced to sell him when he was eight. After five or six years, she made the decision to buy him back and was seeking a boarding stable. She felt that she had given up her best friend; she couldn't bear to visit him. He wasn't neglected. His basic needs were being met. But nobody spent quality time with him. She pleaded with me to take him in as a boarder. At the time I wasn't convinced that I wanted to care for another horse. I also knew how difficult some owners could be if they don't feel their horses are receiving the best care.

One more horse in my barn would bring the total to six, and I wasn't sure if I wanted to handle that many horses next winter. Yet after meeting Irene, I liked her and knew it would be good to have somebody knowledgeable connected with the barn. I told her to make the necessary arrangements to reclaim her horse, Ben. At the beginning of May, my first boarder arrived.

Sadly, we said goodbye to Noah in June. After the long winter, he began to decline rapidly. Most of the day, he remained snuggled up on his blanket in the tack room. On some days, he appeared to rally and left the tack room to forage about the barn. It was hard to tell how he was truly feeling behind his stoic facade.

Meanwhile, Amy and Welby arrived back at Moose River Farm over the Memorial Day weekend for a repeat of their summer before. During Amy's first week back, Noah was suddenly no longer able to urinate. Before I hauled him off to the vet, I decided to see if taking him for a short ride in the car would stimulate him to pee. I covered the backseat with towels. Noah's weight loss made it easier for me to lift him into the car by myself. He still possessed a great deal of strength as he strained his body and verbally protested when I lifted him into the car. My plan did not work. Noah was so upset in the car that I had to turn around and take him home. Once out of the car, he collapsed in the aisle of the barn. Amy and I lifted him to his feet then guided him to his nest in the tack room where he collapsed for the last time. I stayed with him for a while, stroking his face and kissing his snout.

"I love you Noah B, Pigiletto," I cried. Within one hour he was gone.

Shortly after Noah's death, Spy began to exhibit some peculiar symptoms. In fact they were so peculiar that I was at a loss to describe them. All I knew was that something was different about him after the long winter. He began to spend a longer time lying down in the paddock he shared with Windy. His body shook with tremors from time to time, and he stood with his head low to the ground. I began to ride and condition him out on the trails for the upcoming lesson season. I noted nothing strange while I rode him except that he appeared lethargic. I passed it off to his advancing age. During my last ride on Spy, I led Windy alongside. As we galloped down the stretch, I thought about how much these two horses had enriched my life and the lives of so many others, for almost twenty years.

June and the end of the school year came into view. My family was off to Seattle, Washington, where we boarded a cruise ship and traveled up to the lower panhandle of Alaska. Rod and I were disappointed by the lack of wildlife. Aside from Bald Eagles, which are as common as robins in the Adirondacks, we saw no other native species. Although the fjords, glaciers, temperate rainforest and lush green mountains were breathtaking, by the end of the week, I was ready to get back home with my animals.

Cindy had offered to take a week off from work to stay at the farm. While we were exploring Alaska in turtlenecks and sweaters, the Adirondacks sweltered in a heat wave. Poor Cindy cared for all of the animals in temperatures that only dropped to eighty-five degrees come nightfall. The daytime temperatures soared above 100 degrees, unheard of for the North Country. After several days of sustained high temperatures, it became difficult for Windy to breathe. By the time we arrived home, he was suffering from a severe respiratory infection. Our vet had prescribed antibiotics to fight the infection before the heaves could be treated with steroids. It was difficult to watch Windy gasp as his entire body fought to breathe.

The morning after we arrived home from the cruise, I was eager to get back into my barn routine. Regardless of Windy's condition, the euphoria of being home energized me despite the oppressive heat. The goats, Hannah and Lacey, were out of their stall, seeking refuge in the cool barn. Hannah, now sixteen years old, looked ancient. Lately, she had been choosing to stand quietly off on her own, not seeming to care where Lacey was.

Late on a Sunday afternoon before school ended, Amy and I headed out with the goats and the dogs for a walk. The deerflies nagged us. Lacey and Hannah turned back, but Amy and I kept going. When we returned, Hannah was nowhere to be seen. Lacey was back in the barn, but Hannah had simply vanished. For two hours we searched the woods and trails. With nightfall looming, we had no choice but to abandon the search. And then Hannah came strolling out of the woods. Where had she been?

After her disappearance, Hannah began to age rapidly. She spent more and more time standing quietly in the cool wash stall or feed room where she could catch a breeze through the open door. Sometimes she bleated softly to herself as if she was in pain. Through it all she continued to eat and function normally.

When the phone rang, I answered. Rod was working on one of the stall doors that needed an adjustment at the far end of the aisle, and Irene had just arrived in the barn to see Ben. While I continued my conversation on the phone, Hannah approached me and leaned her whole body against my leg. I reached down to cup her head in my hand and hold her for just a minute. She bleated softly as I stroked her face. Still talking on the phone, I didn't pay attention when Hannah pulled away and walked into the feed room. Within a minute, the call ended and I went into the tack room to hang up the phone.

"What's wrong with Hannah? Anne, I can't get her up. She's not responding," Irene called urgently as she tried to pull Hannah to her feet.

I rushed to help, but it was clear that Hannah was gasping her last breath. Her body went limp. Irene then gently lowered her to the concrete floor.

"There was no warning! No sign! Just a minute ago she was leaning on me," I sobbed as Irene held me. At Irene's urging, I knelt and put my hands on the dead goat. I bent to kiss her and whisper that I loved her. Rod, drawn by the commotion in the feed room, joined us. He had just witnessed Hannah pressing against me. We stood in disbelief at our beloved dead goat. I told Rod that I wanted to believe that when she pressed against me and bleated softly in the moments before she died, she was saying goodbye.

We decided that, since Amy was graduating after the next year, there was no need for Welby to travel all the way home come fall. He was more useful to the lesson program than he was hanging out in his pasture at home. My sister and her husband were done with horses since their youngest daughter Megan preferred raising chickens, ducks and a guinea pig.

The two summers that Amy spent at Moose River Farm created a significant bond between us. Her life experiences since graduation from college have included two years of teaching in Mississippi through Teach for America and two years teaching in a Charter school in Boston. Today she is a first grade teacher at a Charter school in New Orleans. I am proud of all that she has accomplished and of the adult that she has become. Once a year, Amy takes time out of her busy life to visit Moose River Farm and to check up on Welby. During those visits she revisits her own childhood while riding him through the Adirondack woods.

FRIESIAN FEVER...

In the fall of 2005, Friesian fever took hold of me with the strength of a flu bug. I was exposed to the Friesian virus at Dressage at Devon where Sabine Shute-Curry and her beautiful Friesians provided the entertainment at intermissions throughout the Grand Prix weekend. The horses' long black manes, flowing feathered legs and fairytale image captivated me. I could only imagine what it was like to sit on all of that energy and movement.

When the barn where the Friesians were stabled opened for public viewing, I stole the opportunity to visit the horses up close. The gentle expressions and placid demeanor of the stallions were impressive as they stood patiently with masses of people mingling among them. They abandoned piles of hay to have their necks stroked and manes tussled.

When the weekend ended, I returned home on a mission to find out all that I could about this breed. I learned that the Friesian was originally bred for driving in the Netherlands. Lighter and smaller than typical draft horses, they possessed the strength and sensibility to pull carriages with a graceful flow of motion. The Friesian is fairly easy to train and maintains its bulk on relatively little food. After years of feeding Thoroughbreds, this piece of information was of critical interest.

There were several obstacles standing in the way of obtaining a Friesian of my own. At the top of the list was the fact that I was already facing the winter with seven horses to care for. Since I worked full time as a school teacher, my barn hours were limited to afternoons and weekends. More horses to care for meant less time to ride. The reality of my situation cooled my desire to purchase a Friesian before the winter months took hold.

As fall blazed in mid-November, I attended Equine Affaire in West Springfield, Massachusetts, where the Friesians appeared to be the flavor of the month for middle-aged professional woman like me. The Friesian area of the sale barn was well represented by several farms. It appeared that they all brought their weanling crop with them to tempt potential buyers. One farm selling fourteen weanlings already had a sold sign on each stall. So where was my Friesian?

The second obstacle to owning a Friesian was the price tag. A Friesian already started in training was way out of my checkbook's league. I have never been one to justify the high price of well bred horses; in my life, horses are basically recreational companions. I couldn't accept the risk of paying high prices for flesh and blood so vulnerable to death. When I began to

Finding My Way to Mountain View Farm

investigate horses with partial Friesian breeding, I discovered many beautiful crosses who carried only half of the Friesian's majesty and, therefore, half the asking price. What I really wanted, however, was a Friesian, pure and simple. How could I possibly justify the money for a magnificent horse to play with in my backyard?

The internet is a useful yet surreal world where searching seems as innocent as window shopping until one sends e-mails to inquire about prospective horses. As soon as I hit the "send" button, I plunged into the buyer's market and was struck at how willing Friesian breeders were to whet my appetite with (in their words) great deals and pictures of available Friesians floating on air. Still, no bargains presented themselves. Besides, I still hadn't sold the idea to Rod who had endured the "just one more horse" in the barn plea over and over again.

What did strike me was the huge price difference between Friesian babies and adults in training. Weanlings were available at a fraction of the adult price. What if I bought a weanling and waited two years to ride it? Two years was a long time to wait for the opportunity to go floating off on my Friesian. However, a weanling was affordable, and I had never had a baby horse before. Perhaps this was the solution. The barn was full of project horses that would keep me working in the saddle for two years while waiting to ride the baby Friesian.

My next email was to Iron Spring Farm in Coatesville, Pennsylvania. Known for their extraordinary warmblood stallions that stand at stud there, ISF also breeds Friesians. Being the well-oiled professional organization that it is, ISF returns email inquiries as quick as lightening. They also get right to the point when they can sense a forty-something female buyer at the other end of the internet.

"…But we do have some weanling foals available from last spring that might be of interest to you." ISF replied to my quest for information about the next season's crop of expected foals. That meant that there were weanlings already on the ground looking for good homes. Perhaps, my Friesian was among them! Unfortunately, the holidays were just about to get in the way of foal shopping. I would simply have to do with a video of the perspective foals to tempt my imagination.

A video that arrived shortly before Christmas showcased two weanlings, young adults ready for training, and a slew of horses already competing at various levels of Dressage. I must have watched the two weanling videos one hundred times before calling ISF with my offer. One of the babies was an expressive colt with flowing feathers that shimmied around his ankles as he trotted across the paddock. His knees snapped up to his nose with little effort and tons of grace. He was extraordinary. The other was a filly with less brilliant movement. She floated around the paddock with more control of her physique but less expression in her gaits. The filly also appeared to run out of gas after a few laps. Needless to say, the colt captured my interest although his price tag was higher than the filly's.

I called ISF and made an offer on the colt that was not too far below his asking price. The Christmas holiday prevented a speedy reply to my offer, so for two weeks I waited to hear if the colt was to be mine. In that time, I continued to view the videos of both Friesian foals. My preference began to switch from the colt to the filly. The video showed her calm temperament, allowing me to imagine a breaking process without incident or injury. The fact that she ran out of energy quickly indicated to me that with a bit of lunging and preparation, sitting on her would be easy. As the days passed and I waited for ISF to respond, I began to hope that my offer on the colt wouldn't be accepted.

The call finally came and played out exactly as I had hoped. My offer for the colt was too low. With no sign of disappointment or attempt to up my offer, I explained my change of heart and placed an offer on the filly. Within twenty-four hours, the offer was accepted. I was going to own a little girl Friesian. Within two weeks, I was on my way to Philadelphia to see the filly at ISF. I arranged for my sister and three friends to come with me. What a day we had touring the beautiful facility in the lush landscape of southern Pennsylvania. A slew of employees attend to every detail of horse management. The farm is not glamorous, but it is impressive with its old barns and rolling landscape of hundreds of acres where some of the finest warmbloods and Friesians in the country are bred.

Shortly after our arrival, we piled into the farm's Blazer and headed over to the foal barn. My level of excitement was over the top as the car entered the driveway where my Friesian resided with all of the other weanlings. Once out of the car, I was distracted by a field of Dutch Belted cattle that were grazing close by. As I commented on them, my sister asked excitedly, "Is that your baby?"

I turned around mid-sentence and there she was being led out by the farm's weanling manager. Only eight months old, the filly was not very big. Her tail was nothing but a flat mat of short spikes. I approached her head and gently put my hands out to stroke her neck. With bulging eyes and flaring nostrils, the filly strained at the tiny leather halter around her head to assess the stranger who was touching her. I walked the circumference of her body and wondered at the way she was put together. The youngest horse I had purchased to date was a two-year-old. This was like having to pick a caterpillar before it turns into a butterfly.

I asked if I could lead her out to the paddock where my captivated entourage and I could watch her move. As we walked farther away from the barn, she became agitated, clearly indicating that she was not happy to leave her herd mates back in the barn. With a little coaxing, the filly allowed me to guide her out to the paddock. Several human bodies formed a fence to prevent her from leaving a small area of the paddock. We all clucked at the little filly as she dutifully trotted, demonstrating the floating gait I recognized from the video.

When we walked the filly back to the barn, I noted her calm demeanor in the company of her companions. In the safety of her stall, she relaxed. With great interest, she poked her muzzle into my hair, hands and all over my jacket. Fifteen years and eight geldings later, I was going to have a girl in my barn again.

Before she could make the long trip to the Adirondacks, we had to attend to Iron Spring Farm's strict protocol. Vetting, payment and shipping all had to be coordinated within a limited time period. In dozens of phone call over the next three weeks, we ironed out the details of the Friesian filly's purchase.

The vetting exam resulted in some questionable blood work that turned out to be nothing but threw obstacles in the way of shipping arrangements. Finally, three weeks after I met Piepelotje (Pip-a-LOW-cha), she loaded onto a large shipping van and headed north to her new life. For nine hours, I kept myself busy around the barn with butterflies dancing in my stomach. The moment she stepped onto the horse van she became mine; if anything happened to her in transit, I was out of luck. It was the last day of January, 2006. Although the weather was clear, our driveway was a sheet of ice from a week of freezing rain.

While I mucked and bedded the stalls, cleaned water buckets, swept the tack room, tackled the cobwebs, stacked hay, groomed horses, pulled manes and basically used up time, I tried to figure out what our little girl should be called. Her formal name was an awkward mouthful. I didn't like Pippy, Pippin or Piper. As I twisted the name backwards and forwards on my tongue, the name Lotje came out. That sparked my brain to say and spell it phonetically resulting in "Lowtchee." I loved the sound of it.

The evening hours dragged while I waited and waited for lights to appear in my driveway. I tried to watch TV, write emails, read a book, but nothing could speed up the clock. Finally, just after midnight, hours after Rod had gone to bed, lights pierced the darkness. She was finally here!

The icy condition of our driveway was the next obstacle in addition to a jammed ramp on the large gooseneck trailer. Because of her youth and small size, Lowtchee shipped in a box stall rather than a tie stall. With the ramp stuck half open, I could just see the tops of her little Friesian ears pointing inward at each other over the edge of the door. Her high-pitched whinny made it clear that she was ready to get off the trailer. A low rumbling chorus answered her from the barn as the horses began to show interest in the activity taking place in the driveway. Rod came up behind me to video-tape her arrival as she made her way off the trailer and into her new life.

Finally, as if the director yelled "roll film," the ramp was lowered to the ground, and the van driver led the little filly off the trailer and into the glowing light of the barn. From there he walked her to a stall at the middle of the barn and led her through the door. Next to my horses (now all "apuff" and desperately trying to read the messages sent by the stranger), she looked so tiny with her flat stubby tail and short fluffy mane. Her soft brown eyes showed no nervousness about her new surroundings. Her first order of business was to plunge her delicate muzzle directly into the pile of hay waiting in the corner of her stall.

I settled up with the van driver and sent him on his way to Massachusetts where the other horse on the van would not arrive until close to 5 a.m. I wondered what kind of night his new owner was having, a sleepless one for sure.

Although it was late and I had to get up for school in just a few hours, I couldn't leave my filly just yet. She seemed to welcome me into her stall for a visit. Welby, in the stall next to Lowtchee's, squeezed his nostrils through the bars to get as much information about the filly as he possibly could. She showed little interest in her new neighbor, only pressing her little ears forward to introduce herself. I was sure I had purchased a confident little filly who was going to mature into a lovely riding horse and companion. While stroking her neck and combing my fingers through her mane, I understood that the only cure for Friesian fever was simply to buy one.

Farewell to Spy Hopes and Windy...

The next summer Spy was still with us but showing signs of a weaker hind end as he roamed freely around our property, grazing the areas of our lawn where the other horses were not allowed. I began to separate Windy from Spy during the day, preparing them and me for the inevitable. In the evening when they were reunited back at their "suite," they greeted each other with anxious "where have you been" whinnies.

As the summer days began to shorten, Spy's back end weakened noticeably. I had to make a decision. Winter comes early to the Adirondacks, and the thought of finding Spy too weak to rise on a frosty morning was more than I could bear. Our vet agreed to call me later when he had time to come out to euthanize Spy. This way, I would not have to think about it. It would just happen. After the plans were made, I began to see Spy in a different light. I realized how much horses mean to me and how every single one of them has helped shape a piece of who I am. I hugged and kissed him every chance that I got and tuned into the time I spent brushing him, often burying my nose into his neck and mane. I wanted to inhale everything about him, to fill myself up with him. I clipped a piece of his tail and wished my hair were longer so I could braid a piece of it into his mane.

In the middle of October, Dr. Hausermann called to say he would come the next day, Saturday. His call caught me off guard; I was teaching in school when the call came. I vowed to call him back at the end of classes to cancel the appointment. As the day wore on, I realized I was not going to make that call. Cindy drove up from Saratoga on Friday night to stay with me to witness Spy's death. The next day she groomed him, readying him for his journey. I ran a mandatory errand Saturday morning, the trip a welcome distraction. When I arrived home, I learned that the vet was only half an hour away. I took my freshly coiffed Spy for a walk. Without words, I shared my thoughts with him. I shared how much he was loved, thanked him for all of the wonderful memories, and wept while he stood patiently supporting my weight around his neck.

The vet arrived. Quietly, we walked Spy out to the field with Windy in tow. Rod held Windy while we positioned Spy near his burial site. Our compassionate vet waited through more hugs, kisses and tears. Then Spy slipped quickly and quietly out of my embrace to the earth. The last thing he heard was a chorus of "I love you." When he was gone, my friends and I commented on how beautiful he was. His chestnut coat shone like polished copper and his two hind socks beamed in the sun. As his mane blew gently in the breeze, the rest of his body remained perfectly still.

At this point, Rod released Windy, who had been standing stoically, staring at his fallen companion. Windy galloped over to the body and stood between Spy's front and hind legs. He lowered his head to smell Spy and stood with his head bowed. He seemed to be absorbing Spy's death. It was peaceful, it was perfect and it explained so much about the powers of acceptance that animals have. This scene lasted for over an hour. Fascinated,

Finding My Way to Mountain View Farm

we watched to see what would happen next. Occasionally, Windy left Spy to graze briefly before returning to the same spot between Spy's front and back legs where once again he would take up the vigil. Eventually, Windy lay down near Spy. Through the whole ordeal, Windy never acted fretful. He was clearly at peace, as was Spy, as was I.

Later that afternoon, we returned Windy to his stall and small paddock. From the fence, he watched as Rod worked the backhoe and buried Spy's body. I checked on Windy often and never once witnessed any sign of stress. He watched quietly but deliberately for the duration of the burial.

As the months passed, the void that was Spy's absence began to heal. I had no regrets for deciding to end his life. I gained a deeper acceptance of his death, thanks to Windy. But most of all I felt a greater appreciation for those still living in the barn and looked forward my future with them.

For a long time after Spy's death I was unable to listen to the Riverdance song, *Harvest*. I avoided the CD altogether as if riding to it might somehow show disrespect for the horse whose theme it had become. Although Windy helped me to accept Spy's death, the truth was I had a hard time recovering from it. But time eases pain, eventually.

A year or two later, in need of a change from the music we had listened to all spring, I chose the Riverdance CD and four others to fill the CD player, then hit the random button. Several days passed before Spy's song finally visited us in the outside ring. It caught me off guard as I was riding Easau. All of a sudden, the familiar introduction to Harvest flowed from the speakers. I remembered what a thrill it was to ride Spy in sitting trot as he established the beat through his own gait. Although my eyes welled up, they were tears of joy as I relived the vivid memory.

Almost four years after Spy was euthanized, Windy's breathing became difficult to manage with daily steroid medication. In early spring and after another tearful goodbye, the vet inserted two syringes into Windy's jugular vein, sending him off to where, I like to think, Spy was waiting for him. Now, together, the two of them watch over Moose River Farm.

PROFOUND LOSS...

"What?" I gasped in disbelief at the news that came crashing through the phone late on a Monday night in May.

"Perry and Dylan were killed in a car accident today," Michele repeated choking on her own words.

I waited for my brain to process this information.

Dylan, now eighteen, had been practicing his driving skills with Perry, his step dad. Apparently Dylan miscalculated a right hand turn and ran into a huge dump truck that tried desperately to stop when the truck driver saw the little Toyota Corolla coming at him. In an instant, Perry and Dylan were killed. Cindy's life, along with the lives of her two girls, changed forever.

When Michele called with the shocking news, I was conducting the nightly ritual of "cookies and carrots" in the barn. After I hung up, I returned to dispensing hay and picking manure from the stalls. Usually, this is a comforting end to my day. Tonight it seemed obscene for me to attempt to seek the comfort of routine while Cindy had suffered such a cruel loss.

It had been almost two weeks since Rod's mother Rachel had been diagnosed with ovarian cancer that had spread throughout her abdomen. Rachel had fought with all her might not to burden anybody in her twilight years. Since Big Rod had died seven years before, she appeared to be in slow decline as she moved to a retirement villa and then into assisted living. Rod's sister Donna was nearby to attend to the specifics of her care and to ensure that she was provided for in every way. His sister Dodi also provided assistance in looking after Rachel, despite her own array of health issues.

The cancer prompted immediate surgical removal of an ovary and the de-bulking of tumors that had spread. The oncologist was confident that surgery and chemotherapy would improve the quality of Rachel's life in the time that she had left. This information made me uneasy. My father's own mother had required surgery to remove a benign bowel obstruction when she was in her mid-eighties. Going into surgery, she was strong and optimistic, but she never recovered from the anesthesia.

Finding My Way to Mountain View Farm

Although Rod had intended to visit his mother at some point during the previous winter, extended harsh weather had prevented him from making plans to go. It was now the end of May. Without hesitation, he booked a flight for early Sunday morning and headed to Florida, hoping to lift his mother's spirits.

I lay in bed, unable to fall asleep despite the canine sentinels snoozing close to me. News of Perry's and Dylan's sudden deaths prevented me from concentrating on anything else.

Apparently, Cindy had gone ahead of the men in her own car and planned to meet up with them at Perry's place of work. When they failed to show up, she made several attempts to contact them on their cell phones. No one answered. Then a co-worker told Cindy about a horrific fatal accident that had just been reported. Perry and Dylan were the victims. With this image etched on my mind, I fell into a fitful sleep. I awoke several times during the night, sadly realizing that Cindy's tragedy was not a bad dream.

Meanwhile Rod was with his mother who was still in the hospital. Despite pain from her surgery, she was improving slowly each day. On Tuesday evening, I sent Rod an email about Perry and Dylan. By then he was able to access several articles on the internet about the accident. A day later, the tone of the articles began to change from tragic to tribute as both Perry and Dylan were remembered fondly by so many people in Australia and the United States.

On Wednesday evening, Rod returned home to Moose River Farm, having cheered his mother with a visit from her only son. Teaching and caring for the animals had kept me busy over the past three days. I still felt as if I was only half of a person waiting for the other half to return so I could resume living whole. Would Cindy ever feel this way again? Every time this thought occurred to me, I cried.

On Thursday, an emailed update arrived from Florida to share that Rachel's abdominal drainage tube was going to be removed and, as a result, she would be able to take food by mouth. Since the surgery, she had only received nourishment intravenously. When the phone rang Friday morning at 6:30, I was not prepared to handle more sad news.

"Anne, this is Donna," a voice sobbed on the other end. "Mother is not doing well. They called me in the middle of the night to say that she was failing quickly and will not live much longer. I wanted Rod to know before she is gone."

Apparently, Rachel had been given some light chicken broth the night before and had vomited in the middle of the night. Her weakened condition prevented her from being able to clear her lungs; her body began to shut down.

"I will call you later after she goes." Donna promised. "Anne, take care of Rod."

Her final statement broke my heart. I hoped that I could offer comfort to this man who had never let me down. I hung up and returned to the house to give Rod the latest information.

Four hours later, Rachel died. With her went one of the Adirondacks' most indelible spirits, one who, I am convinced, dwells in our majestic mountains and lakes. I see her in hummingbirds, deer, loons and black bears. With each sighting, Rod and I are reminded of this gracious woman who loved us so.

With Rachel's death came the end of the saddest week in my life. The contrast between these losses has left me to question God's motives. Perhaps Rachel's death was merciful considering the alternative—a long drawn out battle with cancer that she would ultimately lose. But Perry and Dylan's deaths left me unable to imagine a single justification that might bring comfort to Cindy and her girls. They were left behind to pick up the tragic pieces of their own lives.

The melancholy events of the spring transitioned into a summer of reflection. Friends and family who also enjoy interacting with the animals filled our calendar with visits that lifted our spirits urging us to move forward. All too soon the new school year began and summer's lush green landscape faded into memory. The warm days were replaced by crisp cool air announcing the arrival of fall.

Finding My Way to Mountain View Farm

A Walk in the Woods...

"Wanna go for a walk?" Rod calls as he slips his feet into hiking boots and bends down to tie the laces.

Suddenly toenails scramble to grip the wood floors and race to the back door. Nina and Niles, our Westies, are whining, almost howling, as Rod grabs the handle and swings open the door before those same toenails assault it with more scrapes and scratches. A young long-haired Dachshund, Hayden, begins a chorus of barks that pierce our eardrums in the confines of the laundry room. He exits through the same door to the backyard to join the bouncy Westies, now scratching at the gate.

Huxley appears at the door. Apparently, he wants to join us on the walk but lacks the other dogs' enthusiasm. They are now through the gate and zooming across the driveway towards the barn. Hayden holds Nile's tail in his teeth and Niles growls angrily as he pulls the younger dog along.

The autumn chill requires me to climb reluctantly into my brown barn coat for the first time in four months. After the short summer, I resent the inevitable arrival of winter. Today the leaves display a spectacular bouquet of autumn colors glittering in bright sunshine. Saffron, gold, burgundy, and evergreen form the backdrop of every view on the farm. This afternoon we will walk in breathtaking beauty while mourning the passing of summer.

Before stepping through the gate, I place Rosemary on the patio to catch some rays while we are out walking. Nothing rejuvenates a reptile more than unfiltered sunlight. In just a few weeks, the cold weather will end her sunbathing days. On my way to catch up with Rod who is waiting at the head of the trail, I stop at the barn to release the three goats from their stall. They anticipate the walk as much as the dogs do. Liam, Lilly and Lacey bounce out across the concrete aisle into the sunshine where they stop and stare back in the barn to see what I will do next. For some reason the goats only participate in a walk if I go along.

Huxley has now caught up after taking his time to stroll from the house. I pick him up and zip him into my jacket where he will spend most of the hike. I wrap my arms around the bulge he makes in my coat. While

I hurry to catch up with Rod and the dogs, I hear Fiona's soft grunting behind me. Once every four weeks, Fiona comes into heat for two or three days. Only then will she follow along on the walk. Today she is trotting to catch up. With everybody accounted for, we begin one of my favorite activities.

Many animal-loving guests have participated in this simple pleasure, marveling at the joy of this daily ritual. While Rod and I define the route and set the pace, three of the dogs drop their noses to the ground, zigzagging across the trail and into the woods to search for the source of good smells that tell stories from the night before. Once in a while, Nina doubles back, making sure she can find me, (called the "Mommy check"), before taking off again to sniff out the story's plot. Hayden, too, does not like to be too far ahead or behind, but he must remain in perpetual motion, visiting us frequently on his spiral tour. Niles keeps to himself, sometimes needing to be called firmly when he lingers too long with his nose at the base of a tree.

Occasionally, I peel Huxley's warm body away from mine and pluck him from inside my coat. Once on the ground, he scampers ahead to join the squad of canine detectives with his own nosiness. After a few minutes,

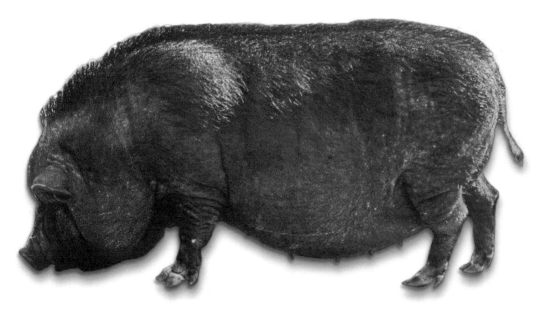

Finding My Way to Mountain View Farm

he slows down and begins to shiver, an indication that it is time to zip him back inside my toasty jacket. I oblige and hold his vibrating body tight, kissing his head as he rests under my chin.

The goats prefer to walk directly in front of me. If I try to pass them or at least move to the other side of the trail, they will immediately relocate so that they are again directly in front of me. They walk single file, taking turns as leader. The other two goats remain at eye level with the rump of the one in front. In this position they are missing the glorious view across the mountains toward Independence Lake or the blazing tunnel of our woodsy portion of Trail 5. Occasionally, they stop to nibble on fallen branches or worse, the bark of viable trees.

"Get out of there," Rod yells.

This one act of environmental vandalism has caused more conflict in my marriage than any other. Despite Rod's concerns the goats can't do much damage in the short time that they stop to sample the bark. If I keep walking, they will eventually abandon the tree and bounce on all fours to catch up and reestablish their line.

The dry leaves crunch, releasing the familiar scent that signals the death of summer. After four months of waving in the breeze and shading the farm, the leaves have exploded into brilliance before tumbling to the ground. I try to take snapshots with my eyes. Unfortunately, rain and heavy winds are predicted tonight.

Once in a while, I retreat to check on Fiona's progress.

"Urmph, Urmph, Urmph," she calls, maintaining the rhythm that beats throughout Moose River Farm. My purpose here on this farm is to keep that beat strong and consistent while thwarting possible threats to its peace and contentment. This is the rhythm of my life.

ABOVE.
Lacey provided company for our elderly Hannah.

ABOVE. *In 2006 baby Fiona arrived to fill the void that Noah left behind.*

RIGHT. *When our puppy, Huxley, arrived, a new generation of dogs began.*

Lowtchee was only nine months old when I saw her for the first time.

BELOW. *Windy and Spy were constant companions for eighteen years.*

BELOW. *Cindy and her whole family.* (2004)

BELOW. *Another great shot of the whole family.*
PHOTO BY MICHELE DECAMP, 2005

ABOVE. *Who wouldn't want to join in the goatie dance?*
SUSAN KOZLOWSKI, SUSANKOZLOWSKI.BLOGSPOT.COM

BELOW. *More than twenty years after working for Olympian Michael Matz, I caught up with him in Saratoga.* 2006

Finding My Way to Mountain View Farm

Part IV

Hoofbeats in the Adirondacks

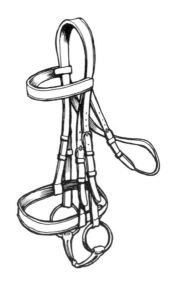

Finding My Way to Mountain View Farm

MUSIC AND HORSES...

Five years after moving to Moose River Farm, I began to consider options for keeping my riding students motivated. While students progress through the skill levels, it is important to set goals along the way. It had been more than thirty years since Promise arrived in my life. Riding her gave me opportunities to develop my character and build my self-esteem through competition. So much in the horse industry has changed since that time, yet so much remains the same. The cost of owning a horse, particularly if it has to be boarded on someone else's property, has skyrocketed due to insurance fees and rising feed costs. The expense of keeping a horse's feet shod or trimmed is equivalent to almost one third of the monthly board fee. But little girls, and some little boys, still fall madly in love with horses and beg their parents for a horse of their own. Parents dig deep into their pockets to pay the whopping weekly riding lesson fee, but they can't afford to own a horse. How well I remember suffering through those ten years of wanting a horse. I have never forgotten the ache left after I squeezed my eyes shut and pleaded with forces of the universe, God and my parents to please, please, please let me have a horse of my own.

As a child, I had the privilege of competing in horse shows before Promise arrived and with her during my last year in high school. The area where I lived provided several horse show venues within my budget. Although my competition achievements would never have taken me to Olympic glory, horse shows gave me a focus for Promise's training. I took competition seriously. I understood that the more time I put into riding Promise between horse shows, the more proud I was of our performance on show day. Winning ribbons boosted my confidence; if I felt we had ridden well, I was proud of my horse and of myself.

There are few horse shows within an hour of Moose River Farm. Most local horse shows are out toward Syracuse, well over two hours away. Travel expenses add to the cost of showing, not to mention the ten hours or more that I would have to be away from chores. To be honest, I don't like to leave the farm. Everything I have dreamed of is right here. I would rather spend a day puttering about the barn than leaving it for extended periods to compete on horseback.

However, I do recognize a need for my students, particularly those who have taken riding lessons summer after summer, to experience the thrill of riding in front of a crowd. There is nothing like having butterflies in the stomach as horse and rider combine all of their training into a ride that inspires an audience. Add a bit of energetic or ethereal music to the mix and the feeling is indescribable.

I needed to come up with some sort of compromise between competition and the redundancy of weekly riding lessons. Once again fate grabbed me by the shoulders and pushed me on my way into a new frontier of equestrian territory.

"Music?" I muttered to myself. "Really? Who would believe that my strongest 'cognitive ability' is music?"

Although I love music, I hardly believe that two years of piano lessons and one year of ballet define the strongest area of my intellect. But based on Howard Gardner's test of multiple intelligences, it is. As the presentation continued, I began to understand that, yes, indeed, music is the variable by which I retain information that translates into learning.

During a session on diverse teaching strategies at one of our superintendent's conference days, I was enlightened by this information. I have always been aware of the different ways in which students learn. Some children retain information more efficiently while fiddling with something in their hands; others absorb the content while doodling with a pencil, while others need to quietly tap a foot or finger. The challenge is to identify the areas of strength in each student and customize learning strategies.

As I pondered the results of the quick little test that the facilitator gave us, it became perfectly clear to me why music surfaced as my strongest cognitive ability. Despite my educational focus, degrees in science and love of synthesizing words, music is and always has been a constant in the background. Music, for me, has more to do with mode of learning rather than content learned. Therefore, I began to see why, despite my lack of training in music, I still possessed an innate musical ability to learn.

Growing up, I needed to listen to music. While I was yearning for a horse, music played in the background, either from the stack of forty-fives that dropped one at a time onto our family's turntable or from the transistor radio that I kept next to my bed. I have been able to chronicle most of this book from my memory of the popular music that I listened to over and over again.

Sue and I traveled in the Lost Acres Day Camp's Volkswagen van as The Grass Roots belted out "Wait a Million Years," and Tommy James and the Shondells crooned "Crystal Blue Persuasion." At Diane's Was-A-Farm Day Camp, James Taylor, Carol King. The Carpenters, Seals and Crofts and Crosby, Stills and Nash blared from the barn radio all day long as I cared for Missy, Merrylegs and eventually Beau. When I attended Camp Equinita, Elton John was riding high on the success of his legendary album, *Captain Fantastic and the Brown Dirt Cowboy*. By the time Promise came along a few years later, we were often listening to Billy Joel, and Philadelphia's own Hall and Oats on the radio at Triangle Acres. I can still remember riding Royal Rouge while listening to *Eye in the Sky* by The Alan Parson's Project from a radio that broke up the daily monotony for two young men hired to paint the enormous Dressage barn my first summer at Erdenheim Farm. The Erythmics sang *Sweet Dreams* at least once an hour, and just about every song on Michael Jackson's album *Thriller* was a hit that summer.

Now as I ride horses to music every day, I am intensely aware of how the combination soothes me and clears my head so that I can let go of the stress from my school day. The effect is magical. Before the construction of my indoor arena, several weeks went by without riding during the long winter. I felt like a caged animal who needed to spend pent up frustration and energy before I unleashed them on my loved ones. Simply put, music and riding horses are a therapeutic mix.

In late winter of 2009, an idea began to emerge; the more I pondered it, the more I liked it. The more I rode to music, the more I wondered how I could show off my students' progress on the horses.

"Val, how do you run your piano recitals?" I asked our choral music teacher one hot sticky day near the end of the school year. She taught piano lessons after school in her own living room.

"Each student plays a couple of different songs that they have been working on during the year. Afterwards we celebrate with refreshments," Val replied.

"I want to have a riding recital for my students so that we can bring the parents out to watch and also celebrate the riders at the same time," I said.

My brain was more or less putting together thoughts as I spoke them; for the first time I could picture what a riding recital might look like. Lots of riding stables have horse shows in which student riders compete against each other for ribbons and other prizes at their own barn. My eclectic and quirky collection of horse flesh, not to mention the range of riding abilities among my students, eliminated fair competition. Besides, I had groomed my students to be effective riders, not necessarily "show" riders who sit in the saddle looking pretty. To encourage them to compete against each other seemed anticlimactic to all the hard work they had been doing with the horses in the ring. Instead I wanted them to show off what they had learned without competing against one another.

In mid-July, *An Evening at Moose River Farm* demonstrated each student's riding skills for an audience that included family and friends. The evening followed a long day of bathing and grooming that exhibited the horses at their very best. Every white sock and blaze glowed in the evening sunlight. Every tail, shampooed and detangled, bounced behind a shiny set of hind quarters. The saddles and bridles were cleaned and oiled. I pulled my collection of white Dressage pads out of storage and attempted to bleach them into blinding perfection. Just before show-time, we sprinkled the horses with shimmering glitter. The students rode their best and the crowd cheered for each of them.

We concluded the recital with three rehearsed performances that demonstrated higher levels of riding skill. A four-horse drill team or Quadrille displayed the complexities of riding in military precision to the theme from the movie *Spirit: Stallion of the Cimarron*. A young girl demonstrated the innate equine behavior of Join-Up with our oldest school horse, Sandi to an ethereal selection by Enya. In a third performance this same student danced while her sister rode Zambi to correlate human dance with Dressage. Their music was upbeat, contemporary, and inspiring.

Finding My Way to Mountain View Farm

Afterwards we served lemonade and desserts on the knoll in the middle of the driveway. The recital was deemed a huge success. We all looked forward to making it a little bit bigger and a little bit better the following year.

In 2010 the recital performances boosted our confidence even more. Michele and I decided that in 2011 we were going to break the recital up into two events. The riders would still perform for their families at a regular riding recital, but we wanted to save the performances for an exhibition/ fundraiser for the new home of the Old Forge Arts Center. People would actually pay to watch the performances this time. Shortly after the 2010 riding recital, we christened the future event *Hoofbeats in the Adirondacks*. We felt a new layer of anticipation and stress blanket Moose River Farm in the months before July 7th, 2011.

To get ready for *Hoofbeats*, we had to attend to an endless "to do" list. Rod needed to build bleachers. A Quadrille needed to train and work harder than ever on precision because this time it DID matter. We needed to design a logo and a web site. We had to order T-shirts. We had to solicit sponsors to support this unprecedented event. We had to think through and organize the logistics of parking, farm safety, bathroom facilities, volunteers, riders, horses, performances, a dancer, choreography, and music to ensure that our show was worth the $20.00 price of admission. Before Christmas, two FEI, or Federation Equestrian International Grand Prix Dressage riders committed to bring their fancy horses and perform for us. That way if the Moose River Farm performances proved to be too amateurish, at least we could show the crowd what real Dressage looked like. Why stop there? Having just attended a book signing by Susan Richards, author of *Chosen by a Horse* and other titles, I decided to assert

my confidence in *Hoofbeats* by asking her to attend and sign copies of her books. The *New York Times* bestselling author graciously accepted the invitation.

After the show, I wanted to throw an informal dinner party in my backyard for all the riders and volunteers who participated. I imagined us all casually arriving in the back yard for dinner after we had taken care of the horses' needs and turned off the lights in the barn.

My level of anxiety, (and blood pressure), rose every time I wondered about the weather, the flies and mosquitoes, horse soundness, insurance, the sound system, the weather, the flies, the footing, disturbance of barn rhythm, the weather, the flies, and whether or not anybody would actually buy a ticket to watch horseback riding.

In March, Michele sent invitations to every horse person we knew in Old Forge and outside of town. We contacted every family associated with Moose River Farm and just about anybody else we knew in the industry. Her effort paid off. I felt a conflict of emotions by the middle of May when we had sold forty-two tickets and were guaranteed $1500 worth of sponsors who apparently believed in our vision. *Hoofbeats* hadn't even been advertised beyond the web site, and already we had accumulated an audience curious to see horseback riding as an art form. As the weeks evaporated, I prayed that we could pull it off. During the four weeks that preceded *Hoofbeats*, various challenges preyed on our preparations. All we could do was solve each problem and wait for the next.

SETBACKS...

I promised the four teenaged girls who volunteered to ride in the Quadrille that practice would begin Memorial Day weekend and that before school ended four weeks later, the routine timing and movements would be established and in place with the music. Therefore, we would spend the two weeks before *Hoofbeats* practicing with few changes to the routines. The routine was never an issue. The selected horses, however, proved to be more of a challenge than we anticipated. A combination of shoeing problems and minor lameness demanded a rotation of horses at each of the initial practices. While waiting for Zambi's tender bare feet to toughen up, one rider had to make do with riding the arthritically challenged Murray. She had her heart set on riding Zambi and hoped that by the dress rehearsal date, Zambi would be able to perform.

Then I received word that one of the Grand Prix riders initially planned to perform with her Lusitano stallion. On hearing this news, my mind flashed back to several years before when I had boarded Zambi in a barn that housed a Thoroughbred stallion. My mild mannered and easy going gelding to whom I entrusted my life became a deviant lunatic stallion wannabe in the presence of the full male horse. For the first time, I became afraid of Zambi who whinnied piercingly, reared and bucked whenever the stallion came near him. On one occasion, the stallion's owner brought him with her down to the field where I was schooling Zambi. After a brief conversation, the owner retreated with the stallion in tow. As they disappeared behind the house on their way back to the barn, "stallion" Zambi invaded mild mannered gelding Zambi. Before I could react, Zambi began to scream and pull me up the hill to follow his protégé. When I pulled on the reins to slow him down, he bucked and reared in total disregard of my correction. I had no choice but to keep him moving forward while trying to maintain some degree of control over him. He did not calm down until the stallion disappeared into the barn. The incident spooked me. How had my most trusted partner turned into such an unpredictable monster? Fortunately, once he returned home to testosterone-less Windy and Spy, Zambi reverted to the mild mannered gelding horse I knew.

The next crisis began the first morning of summer vacation when I arrived in the barn to feed breakfast. The horses greeted me with hungry whinnies while I tossed hay into each stall. As I approached Welby's stall, it occurred to me that I couldn't see him through the bars. When I opened his door, I found him lying flat out on his side, completely still with eyes open staring at nothing. Unable to comprehend what I was looking at, I entered the stall and pushed at his hind quarters with my foot. He did not move. I took off for the house.

"Rod, Welby is dead in his stall!" I shouted as my husband came out through the door, alarmed by the sound of my voice. "I can't believe he is dead in his stall!" I cried. Back to the barn I ran as Rod collected his thoughts and dressed for the trek out to the barn.

At Welby's stall, I stared at the form lying deathly still in the shavings. With my hand over my mouth, I entered the stall and approached his head. I squatted down next to him and stroked his face. My only thought was sadness that he had died alone. I told him how much we loved him, how much Amy loved him.

Then an ear moved. As it rotated back and forth to capture my voice, his eyes moved. He sat up on his chest, groggy but very much alive. I moved to the other side of his body and began to push on his back and hind quarters, encouraging him to get to his feet. He wasn't inspired to rise. By now Rod had arrived in the barn. He approached the stall, expecting to see a carcass and wondering how on earth he was going to remove walls to get Welby out of the barn.

"Well he's not exactly dead," I giggled through tears as I realized how absurd I sounded in my initial panic. "Something is still not right about him."

With both of us coaxing, we managed to encourage Welby to his feet. He had no appetite, but there were several piles of manure strewn about in his stall. We surmised that the new green hay delivered just a few days before had probably given Welby a gassy bellyache. He spent the day quietly in his stall and did not eat much until later in the afternoon. By the next morning, he had recovered completely. After a few days' rest, he was as good as new.

With every performance practice, our excitement grew. The riders and horses were beginning to look polished as the choreographed sequences of their rides fell into place. Rod perfected the sound system out at the ring so that the music, as much a performer as the riders, would inspire the audience.

Two days before *Hoofbeats,* we had scheduled a dress rehearsal of sorts for three of the performances, the ones that involved Moose River Farm riders. We wanted to give the riders a chance to perform in front of a crowd before the big day. Our good sized audience that evening was composed of about sixty Woodcraft campers and staff who walked down the dirt road to our farm.

Finding My Way to Mountain View Farm

On the morning of the dress rehearsal, Rod and I were awakened early by a strange banging sound. Rod rose quickly and ran to the balcony door that offers a view of the entire barnyard from our bedroom.

"A horse is hung up in the fence," he affirmed on his way down the stairs.

Fueled by pure adrenalin, both of us hurried out to the paddock.

The scene sent shockwaves through my brain. Easau was hanging from one hind leg that was stuck between the highest rails of the fence. The other hind leg swung back and forth about ten inches from the ground as he desperately tried to locate a place to put his foot down. I was certain that the other leg was broken for it was coiled in the fence and squeezed up tight under Easau's hind quarter. With bugged eyes and a look of sheer terror, Easau tried desperately to pull himself free from the noisy fence. And then something miraculous took place. This big spooky horse took one look at us approaching him and relaxed; he recognized that help had arrived.

Rod was able to get a good look underneath him to see just how the leg was anchored in the fence. Unfortunately, there was no way that we could lift him up and out of the trap. Rod began to shout at him in an attempt to get Easau moving again. Easau tried one more time to hoist himself and finally pushed against the fence with the swinging foot. With a tremendous clatter that echoed through the woods, he kicked the fence and pulled his haunches forward. He was free.

With adrenalin coursing through his veins, he exploded into a gallop to get as far away from the offending fence as he could. When he calmed down, I approached him to assess the damage. Aside from a number of minor lacerations on the inside of his hind legs, nothing else seemed out of place. He was, however, very stiff in the hocks and ankles. I took him to the barn and began a regimen of cold hosing, Bute for pain and general first aid. Each time I looked at the cuts on his legs, I was amazed that he had fared so well. Easau was unable to perform at the dress rehearsal, but with aggressive care, his stiffness subsided by the day that *Hoofbeats* finally arrived.

HOOFBEATS...

When July 7th dawned, my prayers had all been answered. The day was bright and sunny with a high in the mid 70s. The flies remained at bay as well. Finally, the two o'clock hour ticked into sight. Shortly after 1:00 p.m., spectators began to make their way through the woods between the designated parking area and the barn. They followed a trail of discarded horse shoes spray painted gold that led to the seating area at the front of the arena where the horses and riders were about to perform. By 2:00 p.m., more than 200 people had assembled in anticipation of the spectacle about to emerge from months of preparation and weeks of practice. It was show time!

After a brief introduction from Mike Farmer, the President of the Old Forge Chamber of Commerce, Miriam Kashiwa, the founder of the Old Forge Arts Center, spoke about the connection between horseback riding and performing arts. She graciously welcomed all who had come to watch various levels of Dressage set to music. I couldn't think of a better way to set the audience up for what they were about to witness.

Central New York news anchorwoman Laura Hand took the microphone from Mike Farmer and began to announce each of the performances. Her knowledge of sport horses educated the crowd between acts.

The intense time and training that went into each of the three Moose River Farm performances for *Hoofbeats* paid off as the show opened with a tribute to the horse-human bond in *A Dance Between Species*. Dancer Roy Tracy and accomplished rider, Chloe Pedersen astride Joshua performed to *Glitter in the Air* by Pink. The contrast and similarity between the equine and human athlete evoked the desired emotional response from the audience.

Next, rider Courtney Holt demonstrated "join-up," the unique trust that builds between horse and human. As Colbie Caillat sang *Fallin' for You* in the background, Courtney and our aged gelding Sandi began with a playful chase that sent him galloping exuberantly around the ring. After a few minutes he stopped, approached, and followed at her shoulder as she

Finding My Way to Mountain View Farm

walked about the ring. Then she climbed up on his back and proceeded to ride him sans saddle for a brief demonstration of their mutual trust.

Join-up was followed by a duet between two Friesians. In this act I enlisted the help of trainer Julie Fisher to ride a Friesian mare named, Herlijk, (rhymes with curly) while I rode Lowtchee. To a majestic piece called *Conquest of Paradise* by Vangelis, we displayed the sheer vibrancy and raw power of our gorgeous black horses with their flowing manes and "feathered" ankles.

Finally, the Quadrille performed flawlessly to the theme from the motion picture, *The Magnificent Seven* before intermission.

At intermission author, Susan Richards read an excerpt from one of her books, allowing time for the FEI riders to prepare for their performances. The crowd took their seats and prepared for the second half of the show.

First, Cowboy Will Hollister, riding his wooden hobbyhorse named Moose as a prop, and Laura Hand educated the audience about Dressage. In addition to explaining military origins that trained horses to be obedient, Cowboy Will demonstrated many of the high level movements to Van Halen's *Jump* as Laura Hand requested them.

"Can you show us some tempi changes, perhaps every stride?" Laura suggested.

After a brief scan of notes that Cowboy Will had jotted down for reference, he addressed the audience in words easily understood by those not familiar with technical Dressage jargon.

"Oh that's just when the horse goes off skipping," he affirmed. "Come on Moose, let's show them how we skip." Cowboy Will then took off at the "skip," changing his lead every stride with a swish and a flare. The audience reacted in gales of laughter.

When the FEI riders took over the ring, they brought a whole new level of a horse's capabilities to the stage by performing high level movements such as piaffe, passage and tempi changes to moving music. Catherine Howard rode her Lusitano gelding, Xerife, not the stallion she had originally planned to ride. Dressed as a pair of swashbuckling pirates, they performed to the *Theme from Pirates of the Caribbean* by Hans Zimmer.

Rider Darleen Callahan demonstrated these same movements with her horse Adrianne Adel to circus music.

As the spectators headed back through the woods to their cars, the organizers and I took a quick glimpse into the future and were ready to plan for *Hoofbeats in the Adirondacks, 2012.* The success of the show proved to me that horses and riders can put on a popular performance without competing for prizes or awards.

TIME TO RIDE...

Hoofbeats, now behind me left the rest of the summer wide open to indulge myself in my favorite form of daily exercise.

With the reins in my right hand, I lead Zambi out into the driveway and prepare to mount. The mounting block wobbles as I ascend the three steps that will place my foot at the same level with the stirrup. Once my left foot is secure in the stirrup, I pull my body up and lift my right leg over the saddle. My right foot makes a quick and successful search for the stirrup as Zambi begins to move away from the mounting block. As a common courtesy, I allow the horse to walk four or five strides before lightly placing my seat in the saddle.

The familiarity of the saddle, length of my stirrups and steady swinging gait of the horse encourages my body to take up the position it has known so well for more than forty years. By shortening the contact on the reins I steer Zambi out to the trail that leads into the woods. Every ride begins with a stretchy walk, (referred to as a marching walk when I teach lessons). It enables the horse to loosen up under a tight saddle and girth before being asked to exert himself. Zambi knows the drill. He moves in big strides across the ground. My legs on either side maintain contact with his barrel to prevent him from drifting left and right as we forge ahead.

Zambi can't resist helping himself to a balsam branch that teases him at the side of the path. He grabs it with his teeth, then sucks it into his mouth. The piney aroma tickles my nose as I kiddingly scold him for the deed. From the saddle, I view the Adirondack woods between his two swiveling ears. Like my position in the saddle, this view is familiar. The scene reminds me of the thousands of hours I have lived my life on the back of a horse. Such a privilege!

After a long walk, Zambi and I are warmed up and ready for a workout. One of the most amazing features of our farm and the adjacent Adirondack Woodcraft Camp is the natural sand base that covers the trails. Thanks to a receding glacier from long ago, most of the rocks were deposited on the other side of the Moose River. On our side there are very few stones, so there is good footing for trotting and cantering on a horse. I shorten the reins and nudge Zambi into a trot with my calves. He obliges. Soon we are clipping along in the two-beat rhythm of the trot. Trail Five is well defined under a canopy of sturdy maple, birch and spruce trees. The only artificial items out here are the posted signs that protect Moose River Farm from trespassers.

Zambi is eager to go faster. I compromise by letting him canter slowly. My hands creep up the crest of his neck while I lift my seat out of the saddle and stretch my weight deep down into my heels. Two-point position gives Zambi complete freedom of his back and hind quarters while my legs and hands still maintain control of our speed. A "hand" gallop rather than a full gallop is established as I steer Zambi around a corner and off of Trail Five toward camp. His hooves pound the earth in a three-beat rhythm as the woods give way to a grassy clearing that is the camp parking lot. It is early June so the lot is empty except for a line of logs that separate the dirt road from the lot. I steer Zambi to one of the logs and stare straight between his ears as he sails over it. The thrill awakens the young girl in me who used to love to jump. She has aged into a woman who is terrified of suffering an injury that will prevent her from teaching at school and caring for eleven horses.

Zambi and I continue our gallop into camp passed the dining hall, basketball court and soccer field. The scenery changes from dark woods to open fields and back to woods again. Zambi doesn't seem to notice the shadows that wave with the potential to spook a horse. After all, this is my trusted and true partner who exudes confidence, thereby elevating mine. It is the essential ingredient when riding horses safely, whether the rider is participating in her first lesson or the Rolex Four Star Three-Day Event in Kentucky. She must trust her horse and vice versa.

Zambi and I press onward. He has to adjust his frame to maintain balance as we go down a small hill. I stay out of his way. My job is to monitor our speed. Zambi is so focused on the trail that he startles only slightly when a deer suddenly crashes through the woods, flagging a warning with her white tail to three other deer following behind her. My heart skips a beat at the potential disaster that might have occurred if I had been riding some of my other horses. Anxiety ebbs when I remind myself that I would never even consider this activity on those horses. Zambi and I continue our steady pace.

Eventually, we approach one of the kettle lakes, (another remnant gouged out by the receding glacier), at camp. The shimmering water distracts Zambi for a split second before we enter another wooded section of the trail created by a stand of tall Hemlock trees. We gallop for one more minute before I am forced to pull him up at the camp road. We are both breathing heavily from our effort. My thigh muscles burn from supporting my weight in two-point position for so long. I reach down to stroke his neck.

"Good boy, ZZ, good boy," I tell him. "Didn't that feel great?"

I release the short contact of the reins, allowing him to walk "on the buckle" across the road and into another section of wooded trail. Walking allows us to catch our breath and rest before we take off again.

My mind begins to wonder about the debt that mankind owes to horses. They have provided and sacrificed so much over many thousands of years only to be replaced rather quickly in the last century by motorized technology. Did the soldiers of the Civil War and World War I ever have a chance to bask in their relationships with the horses who served them? Or were the horrors witnessed during wartime just too traumatic and numbing, thus preventing them from connecting with their horses emotionally? This is not a criticism. I only question if there had been emotional connections, would a soldier have derived some degree of comfort from his horse?

At the end of World War I, tens of thousands of war horses were slaughtered to provide much needed protein for nations all over Europe ravaged by and recovering from a devastating war. This is just one more example of the gift God has provided for mankind in the horse.

Perhaps I am most thankful for the fact that I live in an era when horses owe humans nothing and horse ownership is a privilege rather than a necessity. It takes hard work and a huge financial commitment to keep horses in my life. Although what Zambi and the other horses give back to me is difficult to articulate, it is priceless and worth every bit of the effort.

Eventually, Zambi and I pass the trail that leads back to the barn. With my right leg I persuade him to keep going straight despite his desperate attempt to make the turn that will ultimately reunite him with a pile of hay at home. We continue on the path along a fence line that keeps snowmobiles out of our sandpit during the winter. A Red-tailed hawk sits at the top of a tall spruce, like the star on top of a Christmas tree, surveying the open field for his next meal. Adult ravens scream at him in an attempt to distract his attention from considering a raid on their fledgling young.

Zambi and I turn right at the bottom of a stony hill to the "stretch," a long section of Trail Five that is wide and straight like part of a racetrack. At the top of the hill the stoniness ends, and I gather my reins in preparation for a long, fast gallop. Zambi senses my intention and begins to anticipate my aids. He leaps into the canter by tugging at the reins and ducking his head in excitement. I want to let him go, but it must be on my terms so I hold him steady until he is back under control. Once my galloping position is established, I allow him to go faster and faster until we are galloping flat out. Zambi's fastest gallop is nothing like the filly in Michael's barn all those years ago. Although it is speedy, I feel completely in control and know that I can slow him down at any time. We gallop over a quarter of a mile before I ask him to slow down at the Woodcraft entrance. Then I change directions and gallop back down the stretch for one more exuberant rush.

Just before the stony hill, I pull Zambi up so we can walk down carefully. At the bottom he turns sharply left to find the hidden path that will take us around the fence and into the sandpit. He is certain that we are headed home this time; and although he is walking, his strides are big and bouncy as he hurries toward his destination. I steer him to a large temporary pond at the base of a huge hill that leads to the barn. Although it is early July, the pond is a remnant of runoff from melting snow. The water will remain until the Moose River recedes over the next few weeks. Without encouragement Zambi plunges into the water until it is about two feet deep around his legs. Instinctively, he strikes the surface with his right hoof. The water sprays up onto my gloves, half chaps, boots and helmet. The girth around his belly is soaked along with Zambi's chest and all four legs. Once in a while, he stops to sample a drink from the churned up murky water. He shifts his weight and begins splashing again with his left hoof. I indulge him for a few more minutes until I clearly read from his actions that he is considering lying down in the water. I nudge him with my legs and we exit the pond. I crawl up into my two-point position one more time and steer Zambi to the big grassy hill. He climbs upward, disappointed that he was unable to complete his mission back in the pond.

At the top of the hill, we hear Easau's loud whinny from a paddock near the barn. Zambi announces shrilly that we are on our way home. At last the barn comes into view, and we see Easau relax his vigil now that he knows Zambi has safely returned. Finally, I dismount Zambi at the barn entrance. He yanks at the reins in an effort to rub his muzzle on his wet front legs. This time I am not joking when I firmly scold him. In his new role as a school horse, he has been allowed to get away with some undesirable behaviors. This is a minor one.

Before leading Zambi into the barn, I pat his face and kiss his nose. Then, wrapping my arms around his neck, I squeeze him against me. I bury my nose in his damp, warm coat and inhale. It's not just Zambi I am hugging. Hopefully, Missy, Never, Beau, Windy, Spy and Promise can all feel my embrace too.

INTO THE FUTURE...

Moose River Farm is more than a physical space. It is a lifestyle, a church, and a state of mind. It is, for me, where peace abounds and all that is bad in the world is dominated by all that is good. There is a rhythm here that never stops, although it does change throughout the year. In the winter, that rhythm is muffled by a blanket of deep snow that encourages us to slow down and recharge our batteries. With the coming of spring, the rhythm picks up tempo and finds accompaniment in the beautiful birdsong that welcomes new life all around the farm. In the summer, the rhythm is established by buzzing insects, garden bounty, and gentle breezes rustling the trees. Come fall, the rhythm is overwhelmed by the brief and dramatic crescendo of color that accentuates every view on the farm. After the rich tones vanish, the beat softens as winter takes hold once again.

At present, eleven horses live in the impressive barn that Rod built. Zambi, Lowtchee, Welby and Easau are among those still with us. The others have found their way to the farm through a variety of unique circumstances, providing material for a future book.

Thanks to the addition of an indoor riding ring in 2007, it is possible for me to ride just about every day during the year. With the evolution of computer technology, it is also possible for me to listen to an endless custom play list of music from the past and present while riding indoors and outdoors. Therefore, my old friends James Taylor, the Carpenters and of course, the Bee Gees visit from time to time and sing for me while I lose myself in the rhythm of Lowtchee's floating trot or Easau's smooth canter. Riding to music increases my heart rate and centers me in the moment.

The goats, Lacey, Liam and Lilly, occupy one of the stalls but spend some of the day browsing the landscape around the barn. One wind gust or snap of a twig sends all three bouncing back to the safety of the barn to wait for any pending danger to pass. Occasionally, they make their way to a stand of trees out near the ring. For the sake of the trees, the goats are rounded up and sent to their stall for time out before they can begin gnawing the bark.

Our middle-aged pig, Fiona, is the one farm resident who bridges the gap between barn and house. Although she sleeps in the house at night, we encourage her to spend as much time outdoors as possible. The barn provides a suitable physical workout for her as she scavenges among the stalls for grain and hay. To escape the hot summer sun, Fiona beds down for a mid-day nap in the cool ferns that form the perimeter of our lawn. She can also be found hiding from the heat under the deck by our back door. On occasion she may wallow in wet sand after a rain shower. However, she doesn't seem to enjoy the warm sponge baths that I try to give her from time to time.

Rosemary, now in her late teens, is the oldest member of our household menagerie. Her menu of fruits and vegetables is at the top of my grocery list every week. In addition to kale and zucchini, she feasts on tofu, broccoli and scrambled egg. She spends her summer days in the backyard with the dogs and Fiona. Favorite treats for Rosemary include petunia blooms that I pick liberally from the window boxes for her to enjoy.

Our pack of dogs still includes Huxley, Niles, Nina and Hayden. Although Huxley ignores Hayden, Nina and Niles have taken to the young Dachshund with great enthusiasm. Their playful antics are a joy to watch as both Westies take turns rolling Hayden in the grass or delighting him in a game of chase around the yard. With his nose to the ground, Hayden traverses three times the distance we do on our daily walks.

The latest additions to the family are two miniature baby donkeys named Frank, (Sinatra), and Bing, (Crosby). These two equids have brought me great joy through their friendly personalities and sweet dispositions. With little coaxing, they have become regulars on the daily walk, accompanying the goats, dogs, Rod and me. Since their arrival I am simply crazy about donkeys; wondering why it took so long to acquire them.

Recalling all of the wonderful memories from the past has been comforting and cathartic at the same time. Reliving the years before and after Promise has encouraged me to accept that my life has been lived the way I envisioned. Who could have predicted that all the decisions made along my path would bring me here?

I am entering my third decade of teaching at the Town of Webb School in Old Forge. In the warm weather months, I teach horseback riding to students of various ages and abilities. Rod spends his day on the farm and tends to an endless list of maintenance tasks—fixing fences, clearing paddocks and hauling manure for compost.

Michele, Jean, and Irene are still constant fixtures in the barn. In June, 2010, I hesitantly accepted another boarder. Could I be lucky enough to add another great owner/horse combination to the barn? I was. Vicky and her Paint, Tango love Moose River Farm as much as the rest of us do.

Through every season, Moose River Farm's remarkable rhythm encourages all of us who reside here to hum along. Friends, animals and other family members feel it too. I like to think that loved ones, human and animal, who are no longer with us exist as residual energy that fuels the tempo.

ALL IS WELL...

Late evening is my favorite time to visit with the horses, donkeys and goats. After dinner, I tend to fall asleep in an overstuffed leather chair with at least three dogs piled on top of me. Sometimes it is as late as 12:30 a.m. before I wake up and head out to the barn. While I pull on my warm jacket, wool hat and gloves, the Westies make one more visit to the yard to take care of their bedtime business. They return to the house quickly just as I am slipping my feet into barn boots. A blast of cold air assaults my face as I close the back door behind me.

Fiona isn't with me. During the winter, she goes to bed around 4:00 in the afternoon. At that time she comes in from her last visit to the barn glistening with snowflakes that melt quickly when she enters the warm house. She heads for her bed in the room where Rosemary sleeps on her electric heating pad. Fiona gets right into her bed and begins scratching at the assortment of ripped saddle pads, blankets and towels. All of these items were once whole, but Fiona likes to tear them up with her strong snout and teeth. Eventually she lies down, satisfied with the nest she has made. "Umph," is the last syllable she speaks. Soon her deep rhythmic breathing signifies that she is fast asleep. When the temperature dips to bitter cold, I stop in to cover her with an extra blanket.

On my way to the barn, I glance up at the stars that twinkle so brilliantly in the black Adirondack sky. The crunchy snow beneath my feet sparkles. Despite the bitter cold, it is a beautiful night.

At the tack room door, I stomp my feet before I turn the knob and enter the heated space. The horses hear me coming and begin to whinny and nicker in anticipation. I grab several carrots from the refrigerator and open another door into the cold barn. The aisle floods with light when I flip on the switch. Every head sticking out to greet me squints and blinks in the glare. Starting with Target and working my way clockwise, I stop at each stall and offer a piece of carrot to the occupant. Next, I deliver one flake of hay to each horse as a midnight snack. Luckily, I have several buckets of water on reserve in the tack room and use them to top off the heated buckets hanging inside the stalls. That way I don't have to waste time dragging the hose out of the tack room and then draining it after use. For the final time today, (or first time, considering what time it is), I visit each stall with the wheelbarrow and a pitchfork to remove manure produced since dinner six hours ago.

Out to the indoor ring I carry a small flake of hay and two little pieces of carrot. My sweet baby donkeys, Bing and Frankie are bedded down in there. Their wheezy greeting through the bitter cold air is soft music to my ears.

"EEEEEEww ong ong ong," they sing to me. I respond by offering each tiny muzzle a treat. While I pick the minute manure balls out of their stall, they stand close to me. So far their long ears have avoided frostbite this winter. With one arm around each tiny equid, I hug them at the same time, then turn off the light.

Before shutting off the lights in the main barn, I divide one flake of hay among the three goats and offer each of them a mint.

"G'night, goaties! G'night, donks! G'night, horsy boys and girls," I whisper on my way out of the barn. Light glowing from the living room windows beckons me back toward the warm house. Once inside, I peel off my winter uniform and head up to bed. On the way, I pick up our long haired Dachshund puppy Hayden and turn off the lights.

"Vrrr, rdddr, frd d fr," Hayden sighs. I carry him in complete darkness up the stairs with Nina and Niles in tow to our bedroom. Sixteen hours ago my day began here.

I place Hayden and Niles on the bed and head to the bathroom to change. I replace my fleece riding tights and wool sweater with cotton pajamas. With face washed and teeth brushed, I make my way to the bed in the dark. As I slide into the flannel sheets, Huxley, who came to bed with Rod three hours earlier, presses his whole body against my chest. Niles curls his little body up on the edge of Rod's pillow above my head. Nina jumps up on the bed and nudges her way under the sheets to her assigned spot between Rod's feet. The puppy, too hairy to find comfort under the sheets, lies on his back against Rod's leg and sighs.

As I drift off to sleep, I take a mental inventory of our family and their whereabouts at the moment. Satisfied that everybody is safe, I allow myself to let go and fall into a deep sleep. Eventually, my breathing synchronizes with the rhythm of Moose River Farm. In that rhythm there is promise that all is well. All is well...

ABOVE. *Hoofbeats in the Adirondacks is a spectacle that combines equestrian arts with music. Rider; Chloe Pedersen, Horse; Partly Cloudy, and Dancer; Roy Tracy.* PHOTO BY MICHELE DECAMP, 2011

RIGHT. *CNY news anchor, Laura Hand poses with trainer Julie Fisher and Heerli.* PHOTO BY MICHELE DECAMP, 2011

ABOVE. *Darleen Callahan performs with Adrienne.* PHOTO BY MICHELE DECAMP, 2011

Finding My Way to Mountain View Farm

ABOVE. *Lowtchee expresses her exuberance after performing at Hoofbeats.* PHOTO BY DON ALLEN, 2011

BELOW. *The 2012 Moose River Farm Quadrille consists of Ashley Herroux/Murray, Courtney Holt/Eastern Salute, Jessica Hannah/Supreme's Golden Spirit, and Lauren Holt/Partly Cloudy.* PHOTO BY DON ALLEN, 2011

GLOSSARY

A Moose River Farm Glossary of Horsey Terms

Aides: Any part of the rider's body or equipment that is used to communicate with the horse.

Dressage: The formal training of horses with emphasis on athletic control and execution of natural movements. Cavalry soldiers used Dressage training methods to establish obedience from the horses their lives depended upon.

Equitation: The combination of a rider's skill and knowledge when riding a horse.

Eventing: Otherwise known as combined training, eventing is an equestrian discipline that combines Dressage, cross-country, and stadium jumping in an extreme form of competition.

Farrier: A trained craftsman who custom fits and applies horse shoes after trimming the hooves. May also be referred to as a blacksmith.

Footing: Material such as sand, shredded rubber or fiber that provides the base for horses to train on in a riding ring. Any terrain where horses are worked.

Hock: The joint in the middle of the horse's hind leg that is analogous to the human heel.

Leg: The amount of pressure applied by the rider's leg against the horse's side.

Shod: A horse who wears shoes is said to be shod.

Warmbloods: A number of different horse breeds developed centuries ago in Europe from the breeding of racing stock, (hot bloods), with work horses or drafts, (cold bloods). Warmbloods possess both athleticism and stamina which is why they are employed as show jumpers, Dressage horses, and eventers at the world class level. Trakehner, Hanoverian and Oldenburg are three warmblood breed examples.